Ireland
1905 - 1925

Volume 2

*Documents
and
Analysis*

A C Hepburn

Colourpoint

To all those who have suffered in the recent Irish troubles on account of the failures of 1905-25.

Published by Colourpoint Books
© A C Hepburn 1998

6 5 4 3 2 1

A C Hepburn studied at the Universities of Cambridge and Kent, and is now Professor of Modern Irish History at the University of Sunderland. Previously he lived in Northern Ireland for nearly twenty years, holding posts at the University of Ulster and at Queen's University, Belfast. He is author of **The Conflict of Nationality in Modern Ireland** (1980); **A Past Apart: Studies in the History of Catholic Belfast, 1850-1950** (1996) and (with E Rumpf) **Nationalism and Socialism in Twentieth-century Ireland** (1977). He is currently working on a comparative study of divided cities in modern history.

Designed by Colourpoint Books
Printed by ColourBooks

ISBN 1 898392 20 X paperback
ISBN 1 898392 46 3 hardback

Colourpoint Books

Unit D5, Ards Business Centre
Jubilee Road
NEWTOWNARDS
County Down
Northern Ireland
BT23 4YH

Tel: (01247) 820505/819787 Ex 239
Fax: (01247) 821900
E-mail: info@colourpoint.co.uk
Web-site: www.colourpoint.co.uk

Cover Illustration:
Posters advertising the launching of the Irish Volunteers, 25 November 1913 and the anti-conscription poster, 1918.

Contents

3 Nationalism old and new

4 Unionism old and new

5 Labour rise and fall

6 The Ulster crisis

7 The Easter Rising

8 The rise of Sinn Féin

9 The War of Independence

10 The Anglo-Irish Treaty

11 The Irish Civil War

12 The establishment of the Northern Ireland state

Acknowledgements

This collection has its origin in a suggestion from Dr Russell Rees that I might consider preparing a revised edition of my *Conflict of Nationality in Modern Ireland*, originally published by Edward Arnold, and long out of print. In order to make the collection fully compatible with Dr Rees's text it has been necessary to undertake a more radical revision than originally intended. The outcome is a new book, with seventy documents freshly added, a new introduction, and revised commentary. I am grateful to Dr Rees for his invitation, and for the stimulus of his own unfolding text as I prepared my own. I am also grateful to Norman and Sheila Johnston and their staff at Colourpoint for being such helpful and efficient editors, and to Edward Arnold (now a division of Hodder) for agreeing to allow material from *The Conflict of Nationality* to be re-used.

In preparing this collection I have benefited greatly from the advice and assistance of colleagues and friends. In particular I would like to thank Don MacRaild, John Hunter, Gordon Lucy, and Hugh Keegan. Elisabeth Knox worked wonders with scanner and word processor.

Every effort has been made to trace the owners of copyright material, and I must apologise for any unwitting infringement. My thanks are due to the following for permission to reproduce copyright material:

The Controller of Her Majesty's Stationery Office for extracts from Parliamentary Papers, Government Reports, House of Commons debates, Cabinet Papers and Public Record Office material; The Stationery Office, Dublin, for extracts from Dáil Debates; the National Library of Ireland; The Roman Catholic Diocese of Armagh; The Irish College, Rome; the Bodleian Library; *The Times*; *The Irish News*; The Army Records Society; The Ulster Society; Mr Mark Bonham Carter for the Asquith Papers; Fr J Anthony Gaughan for the extract from Jeremiah Mee; MacGibbon and Kee, an imprint of HarperCollins Publishers: Random House (successors to William Heinemann Ltd); William Heinemann Ltd; Oxford University Press; Anvil Books Ltd; The Mercier Press; SIPTU.

A C Hepburn, University of Sunderland

Abbreviations

ADA	Archives of the Roman Catholic Diocese of Armagh
BPP	British Parliamentary Papers
HC Deb	House of Commons Parliamentary Debates (Hansard)
HL Deb	House of Lords Parliamentary Debates
HLRO	House of Lords Record Office, London
HMSO	Her Majesty's Stationery Office
PROL	Public Record Office, London
PRONI	Public Record Office of Northern Ireland, Belfast
NLI	National Library of Ireland, Dublin
TCD	Trinity College, Dublin

Introduction

The years 1905-25 saw the most dramatic political changes in the history of modern Ireland. This was also true of most of the small national states which appeared, or re-appeared, in central and eastern Europe after 1918. On the continent these changes, although they were preceded by important social factors, were permitted to happen mainly because of the defeat of the dominant empires of Austria-Hungary, Germany, Russia and Turkey in the Great War. In the case of Ireland, on the other hand, the British Empire shared in the allied victory of 1918-19, and had no difficulty in having the self-appointed Sinn Féin representatives turned away from the Versailles peace conference in 1919. With the limited exception of Irish-American public opinion, there was no external power which could exercise any serious measure of influence on Britain's Irish policy. The dramatic political conflicts of 1910-14, the tensions and violence of 1916-22, and the emergence of two new states in Ireland in a form which no-one could have predicted a decade earlier, were therefore brought about almost entirely by social, economic and political forces generated within Ireland and Britain.

James Bryce (1838-1921), Belfast Presbyterian, Scottish MP, distinguished constitutional historian and Liberal home rule cabinet minister, was one who found this hard to predict. Writing to a Unionist counterpart in 1905 he conceded that home rule was as likely to come from a Liberal or a Tory government '*if*, an important *if*, the Irish continue to press as strongly for it. That is not so certain. When they have the land, much of the steam will be out of the boiler' [29]. With hindsight we can see that the great man was hopelessly wrong. We do not know what notice he may have taken of a very much more prescient analysis sent to him by one of his former legal advisers a couple of years later, who saw distinct signs of 'a new moving spirit in the country. A younger generation is coming up and no-one can yet tell what the outcome will be' [45]. The story told in these documents attempts to explain how the perceptions of these two Dublin Castle 'insiders' could differ so widely. It shows how the rise of male householder democracy, between the 1860s and the 1880s, ended Ireland's integration with British party-political culture, as the Liberal and Conservative parties (which in Britain were able to ride the democratic storm into the twentieth century) collapsed in Ireland and were replaced by Nationalist and Unionist parties, both of which were firmly grounded in Irish political culture and circumstances. It traces the rise and fall of agrarian nationalism, the transition from plebeian Orangeism to political Unionism, the Catholicisation of Gaelic culture and the utter failure of socialism, despite noble efforts, to subdue national animosities – as has been the case virtually everywhere in Europe except where the stifling blanket of Communism has been applied. It shows how the chance outcomes of British general elections, the failure of politicians to resolve political conflicts and the fortuitous highlighting of senses of national identity by the protracted horrors of European war interacted together to transform the situation in Ireland. They helped create an international frontier in Ireland where none had ever existed, an ill-fated home rule regime in six counties for the very community in Ireland which had so bitterly opposed home rule, and a remarkably bitter and brutal civil war in the south of the country over an oath of allegiance which quickly proved meaningless, fought between former comrades who – we can now see with hindsight – had already in 1921 fully achieved the effective freedom over which they then proceeded to fight. The Boundary Commission, finally, was a highly effective diplomatic device, which permitted a settlement to be made. In this sense it was the cornerstone of peace in Ireland, and it allowed a generation of British politicians to forget Ireland [157]. But, perhaps like all except the most brutal solutions to ethnic conflicts, it was at best a medium-term fix. It drew a boundary round divided Ulster, but it did not address the problems therein. These simmered for half a century, before erupting to blight the lives of another generation.

Most modern-day Irish Republicans acknowledge Wolfe Tone and the United Irishmen as the ancestors, if not the founders, of their movement. Several political organisations line up to take their turn each year to pay homage and deliver speeches at Tone's grave at Bodenstown, Co Kildare. But there are two important gaps in this historiography. The first is that between the world of revolutionary ideology which inspired the Society of United Irishmen and the narrower horizons of landlord and estate which guided the rank and file who subscribed to the Defenders and other agrarian secret society groupings [1, 2]. Just as the French historian Georges Lefebre identified four distinct revolutions which made up the French revolution (the nobility, the bourgeoisie, the Parisian crowd and the rural peasantry), the Irish rising of 1798 consisted of the second and fourth of these. The second and more significant gap is that between the secular, enlightenment ideals of the French revolution – which was the radical bourgeois 'republicanism' which attracted Tone – and the cultural nationalism which in Ireland began with the Fenians and was most fluently articulated a century after Tone by Hyde, Pearse, and Moran [10, 39, 40, 70]. The former attracted Protestant non-conformists and idealistic social reformers, the same groups as joined the pro-revolutionary Corresponding Societies in England; the latter was more closely grounded in ethnic and cultural difference. The reason that the Irish republicanism which so attracted the Dublin Episcopalian Tone and his Presbyterian friends in Belfast failed to attract similar interest during the twentieth century is simply that it has not been the same republicanism.

Modern Irish nationalism, in recognisable forms, emerged during the nineteenth century: constitutional nationalism from the emancipation and repeal movements of Daniel O'Connell, which led the mainstream of the Catholic Church away from a policy of advancing through loyalism [4, 5]; and modern revolutionary nationalism or republicanism, which began with the Fenians. Economic factors, in the form of the land question especially, played a key role in the development of modern nationalism. The great increase in population, from about three millions to over eight millions between 1750 and 1841, produced a pattern of population pressure, sub-division of farm holdings, and overdependence on the potato for food that was not reversed until the disastrous rural breakdown of the great famine of 1845-9. Popular response to worsening conditions was at first seldom tinged by any degree of nationalism, and even during the famine period itself Young Ireland writers who sought to make the connection between land and nationalism were by no means in complete agreement about the nature of the link or its efficacy as an organisational weapon [7, 8, 9]. It was in Ulster, ironically, where Orange Protestants in areas like North Armagh came to perceive land-hungry Catholic peasants rather than rapacious landlords as the main causes of rent increases, that the land question was first perceived in ethnic terms [3]. Elsewhere the connection was not made firmly until the period of the land war, that second decade of rural crisis which began in the late 1870s when American farm competition forced Irish landlords and tenants into a bitter and unequal struggle over declining profit margins [13-19].

'Thank God we're surrounded by water' is the refrain to a well-known Irish song. It provides a handy illustration of the Irish nation's view of its territorial limits, but its cosy certainty obscures a few facts. Those surrounded by water actually include a million who are not 'us' but 'them'. The religiously-mixed areas of Ulster – the six counties plus, before independence at least, east Donegal and parts of Cavan and Monaghan – comprise what Frank Wright (1987) called an 'ethnic frontier', just like the German-Polish, German-Czech or Italian-Yugoslav borderlands, notwithstanding the watery *cordon sanitaire* of the North Channel. Ethnic frontiers are disputed territories where general acceptance of the state's (any state's) right to a monopoly of power is disputed by one or more sections of the population. In Ulster the three main communities were defined by religion – Catholic, Episcopalian or Presbyterian – as was typical of Europe in the early modern period. Cutting across this to some extent were the common 'settler' origins of the two Protestant denominations, but the denominational differences remained of considerable political significance at least until the mid-nineteenth century [3, 11]. It required not only the Protestant denominations, but also the Protestant social classes, to come together before ethnic difference and religious sectarianism could become 'Protestant Union' [46-50]. While these two unifying trends – towards Protestant sectarian and class unity – were necessary before Unionism could emerge as a coherent political force, a disunifying trend – between southern Unionism and Ulster Unionism – was required before modern Unionism could emerge fully as an ethnic movement (indeed a kind of nationalist movement) of its own [51, 57]. Irish Unionism in the democratic age could only ever be a movement to keep Ireland within the United Kingdom; Ulster Unionism on the other hand could and did become the political face of an ethnic group, and could hope to operate effectively within either a direct rule or a devolved or an 'independent Ulster' context.

Similarly, Nationalism was made up of alliances. Firstly it was an alliance of agrarian, cross-class issues around the fudge of 'the land for the people', which only very late in the day did rural labourers, younger sons and smallholders come to realise meant 'the land for the farmers' [27, 28, 32, 109]. Secondly it was an alliance between Catholicism and secular nationalism, within which the Catholic Church gradually conceded its role of community leadership in return for an influence over the policies of politicians and the ethos of political movements which transformed the nature of nationalism [37, 40, 42, 43, 45, 155]. Many, perhaps most, Catholic priests and not a few bishops were quicker than the old men of the Irish Parliamentary Party to catch the new spirit of nationalism as it developed between 1900 and 1916.

Only since the demise of the Northern Ireland Labour Party during the troubles of the 1970s has the hope effectively been relinquished by the liberal left that socialism might end or substantially ameliorate ethnic conflict in Ireland. This is surprising, in that socialism was always a smaller and more fragile growth in Ireland than in comparable central European contexts, where social democratic parties were often quite strong in the years before the national conflagration of World War I. In the north of Ireland, where industrial trade unionism was quite vigorous at the end of the nineteenth century, socialism appeared to promise something, but achieved little so far as the main issue was concerned [60, 62, 64, 152]. In the south, James Connolly's name was honoured, but for his final sacrifice on the altar of militant nationalism rather than for his wider vision [60, 61, 63, 67, 110, 116]. If radical or leftish views advanced at all during the 1905-25 period they did so through the populism of, firstly, republican nationalists like Patrick Pearse [70], which can be traced through as far as the early years of Fianna Fáil after 1927, and secondly through the mirror images of such people on the Unionist side [55, 152]. By far the most effective and successful social radicals in Ireland in this or indeed later periods were in fact the relatively staid, late Victorian, lower middle class figures who made up the Irish Parliamentary Party, supported occasionally by renegade Unionists: between the Land League of 1879-82 and the Birrell Land Act of 1909 they made inroads into the rights of property over people in rural society which were unparalleled in industrial society [16-18, 27, 28, 32, 54].

Most of the developments discussed above derive from the social change engendered by economic change, and the changes in group outlook and political behaviour which followed from that. Chance and individual agency, however, also played a part. If the British electorate, for reasons which had nothing at all to do with Ireland, had not delivered an equally balanced House of Commons in January and again in December 1910 (a 'hung parliament', in modern parlance) then the Irish Parliamentary Party would not have held the balance of power or been able to determine the parliamentary agenda so formidably between 1910 and 1914, leaving the Government no scope for defusing Ulster Unionist resistance or for developing any compromise approach of its own. If King Edward VII had not died unexpectedly in the spring of 1910 the crisis might not have been so prolonged and the build-up of Ulster resistance not allowed such ideal circumstances in which to work towards full inflexibility [71-86].

As in continental Europe, the course of the Great War brought new elements to the development of Irish nationalism. Economically the war brought new prosperity to the farmers which made it financially possible, if not strictly necessary in manpower terms, for farmers to keep their sons at home. In the larger towns and cities, on the other hand, the rising price of foodstuffs drove down the condition of urban labourers, who turned either to the lure of the military band and the 'king's shilling' or, initially in far smaller numbers, to the Irish Volunteers and the path pointed out earlier by Connolly and Larkin [63, 67, 68]. It is surprising but true that the urban-rural factor was statistically far more important that the Nationalist-Unionist or Catholic-Protestant factor in determining who enlisted in the wartime British Army. A Shankill man was slightly more likely to enlist than a Falls man, who in turn was slightly more likely to enlist than a working-class Dublin man, but all of these urban groups were far more likely to enlist than a North Antrim man, who was in turn only slightly more likely to enlist than a Louth, Westmeath or Wexford man.

The War also brought the whole question of national identity into a sharp new focus. In peacetime a man might be a nationalist who regarded himself in principle as 'Irish' and 'not British', but who in practice was someone who had a farm or a shop to run, or a job to do and consequently little time to spare for reflecting on identity. In wartime, on the other hand, as first the recruiting sergeant and then, much more important, the rumours and then the real threats of military conscription came round, the question of Irishness or Britishness came to the forefront of many more Irish minds – it became potentially a life-or-death matter [89, 91, 93, 101, 108]. Still, far more Irish Catholics served in the wartime British Army than joined the Irish Volunteers or participated in the 1916 Rising. But senses of identity can change, or develop quite rapidly in times of great excitement, and the War of Independence of 1919-21 was carried out by many who had been 'out' in Flanders during the war, as well as those who had been 'out' in Dublin in 1916. Doubtless members of the former group sometimes had more in the way of military skills and experience to contribute than the latter [119].

In a sense Ireland drifted slowly into the War of Independence after January 1919. Certainly some Sinn Féin politicians, and many voters, expected passive resistance, direct action or an effective appeal to the peace conference to follow the election victory and the establishment of Dáil Éireann [111, 115]. Others, clearly, had their minds fixed firmly on military action from the start [112, 113]. Sustained, deep-rooted and relatively well-resourced guerrilla warfare was a new experience for an established and powerful modern state in the Europe of 1919. Lloyd George's Government and their police and military advisers had, initially at least, very little idea how to handle the unprecedented situation which unfolded before them. A considerable contribution to the success of the IRA in not losing the war of 1919-21 came from inept or brutally counter-productive security policies – admittedly sometimes cynically provoked by the IRA – on the British side [114, 117, 118, 120, 121]. It was a war which both sides gradually realised that they could not win but which, tragically, had to continue in the South until the Unionist situation in the North was sufficiently secured by new political structures to enable the slightly precarious British Coalition Government to feel that it could enter into political negotiations with 'the murder gang' without being overthrown by its own Tory backbenchers [122, 123, 127, 130].

The period surrounding the Anglo-Irish Treaty of 1921 was Lloyd George's finest Irish hour – after long years of failure which had convinced the old Nationalists of the Parliamentary Party that he was not a man who could be worked with or trusted. For De Valera, on the other hand, the Treaty issue was the beginning of a long period of inept and ineffectual political activity, from which he did not emerge until he led his new Fianna Fáil party into the Dáil in 1927 [124-126, 131]. His strategy of keeping out of the negotiations and remaining in Dublin for decisions to be referred back to him was understandable in that it arose from a recognition of two weaknesses. Firstly de Valera knew that the inflexible demand of the republican movement for a Republic was certainly unattainable through negotiation with a British Coalition Government dependent on the votes of backbench Tories who were itching for an issue on which to overthrow the Coalition. The prospects for success on the 'unity' issue were little better. Secondly there was the fact that Lloyd George and his colleagues were political negotiators of twenty years' experience at the highest level, whereas the Irish team were lawyers, journalists and organisers of guerrilla warfare. It was therefore hoped that, by staying behind, De Valera would give his team support and breathing space. In retrospect it was a piece of poor judgement, symptomatic of the problem of inexperience it was seeking to address. Inevitably the powers of decision gathered in the hands of those who were party to the negotiations, and de Valera's absence only served to weaken the team and force him into the arms of the republican absolutists [128,129, 131-133]. The fail-safe strategy of 'staging the break on Ulster' was circumvented by the device of the Boundary Commission, and the opponents of the Treaty in the Dáil had to fall back on arguing the case for full republican sovereignty, which their previous adoption of the 'break on Ulster' strategy had implicitly acknowledged to be flawed in terms of attracting international sympathy. Nonetheless the southern opponents of the Treaty persevered with this line of criticism, and opposition to the Treaty on anti-partitionist grounds was left to a solitary Northern voice in the Dáil [135].

The Civil War flowed from these earlier diplomatic failings. Great efforts were made by the divided Sinn Féiners to avert it, but to no avail. Collins tried pacificatory policies towards the North in the hope of stabilising the general situation [136]. It also seems fairly clear that he secretly encouraged and supported further IRA activities in the North in the spring of 1922, as an intended diversionary tactic for anti-treaty elements [151]. He also attempted political reconciliation with De Valera in the South [138], but in the end settled for full implementation of the Treaty agreement. This indeed brought, as all had feared, the onset of full-scale civil war, although there may have been truth in Churchill's assessment that an immediate Southern election in February 1922 might have won a strong and early verdict in favour of the Treaty from the Southern electorate, and forestalled the build-up of anti-Treaty IRA feeling [140]. On the other hand Churchill's views do no seem to have been entirely consistent on this subject [137]. Chance again became an important factor in events in August 1922, when the death of Griffith, followed only a few days later by the killing of Collins, gave fresh hope of destabilisation to the reeling anti-Treaty forces. But the longer the war dragged on, the more the atrocities multiplied, and the harder the anti-Treatyites found it to surrender [141-145]. Only after the killing of anti-Treaty military commander Liam Lynch was an effective surrender possible [145].

In the North, meanwhile atrocities continued — on both sides, although he Catholics suffered proportionately far more — from summer 1920 until summer 1922. Only the outbreak of renewed violence in the South brought Northern violence to an end. Amidst all this, the political structures of Northern Ireland were put into operation with surprising smoothness. No Nationalists participated before 1925, and the Boundary Commission indeed lent false hope to those Nationalists who still believed that partition would not actually happen — or at least would not happen to them. The difference in outlook and aspiration between east and west Ulster Nationalists, which had dogged the movement since 1916 [98], had a debilitating effect on the strategy of Northern constitutional Nationalists until it was too late to do anything effective. There is certainly a school of thought which maintains that Nationalists would have got a better deal had their politicians involved themselves in the Northern political process at a much earlier stage. On the other hand, the circumstances in which the Northern state came into existence could scarcely have provided a worse backdrop for any attempt at creating a new harmony between the communities [149-151]. Once peace returned, from 1923, it is argued by many, notably Patrick Buckland (1979) that the Unionist Government ought to have pursued a more conciliatory and inclusive policy, rather than allowing the interests of the state and the interests of the Unionist Party to become increasingly merged in their minds [153, 154]. Certainly any evidence that they tried to do so is sparse indeed. On the other hand it needs to be noted that the Unionist regime did little more than accept and operate the simplistic framework that the British Government thought it had provided — one parliament for the South/Nationalists and one parliament for the North/Unionists. In effect Lloyd George took the Ulster Unionists at their word, as the grouping who claimed to know how to deliver stability to the North, which indeed they did — not fairly, but effectively — for forty-five years. It is certainly likely, within the constitutional structure and political culture of 1920s Ulster, that the outcome of an Ulster Unionist Party which advocated liberal and conciliatory policies would not have been the implementation of those policies but the supplanting of that Party by a more populist style of Unionism. Majoritarian democracy in an ethnically-divided society, especially once it reverted to a first-past-the-post electoral system [153], became merely democracy for the majority.

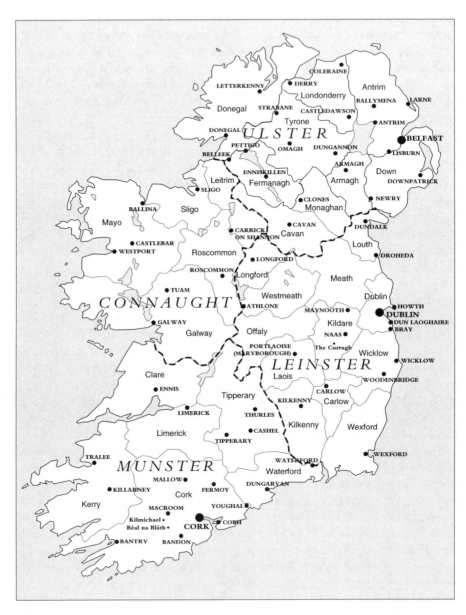

Ireland

Chapter 1
Union to rebellion

1 *Wolfe Tone: An oppressed, insulted and plundered nation*

Wolfe Tone (1763-98) was an Episcopalian by birth, and a graduate of Trinity College, Dublin. After an early career as a law student and would-be colonial adventurer in London, he returned to Dublin in 1788 to practise as a barrister. He soon became active as a political pamphleteer however, and a central figure in the Society of United Irishmen, a body committed to ending British rule in Ireland by whatever means possible. In 1796 he arrived in France, via America, to work for French involvement in an Irish uprising. He was later arrested by the British authorities after a short sea battle with a small French invading force off Donegal, and committed suicide while awaiting execution. Meanwhile a series of uncoordinated uprisings, determined but brutally anti-Protestant in Co Wexford, puny but theoretically non-sectarian in Counties Antrim and Down, had in the absence of French support been crushed with little difficulty and less mercy. These extracts from Tone's posthumously published autobiography reveal the importance to his nationalism of the ideals of the French revolution, his hopes for a revolutionary alliance between the Catholics and the Protestant Dissenters against the Established church, and at the same time his deep distrust of the Catholic clergy.

(a) Animated by their unconquerable hatred of France, which no change of circumstances could alter, the whole English nation, it may be said, retracted from their first decision in favour of the glorious and successful efforts of the French people; they sickened at the prospect of the approaching liberty and happiness of that mighty nation: they calculated, as merchants, the probable effects which the energy of regenerated France might have on their commerce ...

But matters were very different in Ireland, an oppressed, insulted, and plundered nation. As we well knew, experimentally, what it was to be enslaved, we sympathised most sincerely with the French people and watched their progress to freedom with the utmost anxiety; we had not, like England, a prejudice rooted in our very nature against France. As the Revolution advanced, and as events expanded themselves, the public spirit of Ireland rose with a rapid acceleration. The fears and animosities of the aristocracy rose in the same, or a still higher proportion. In a little time the French Revolution became the test of every man's political creed, and the nation was fairly divided into two great parties, the Aristocrats and the

Democrats (epithets borrowed from France), who have ever since been measuring each other's strength, and carrying on a kind of smothered war, which the course of events, it is highly probable, may soon call into energy and action.

It is needless, I believe, to say that I was a Democrat from the very commencement, and, as all the retainers of Government, including the sages and judges of the law, were, of course, on the other side, this gave the coup de grace to any expectations, if any such I had, of my succeeding at the bar, for I soon became pretty notorious; but, in fact, I had for some time renounced all hope, and, I may say, all desire, of succeeding in a profession which I always disliked, and which the political prostitution of its members (though otherwise men of high honour and of great personal worth) had taught me sincerely to despise.

(b) The dominion of England in Ireland had been begun and continued in the disunion of the great sects which divided the latter country. In effectuating this disunion, the Protestant [Episcopalian] party were the willing instruments, as they saw clearly that if ever the Dissenters and Catholics were to discover their true interests and, forgetting their former ruinous dissensions, were to unite cordially and make common cause, the downfall of English supremacy, and, of course, of their own unjust monopoly, would be the necessary and immediate consequence. They therefore laboured continually, and, for a long time, successfully, to keep the other two sects asunder, and the English Government had even the address to persuade the Catholics that the nonexecution of the penal laws, which were, in fact, too atrocious to be enforced in their full rigour, was owing to their clemency; that the Protestants and Dissenters, but especially the latter, were the enemies, and themselves, in effect, the protectors of the Catholic people. Under this arrangement the machine of government moved forward on carpet ground, but the time was, at length, come when this system of iniquity was to tumble in the dust, and the day of truth and reason to commence.

(c) ... Clarke then, after some civilities in reply, asked me what I thought of some of the Irish priests yet remaining in France. I answered, that he knew my opinion as to priests of all kinds; that in Ireland they had acted, all along, execrably; that they hated the very name of the French Revolution, and that I feared, and indeed was sure, that if one was sent from France, he would immediately, from the *esprit de corps*, get in touch with his brethren in Ireland, who would misrepresent everything to him ...

R Barry O'Brien (ed), *The Autobiography of Theobald Wolfe Tone* (Dublin 1893), I, 38-39, 43, 300

2 'If the rich would alleviate the sufferings of the poor ...'

The gulf between Tone's cosmopolitan world of revolutionary enlightenment and the social conditions of rural Ireland was enormous. Rapid population growth, subdivision of holdings, and an exploitative system of sub-letting, produced recurrent waves of protest in the traditional form of intimidation and secret society activity. Most movements in the south of Ireland, like the Whiteboys and the Rightboys (followers of 'Captain Right, who comes by night'), were simply agrarian. In Ulster, as we shall see, sectarian factors caused a nationalistic pattern to be imposed on this background. The Defender movement, originating in Ulster, is credited with having been the Catholic nationalist rival to the alliance of Protestant forces which became the Orange Order. Indeed, known Defender oaths contain garbled republican references – 'The French Defenders will protect our cause, and the Irish Defenders put down the British laws'. But while the Defenders' style caught the imagination of the rural poor and spread throughout Ireland, the. following extract suggests that outside the areas of mixed religion in Ulster, agrarian questions were not readily perceived in nationalistic terms, at least in the early stages of the movement. Lawrence O'Connor, a rural schoolteacher in Co Kildare, was executed in 1795 for administering a Defender's oath. His speech from the dock following sentence was reported in the contemporary press.

... He proceeded in stating substantially that the paper produced in evidence against him and which had been called an oath, was symbolical. Three words were observable in it, Love, Liberty and Loyalty, the meaning of which though well known to his fraternity was not known to their lordships, and he would explain them. By *Love* was to be understood that affection which the rich ought to show to the poor in their distress and need, but which they withheld from them; and here he animadverted with severity upon this subject. *Liberty* meant that liberty which every poor man had a right to use when oppressed by the rich, in laying before them and expostulating with them on their sufferings - but the poor man in this country had no such liberty. Here he stated several grievances the poor laboured under, as landholders refusing them land to their cottages, rackrents and particularly obliging them to take potato ground at six guineas an acre – a rent, considering the price of labour, that swallowed all their earnings and left them in debt and poverty, etc, etc. *Loyalty* he defined as meaning that union which subsisted among the poor – he would die in that loyalty – it meant that the poor who formed the fraternity to which he belonged would stand by each other. He expatiated at large upon this subject, insinuating that he died in a cause which he and many others thought a good one, and held out the admonition that the rich should immediately take such measures as would alleviate the distresses of the poor; that prosecutions were not the means of bringing about peace in the country; but if the rich would alleviate the sufferings of the poor, they would hear no more of risings or Defenders and the country would rest in peace and happiness. He denied any intention of dividing the lands – and as a last request of a dying man, he called upon the judges not to afflict him with a sudden execution, but to allow him some time to appear before his God in a state of repentance for such sins as he had committed.

Hibernian Magazine, November 1795 pp 431-33

3 The emergence of the Orange Order

The unprecedented rate of population growth in late eighteenth century Ireland put an intolerable strain on the resources of the country. In the northern parts of Co Armagh, where many small farming families had the skill and opportunity to eke out their income by the domestic spinning and weaving of linen, the rate of growth and density of habitation was higher than elsewhere. Competition for land among the Protestant descendants of seventeenth century English and Scots settlers was acute, aggravated by a growing Catholic demand for land as the enforcement of the penal laws became less strict. Just as in England and the rest of Ireland during this period, agrarian secret societies proved to be the only effective form of political organisation available to the peasantry. In north Armagh and some other parts of Ulster, bodies like the Protestant Oakboys and Peep O' Day Boys, and the Catholic Defenders, saw their situation more in ethnic sectarian than in class terms. In Co Antrim in the 1770s the Steelboys embraced both attitudes in their bitter complaint that 'some of us refusing to pay the extravagant rent demanded by our landlords have been turned out, and our lands given to Papists, who will promise any rent. Feelings similar to this were the background to the fiercely-fought 'Battle of the Diamond', near Loughgall, Co Armagh, in 1795, where the struggle for what was essentially local economic territorial ascendancy seemed to merge into the wider question of national allegiance. From the victorious Protestant side at this encounter, reinforced by Protestants of a higher social class, sprang a new and far more durable body, the Orange Order. The following narrative by Joseph Atkinson, a local justice of the peace sympathetic to the Protestant side, was recorded in a contemporary account of the battle.

For several days prior to the 21st of September, 1795, this neighbourhood was disturbed by mobs of Defenders. On the 18th they took possession of the gravel pit of Annaghmore, their number amounting to at least 500 men, and they hoisted a white flag, upon which all the good and loyal Protestants of the neighbourhood became much alarmed, and assembled on the hill of Cranagill, opposite Annaghmore. On the morning of that day a skirmish took place in the townland of Teaguy, in which there was a man killed of the name of McCann, a Defender. Some time during the day Mr Archdall Cope and his brother Robert Camden Cope, Mr Hardy, Councillor Archdall, Priests Taggart, McParland, and Traynor, came to my house, and we all went to where the Protestants were stationed on Cranagill Hill. Mr Archdall Cope and Taggart proposed to me to make the Protestants lay down their arms; in reply to which I declared they should not do so, until the others had laid down theirs first, as I considered the Protestants were entitled to carry arms, which the others were not. Upon which Taggart said, 'that they should fight it out', to which I replied, 'With all my heart'. We then rode over to where the priests' party were assembled, when a woman called out, 'There's Atkinson, the traitor'. Immediately one of the party presented his gun at me, when a woman, a tenant on my property, caught hold of the gun, and said, 'her landlord should not be shot'...

On Monday morning, the 21st, I got up at 5 o'clock, and soon after the firing commenced at the Protestant houses at the Diamond ... We did not expect this after what had occurred at my house. A number of Protestants came to me, finding they were attacked. I gave them all the ammunition I had, and set out with my family for the Fort of Charlemont, being well aware their object was to destroy my house, and all who were in it. On the road I heard the Protestants were likely to be successful, and I sent my family home and went on to Charlemont. I got Captain Killeney, and sixty invalids who were stationed there, to accompany me. When we arrived at the Diamond the battle was over.

Reprinted in: M W Dewar, J Brown,
S E Long, *Orangeism: A New Historical
Appreciation* (Belfast, 1967), pp 934

4 *Archbishop Troy: Loyalty and its rewards*

The Catholic church in late eighteenth century Ireland was concerned primarily with rebuilding an ecclesiastical structure which the Williamite period and the penal laws had destroyed. Secret societies, however their oaths might be framed, were denounced firmly by the church, as they were to be in most subsequent phases of Irish history. But senior clerics of the period, especially John Thomas Troy (1739-1823) Catholic archbishop of Dublin, were also strongly opposed to more open expressions of republican sentiment, and even to any kind of nationalist tendency at all – thus providing some justification for Tone's opinion of them. Troy's Pastoral Address of 1798 contained the usual denunciations of Whiteboyism, Defenderism, and oathtaking in general, a long account of the treatment of the continental Catholic church and the papacy by the forces of revolutionary France and, in this passage, a vision of the re-establishment of Irish Catholicism in terms entirely independent of any form of nationalism.

At present, when these kingdoms are seriously menaced with invasion by a formidable and implacable enemy, when too many may have been seduced into a persuasion, that French Republicans are our friends and allies, desirous to fraternise with us, for the sole purpose of delivering us from pretended bondage, and securing our religion and liberty, I cannot be silent, nor withhold my pastoral endeavours to warn the unreflecting, or recall to a sense of duty such as may unhappily, have become the proselytes of that dangerous delusion.

In publishing different pastoral instructions, I have been influenced by no other motive than a conscientious sense of duty, and a most sincere friendship for my beloved flock; not only without pension or other temporal emolument, but without even the expectation or desire of any; neither have I ever published or preached any doctrine at the instance or insinuation of Government ...

Compare your present situation with the past. Twenty years ago the exercise of your religion was prohibited by law; the ministers of it were proscribed; it was penal to educate Catholic youth at home or abroad; your property was insecure, at the mercy of an informer; your industry was restrained by incapacity to realise the fruits of it. At present you are emancipated from these and other penalties and disabilities, under which your forefathers, and some amongst yourselves, had laboured. You are now at liberty to profess your religion openly, and to practise the duties of it; the ministers of your religion exercise their sacred functions under the sanction of law, which authorises Catholic teachers; a College for the education of your Clergy has been erected at the recommendation of his Majesty; it is supported and endowed by parliamentary munificence; the restraints on your industry are removed, together with the incapacity to realise the fruits of it for the benefit of your posterity. What, let me ask you, has effected this favourable change – this great difference between your past and your present situation? I answer: Your loyalty, your submission to the constituted authorities, your peaceable demeanour, your patience under long sufferings ...

You will perhaps reply, that some legal disabilities still exclude the most loyal and peaceable Roman Catholics from a seat or vote in Parliament, from the privy council, from the higher and confidential civil and military departments of the State. I grant it. But, is it by rebellion, insurrection, tumult, or seditious clamour on your part, that these incapacities are to be removed? Most certainly not ...

Reprinted in: P F Moran (ed), *Spicilegium Ossoriense* (Dublin, 1884), iii, 553-9

5 Daniel O'Connell: Towards a friendly connection

The uprisings of 1798, together with Robert Emmet's tailpiece in 1803, became the basis for an enduring republican tradition. But a more immediate outcome was the Act of Union of 1801, binding Ireland to Britain in legislative union. The granting of full civil rights to Roman Catholics, promised as an accompanying measure, did not materialise. For twenty years there was little interaction between the essentially middle-class world of political protest and the crude, direct responses to material distress offered by the agrarian secret societies. Not until 1823 did a Catholic barrister, Daniel O'Connell (1775-1847), member of a gentry family from Kerry, bring together these forces in a formidable new body, the Catholic Association. Co-operating closely with the priests at local level and drawing financial strength from the 'Catholic rent', a penny a month contributed by almost a million peasants, the Association soon had the Catholic electorate sufficiently well organised to return O'Connell to Westminster by an overwhelming majority at the Clare by-election in 1828. Within a year Parliament had given way, and O'Connell was admitted as the first avowedly Catholic MP since the seventeenth century. The political energy and organisation generated by the drive for emancipation was carried on in O'Connell's new movement for repeal of the Act of Union, and so constitutional nationalism was born.

I would not ... fling British connection to the winds. I desire to retain it. I am sure that separation will not happen in my time; but I am equally sure that the connection cannot continue if you maintain the Union on its present basis. What, then, do I propose? That there should be that friendly connection between the two countries which existed before the Union. I propose it not as a resolution; but what I look for is that friendly connection by which both countries would be able to protect each other. As Ireland exported corn to England, so could England export her manufactures to Ireland – both countries would afford mutual advantage to the other. I propose that you should restore to Ireland her Parliament. We have our viceroy and our Irish peers; we only want a House of Commons, which you could place upon the same basis as your Reformed Parliament. This is the claim of Ireland upon you; this is what I ask from you. I have shown you that Ireland is entitled to an independent Legislature. I have shown you the effects of that independence. I have shown you the incompetency of the Irish Parliament to vote itself away. I have shown you that the Union was accomplished by crimes the most unparalleled. I have shown you that the terms of the Union were unjust to Ireland. I have shown you that the Union has been ruinous to us, and that some of its consequences have reverted to yourselves. I have shown you that the legislative terms of the Union were unjust. I have shown you that the Union has deprived my country of the protection of the law and the benefits of the Constitution, and that it has despoiled the people of the means of existence. I have shown you that the English labourers and artisans have suffered equally from the poverty of Ireland. I have shown you the probable consequences of continuing the Union. I have shown, or rather I have suggested, with what facility the connection could be placed on the basis of right and justice. You are unable to govern Ireland, even to your own satisfaction; for two-thirds of the time you have presided over her destinies you have ruled her, not by the powers of the law, but by undisguised despotism. You have not made Ireland prosperous, and her misery has been of no advantage to you. In the name, then, of Ireland, I call upon you to do my country justice. I call upon you to restore her national independence.

Speech to the House of Commons, 22 April 1834,
in M F Cusack (ed), *The Speeches and Public Letters
of the Liberator* (Dublin, 1875), i, 433-34

6 The Nation: a nationality of the spirit as well as the letter

O'Connell was a political organiser, a parliamentary politician and a pragmatist. For him the content of Irish nationalism lay in the redress of practical grievances – Catholic emancipation and the negative impact of the Union on Ireland's material circumstances. Young Ireland represented a different ethos and a different generation. A group of young men centred on Trinity College, Dublin – the intellectual core of the Anglo-Irish ascendancy – they were pamphleteers and propagandists rather than politicians. Mainly upper middle-class Catholics by background, they also included Protestants in their number, notably their sharpest and most eloquent writer, the poet and journalist Thomas Osborne Davis (1814-45), a Co Cork man of English and Irish parentage. Young Ireland ideas built on the non-sectarian approach of the United Irishmen, and added a high-minded romantic nationalism to the practical reformism of O'Connell. The Young Irelanders, and Davis in particular, were important not for their impact on public affairs – which was slight – but for their coherent articulation of moral regeneration through cultural nationalism. The main organ for their views was *The Nation*, a journal for which the following is the prospectus, issued on 15 October 1842. Apart from Davis, the names associated with its foundation were Charles Gavan Duffy, W J O'Neill Daunt, J C O'Callaghan, John Blake Dillon and Clarence Mangan.

The projectors of the Nation have been told that there is no room in Ireland for another Liberal journal; but they think differently. The believe that since the success of the long and gallant struggle which our fathers maintained against sectarian tendency, a NEW MIND has grown up amongst us, which longs to redress other wrongs and achieve other victories; and that this mind has found no adequate expression in the press.

The Liberal journals of Ireland were perhaps never more ably conducted than at this moment; but their tone and spirit are not of the present but of the past; – their energies are shackled by old habits, old prejudices and old divisions; and they do not and cannot keep in the van of the advancing people.

The necessities of the country seem to demand a journal able to aid and organise the new movements going on amongst us; to make their growth deeper and their fruit more 'racy of the soil'; and above all, to direct the popular mind and the sympathies of educated men of all parties to the great end of Nationality. Such a journal should be free from the quarrels, the interests, the wrongs and even the gratitude of the past. It should be free to apply its strength where it deems best; free to praise; free to censure; unshackled by sect or party.

Holding these views the projectors of The NATION cannot think that a journal prepared to undertake this work will be deemed superfluous; and as they labour not for themselves, but for their country, they are prepared, if they do not find a way open, to try if they cannot make one.

Nationality is their first great object – a Nationality which will not only raise our people from their poverty by securing to them the blessings of a DOMESTIC LEGISLATION, but inflame and purify them with a lofty and heroic love of country, – a Nationality of the spirit as well as the letter – a Nationality which may come to be stamped upon our manners, our literature, and our deeds, – a Nationality which may embrace Protestant, Catholic and Dissenter, – Milesian and Cromwellian, – the Irishmen of a hundred generations, and the stranger who is within our gates – not a Nationality which would prelude civil war, but which would establish internal union and external independence; – a Nationality which would be recognised by the world, and sanctified by wisdom, virtue and prudence.

Sir Charles Gavan Duffy, *Young Ireland: a Fragment of Irish History 1840-50* (London: 1880) p 80

7 John Mitchel: The vast brute mass of England

The repeal movement ultimately foundered on its failure to achieve the same kind of rapid results which had been won in the case of emancipation. Its decline, and O'Connell's own death, coincided with an event which was to affect the lives of Irish people in a more powerful way than any political movement had ever done. Between 1845 and 1847 rural Ireland was so devastated by potato famine as to reduce the total population by one quarter within the space of five years, and reverse the general trend of early marriage and subdivision of holdings so sharply that emigration reduced the population from eight millions to four millions by the end of the century. Young Ireland attempted to address itself to this crisis, even though its intellectual middle-class leadership had little direct experience of the problem. The movement's most militant writer, John Mitchel (1815-75), a solicitor and the son of a Presbyterian minister from Ulster, laid the blame for the famine unequivocally at England's door.

The Conquest was now consummated – England, great, populous, and wealthy, with all the resources and vast patronage of an existing government in her hands – with a magnificent army and navy – with the established course and current of commerce steadily flowing in the precise direction that suited her interests – with a powerful party on her side in Ireland itself, bound to her by lineage and by interest – and, above all, with her vast brute mass lying between us and the rest of Europe, enabling her to intercept the natural sympathies of other struggling nations, to interpret between us and the rest of mankind, and represent the troublesome sister island, exactly in the light that she wished us to be regarded – England prosperous, potent, and at peace with all the earth besides – had succeeded (to her immortal honour and glory) in anticipating and crushing out of sight the last agonies of resistance in a small, poor and divided island, which she had herself made poor and divided, carefully disarmed, almost totally defranchised, and totally deprived of the benefits of that very British 'law' against which we revolted with such loathing and horror. England had done this; and whatsoever credit and prestige, whatsoever profit and power could be gained by such a feat, she has them all.

John Mitchel, *The Last Conquest of Ireland (Perhaps)*
(Dublin, nd), p 210

8 Fintan Lalor: A people and a class

A latecomer to the Young Ireland movement was James Fintan Lalor (1807-49), member of a prosperous Protestant farming family in the Irish midlands. Though politically associated with Mitchel, Lalor differed from him in identifying not 'England' but his own Anglo-Irish landlord class as the cause of the famine and of Ireland's national degradation. In a prophetic letter to the editor of a new national journal, *The Irish Felon*, on 24 June 1848, Lalor sought to find in the land question a new and more enduring basis for the national movement.

... It is a mere question between a people and a class – between a people of eight millions and a class of eight thousand. They or we must quit this island. It is a people to be saved or lost – it is the island to be kept or surrendered. They have served us with a general writ of ejectment. Wherefore, I say, let them get a notice to quit at once, or we shall oust possession under the law of nature ... They do not now, and never did belong to this island. Tyrants and traitors have they ever been to us and ours since first they set foot on our soil. Their crime it is and not England's that Ireland stands where she does today – or rather it is our own that have borne them so long. Were they a class of the Irish people the Union could be repealed without a life lost. Had they been a class of the Irish people that Union would have never been. But for them we would now be free, prosperous and happy ... I hold and maintain that the entire soil of a country belongs of right to the people of that country, and is the rightful property not of any one class, but of the nation at large, in full effective possession, to let to whom they will on whatever tenures, terms, rents, services, and conditions they will; one condition, however, being unavoidable, and essential, the condition that the tenant shall bear full, true, and undivided fealty, and allegiance to the nation, and the laws of the nation whose lands he holds, and own no allegiance whatsoever to any other prince, power, or people, or any obligation of obedience or respect to their will, orders, or laws ... A people whose lands and lives are ... in the keeping and custody of others, instead of in their own, are not in a position of common safety. The Irish famine of '46 is example and proof. The corn crops were sufficient to feed the island. But the landlords would have their rents in spite of famine, and in defiance of fever. They took the whole harvest and left hunger to those who raised it. Had the people of Ireland been the landlords of Ireland, not a single human creature would have died of hunger, nor the failure of the potato been considered a matter of any consequence. Between the relative merits and importance of the two rights, the people's right to the land, and their right to legislation, I do not mean or wish to institute any comparison. I am far indeed from desirous to put the two rights in competition, or contrast, for I consider each alike as the natural complement of the other, necessary to its theoretical completeness, and practical efficacy. But, considering them for a moment as distinct, I do mean to assert this – that the land question contains, and the legislative question does not contain, the materials from which victory is manufactured; and that, therefore, if we be truly in earnest and determined on success, it is on the former question, and not on the latter that we must take our stand, fling out our banner, and hurl down to England our gage of battle.

Reprinted in: L Fogarty (ed), *James Finton Lalor*
(Dublin 1918), pp 59-65

9   Charles Gavan Duffy: Creatures of the imagination

The Young Ireland rising of 1848 was stimulated less by any awareness of a widespread insurrectionary feeling in the country than by the excitement of the Young Irelanders themselves at the example of revolution in continental Europe. A series of lame and uncoordinated escapades, it scarcely justified the name of rebellion at all. Many of the leaders were transported, and some later appeared on opposing sides in the American civil war. Charles Gavan Duffy (1816-1903), a Catholic from Ulster, editor of *The Nation*, was in prison facing charges of sedition at the time of the 1848 risings. He later became an MP for the shortlived Tenant Right League, before emigrating to Australia in 1855, ending a chequered career as prime minister of the state of Victoria. His later reflections on this period in Irish politics are frequently to the point, although the assessment of his own role in affairs owes much to the benefit of hindsight.

My opposition to Lalor's policy was based not on moral but strictly on political grounds. I believed it had not the slightest chance of success. His angry peasants straining to break their chains were creatures of the imagination. The actual peasants had endured the pangs of famine with scarcely a spurt of resistance. They had been taught by O'Connell that armed resistance to authority was justifiable under no circumstances; while they were perishing in every county in the island they were still taught that submission was their duty, and they submitted and died. Pauper alms carried to their homes, pauper works, which even to their eyes where worthless, further demoralised them, till the spirit of manhood was almost extinct. Mitchel had never been in Munster or seen the peasants on whom we were bid to rely, and his sincere patriotism and courage were not fortified by practical capacity or the inestimable faculty of knowing what can be accomplished ...

C Gavan Duffy, *My Life in Two Hemispheres*
(London, 1903), i, 242-3

10 Fenianism: The importance of revolutionary mythmaking

The famine did generate mass political bitterness, but its growth was slow. Its fruit was the Fenian (or Irish Revolutionary) Brotherhood, an oathbound secret society founded in 1858 along lines which owed something to the organisation of continental movements like the Italian Carbonari. Fenianism was the first in a long line of Irish nationalist movements to draw strength, especially financial strength, from the feelings of exiled Irishmen in Britain (where it was said to have penetrated the army on a large scale) and particularly in the United States. The American civil war was an added stimulus, bringing military experience to large numbers of Irish Americans. It was hoped in a vague way that such forces might find their way to Ireland. They did in fact stage an 'invasion' of Canada in 1867. In Ireland, the leaders of the movement were a group of journalists associated with *The Irish People* newspaper between 1863 and 1865, and dominated by James Stephens (1824-1901), an indefatigable travelling organiser who built a large network of nominal Fenians throughout Ireland. But the moment for a rising, if it ever existed, was missed, and the movement fizzled out with a series of bombings in England and more escapades on the Canadian border. The long-term importance of Fenianism lies in its creation of the tradition of an Irish Republic 'now virtually established', maintained by a revolutionary elite which had a broader class base than the men of 1848 and which, unlike the men of 1798, survived to hand on that tradition. In America the tradition continued to supply money and advice to Ireland, and also enjoyed reciprocal benefits with aspiring Irish American politicians. The Catholic church in Ireland denounced Fenianism more thoroughly than it had done any other nationalist manifestation since the peasant movements of the pre-union period – ostensibly because it was an oathbound movement. The church's success in maintaining this resolute position is perhaps a measure of the movement's limited popular support. This extract is believed to have been written by the novelist Charles Kickham (1828-82), later Head Centre of the reorganised IRB during its quiescent years.

Nothing would please us better than to keep clear of the vexed question of 'priests in politics' if we could do so without injury to the cause which we are endeavouring to serve. But the question was forced upon us. We saw clearly that the people should be taught to distinguish between the priest as a minister of religion and the priest as a politician before they could be got to advance one step on the road to independence. The people for whom God created it must get this island into their own hands. If they do not the fruitful land will become a grazing farm for the foreigner's cattle, and the remnant of our race wanderers and outcasts all over the world if English rule in Ireland be not struck down. Our only hope is in revolution. But most of the bishops and many of the clergy are opposed to revolution. Is it not then the duty of the Irish patriot, be he priest or layman, to teach the people that they have a right to judge for themselves in temporal matters? That is what we have done. We have over and over declared it was our wish that the people should respect and be guided by their clergy in spiritual matters. But when priests turn the altars into a platform; when it is pronounced a 'mortal sin' to read *The Irish People*, a 'mortal sin' even to wish that Ireland should be free; when priests actually call upon the people to turn informers, and openly threaten to set the police upon the track of men who are labouring in the cause for which our Fathers so often bled; when true men are reviled and slandered; when the uprooting of the people is called a 'merciful dispensation of Providence' – when, in a word, bishops and priests are doing the work of the enemy, we believe it is our duty to tell the people that bishops and priests may be bad politicians and worse Irishmen ...

The Irish People, 16 September 1865

11 Henry Cooke: The pledge of Protestant union

The early Orange Order had been predominantly Episcopalian. Irish dissenters, mainly Presbyterians, were slower than members of the Established Church to achieve that amalgamation of views on religion, nationality, and politics which has characterised Ulster since the mid-nineteenth century. But by the late 1820s the theological struggle between the conservative Presbyterian Henry Cooke (1788-1868) and the liberalism of his rival Henry Montgomery (1788-1865) was beginning to swing in favour of the former. Cooke's famous oration to Ulster Tories at Hillsborough, Co Down in October 1834, at (a) below, was the first major political articulation of the new creed of 'Protestant unity'.

By the middle of the nineteenth century, all the major denominations in Britain, Ireland, and elsewhere began to make serious efforts to proselytise the new urban masses. In Ulster this development built on Cooke's earlier reconciliation of the variety of Protestant doctrines, and coalesced with the national question in such a way as to complete the polarisation between Protestant and Catholic. The second extract is from a sermon delivered by Thomas Drew (1808-70), rector of Christchurch, Belfast, to a congregation of Orangemen on 12 July 1857.

(a) I trust I see more in this meeting than a mere eliciting of public opinion or a mere gathering of the clans. I trust I see in it the pledge of Protestant union and co-operation. Between the divided Churches I publish the banns of a second marriage of Christian forbearance where they differ, of Christian love where they agree, and of Christian co-operation in all matters where their common safety is concerned.

R M Sibbett, *Orangeism in Ireland and throughout the Empire*,
Vol ii (London 1937), p 128

(b) ... He who lives, labours, plans and gives for the prosperity of his own church alone is a narrow-minded Christian. He may be a believer; he may be, to some extent, a good Christian – a pious and generous member of some particular denomination. Let him, however, not dream of taking to himself the honoured name of Protestant. That glorious and eloquent name is reserved for those only who can rise above congregational littleness; who can unite on broad and evangelical principles against the common foe, and who look for what is good in the church of a brother, and care not to know what is uncongenial ... It is a miserable triumph to propagate rancour ... Such troubles in the camp of God's hosts will find no countenance from true Protestants. To the honour of Orangemen, they have always discouraged these internecine clamours which gladden the hearts of Rome's children and subserve the aggression of the ever-watchful Papacy ...

... Thousands have left the errors of Rome for the truth of God's word; and the greater portion of those who remain are of a class so priest-ridden, impulsive, uncertain and disloyal, as to make it wonderful that statesmen should prescribe for Ireland as if it were a Popish, and not, as its real strength, worth, industry and loyalty constitute it, a great Protestant country ... The faint-hearted clergy of the past century have to answer, to some extent, for the race of semi-infidel legislators and pro-Popery legislators which abound. It is not to be credited, if preachers had really been scriptural (and to be really Scriptural they must be really Protestant) preachers, that their flocks, especially the young, would have grown up in such deplorable deficiency of Protestant feeling and conduct ...

Transcription from: BPP 1857–58 XXIV
(Report on Riots in Belfast, 1857),
Evidence, pp 248–52

Chapter 2
Land and Politics

12 Isaac Butt: The home rule idea

In the aftermath of O'Connell's failure to achieve repeal of the Act of Union, and of the ignominious collapse of a new 'Independent' Irish Party following acceptance by its leaders of posts in the Coalition Government of 1852, party politics in Ireland reverted to a more parochial focus, with candidates normally offering themselves for election under the banner of the British parties – Whig/Liberal or Conservative. The primary factor which, in due course, brought nationalism to the fore once more were the extensions of the franchise and redistribution of seats in 1868 and 1885. But the individual responsible for re-starting the nationalist political train was the slightly improbable figure of Isaac Butt (1813-79). The son of a Co Donegal rector, Butt was a Dublin barrister and former Conservative MP who came to prominence through his court defence of several Fenians and his related presidency of the Amnesty Association. In 1870 he founded the Home Government Association, a pressure group whose ideas took such popular hold that, by 1874, more than half of Ireland's members of parliament – both Liberal and Conservative – felt moved either by conviction or by electoral pressure to declare themselves to be 'home rulers'. Butt was ageing, moderate in views, and near-bankrupt; within a few years he was to be swept aside by more militant voices. His great achievement was to articulate, in some detail, a nationalist political demand short of repeal, which many believed might be attainable through parliamentary means.

... I intend to propose a system under which England, Scotland and Ireland, united as they are under one sovereign, should have a common executive and a common national council for all purposes necessary to constitute them, to other nations, as one state, while each of them should have its own domestic parliament for its internal affairs. I say each of them because, although my immediate concern is only with Ireland, I do not suppose that if Irishmen obtain the separate management of Irish affairs it is at all likely that Englishmen or Scotchmen would consent to the management of their domestic concerns by a Parliament in which Irish members still had a voice ...

The Imperial Parliament ought plainly to be the great Council of the Empire, with which should rest the constitutional right of advising the sovereign on all questions of peace and war ... There should be an Imperial Ministry responsible to the Imperial Parliament, and that Parliament should have the power of controlling the expenditure and supplies for Imperial purposes.

The Federal arrangement which I contemplate is one which would preserve the Imperial Parliament in its present form ... It would leave it still the power of providing by Imperial taxation for Imperial necessities, including an Army and a Navy such as it judged necessary for the safety of the country, either in peace or war – imposing only a guarantee in the nature of the taxation that the levy should be one to which each member of the United Kingdom should contribute in proportion to its ability and its means.

The Irish Parliament consisting, be it always remembered, of the Queen, Lords and Commons of Ireland, would have supreme control in Ireland, except in those matters which the federal Constitution might specifically reserve to the Imperial Assembly.

That which is important is that Ireland would send, as we do now, 105 representatives to vote in an Imperial Parliament on all questions of Imperial concern, and in return we would submit, as we do now, to be taxed, but only for certain definite purposes and in a certain definite manner.

At home in Ireland we would have our own Parliament controlling all the affairs of our internal administration.

> Isaac Butt, *Home Government for Ireland,*
> *Irish Federalism: Its Meaning, its Objects and its Hopes*
> (Dublin, 1870, 4th edn 1875)

13 Michael Davitt: A Fenian retrains

Just as the Famine dispersed a wave of Irish emigrants throughout the English-speaking world, so the Fenian movement and its collapse sent forth another group, infinitely smaller in number, but retaining a degree of sustained commitment to Irish nationalism which had eluded earlier Irish revolutionaries. For some the commitment was inseparable from fruitful careers in Irish-American politics; for others it led only to long prison sentences and a subsequent life of bitterness and dependence on the charity of old colleagues. The background of Michael Davitt (1846-1906), which he describes below, was fairly typical of the revolutionaries of the Fenian generation. He lost an arm in a Lancashire mill accident at the age of eleven, and from 1870 to 1877 was imprisoned in Dartmoor following conviction for his part in a Fenian assassination plot. But his subsequent role in Irish politics was to prove very different from that of his early associates. Although Davitt's autobiography exaggerates his role in affairs generally and in particular credits him with a prescience he did not possess so far as the linking of the land and national questions was concerned, there is no doubt that he played an important linking role in 1878-9 between Irish-American nationalists of the Fenian generation and new developments which were taking place in Ireland.

... Almost my first-remembered experience of my own life and of the existence of landlordism was our eviction in 1852, when I was about five years of age. That eviction and the privations of the preceding famine years, the story of the starving peasantry of Mayo, of the deaths from hunger and the coffin-less graves on the roadside – everywhere a hole could be dug for the slaves who died because of 'God's providence' – all this was the political food seasoned with a mother's tears over unmerited sorrows and sufferings which had fed my mind in another land, a teaching which lost none of its force or directness by being imparted in the Gaelic tongue, which was almost always spoken in our Lancashire home. My first knowledge and impressions of landlordism were got in that school, with an assistant monitor of a father who had been the head of some agrarian secret society in Mayo in 1837, and who had to fly to England in that year to escape a threatened prosecution for Ribbonism.

Michael Davitt, *The Fall of Feudalism in Ireland*
(London, 1904), p 222

14 *The priest as landlord: Irishtown, 1879*

During the 1870s, developments in refrigeration and shipping exposed European farmers to serious transatlantic competition for the first time. In Ireland the general slump in agricultural prices was compounded by a series of bad harvests, so that by the end of the decade there were more grounds for concern about the situation on the land than at any time since the famine. The land war that developed was essentially a struggle between a poverty-stricken tenantry and a mortgaged landlord class over a disappearing profit margin, the penalties being destitution or emigration on the one side, bankruptcy or a reduced standard of living on the other. The landlord class, even after the restructuring of the post-famine years, was still largely Anglo-Irish. Thus when Davitt founded the Land League in 1879, to resist evictions and reduce rents, and Charles Stewart Parnell (1846-91) took up the question at parliamentary level, it was not difficult to associate the land and national questions in a way that Lalor had dreamed of thirty years before. It was an irony more apparent to historians than contemporaries that the meeting at Irishtown, Co Mayo, on 20 April 1879, which inspired the birth of the Land League, was directed against the rent levels, not of an Anglo-Irish aristocrat, but of a Catholic priest.

The Dublin press did not report the demonstration, nor even allude to it in any way. It was not held under official home rule auspices, while the fact that one of its objects was to denounce rack-renting on an estate owned by a Catholic clergyman would necessarily, at that early stage of a popular movement, frighten the timid editors of Dublin from offering it any recognition. But the local prestige won by the meeting was enormous. The speeches were fully given in the *Connaught Telegraph*. The meeting had within a few days knocked five shillings in the pound off the rentals of the estate which was singled out for attack. This news flew round the county, and requests for meetings reached the organisers from various districts. It was generally known that the active spirits in the organising of the meeting were members of the Fenian body, and on this account, but chiefly owing to the 'attack' made upon Canon Burke, many of the altars in Mayo rang with warnings and denunciations against gatherings called by 'irresponsible people' and which showed 'disrespect' towards the priests.

Michael Davitt, *The Fall of Feudalism in Ireland*
(London, 1904), p 151

15 *The new departure*

While Davitt was readjusting to the world outside Dartmoor Parnell, a Protestant Irish landlord and a member of parliament for the moderate home rule party, was the central figure among a small group of MPs who were evolving techniques for impeding the business of the House of Commons in order to publicise the nationalist cause. Parnell's arrogant, forceful style won attention not only at Westminster and in Ireland, but also amongst ex-Fenians in Irish-America who had grown up with nothing but contempt for constitutional nationalism. His strategy, in so far as one can be identified in so pragmatic a figure, was to pull together under his control as many strands of the nationalist movement as possible – the moderate home rule party (preferably with more militant personnel) and the respectable forces, clerical and lay, which underpinned it at local level; the re-emerging forces of agrarian radicalism; and the sensitive guardians of the revolutionary tradition and purse-strings in America. Although Parnell was never able to obtain formal support from the old Fenian leadership of the IRB itself, he was able to do for some years what no other constitutional leader was ever able to do – win over the mainstream of revolutionary sentiment in America, in the form of the ex-Fenian John Devoy (1842-1928) and his Clan na Gael organisation. It now seems that Devoy's original telegram to Parnell of 25 October 1878, which initiated the 'new departure in Irish politics', was based on a mistaken assumption that Parnell had broken with his moderate parliamentary associates. It is certainly clear that at a subsequent meeting in Dublin Parnell did not in fact promise what Devoy thought he had promised. But the new link held out more real hope of achievement for Irish nationalism than any previous movement had done.

Nationalists here will support you on the following conditions:

First. Abandonment of the Federal demand and substitution of a general declaration in favour of self-government.

Second. Vigorous agitation of the Land Question on the basis of a peasant proprietary, while accepting concessions tending to abolish arbitrary evictions.

Third. Exclusion of all sectarian issues from the platform.

Fourth. Irish members to vote together on all Imperial and Home Rule questions, adopt an aggressive policy and energetically resist coercive legislation.

Fifth. Advocacy of all struggling nationalities in the British Empire and elsewhere.

New York Herald, 26 October 1878

16 Charles Stewart Parnell: The leper of old

For Parnell, agrarian radicalism appeared at the ideal moment; it provided a burning material issue to stimulate grass-roots organisation, and cut the ground from beneath the feet of his moderate opponents in the home rule party. At the same time it provided a rationale and method of agitation in the countryside which captured the imagination of the revolutionary elements at home and abroad. When the National Land League came into being on 21 October 1879, Parnell was its president. His speeches during the following five years transferred the determination and intransigence which had characterised the campaign of disruption in the House of Commons onto the larger canvas of rural Ireland. In a speech at Ennis, Co Clare in 1880, typical of a number he delivered in Ireland during this phase of his career, he gave support to the techniques of boycotting which had been developed against obnoxious landlords and 'blackleg' tenants.

Depend upon it that the measure of the Land Bill of next session will be the measure of your activity and energy this winter. It will be the measure of your determination not to pay unjust rents; it will be the measure of your determination to keep a firm grip of your homesteads; it will be the measure of your determination not to bid for farms from which others have been evicted, and to use the strong force of public opinion to deter any unjust men amongst yourselves and there are many such, from bidding for such farms. If you refuse to pay unjust rents; if you refuse to take farms from which others have been evicted, the land question must be settled, and settled in a way that will be satisfying to you. It depends therefore, upon yourselves, and not upon any Commission or any Government. When you have made this question ripe for settlement, then and not till then will it be settled ... Now, what are you to do to a tenant who bids for a farm from which another tenant has been evicted? I think I heard somebody say shoot him. I wish to point out to you a very much better way, a more Christian and charitable way, which will give the lost sinner an opportunity of repenting. When a man takes a farm from which another has been evicted, you must shun him on the roadside when you meet him, you must shun him in the streets of the town, you must shun him in the shop, you must shun him on the fairgreen and in the market place, and even in the place of worship, by leaving him alone, by putting him into a moral Coventry, by isolating him from the rest of his country, as if he were the leper of old, you must show him your detestation of the crime he has committed ...

The Times, 20 September 1880

17 The rule of the Land League

The Land League alarmed government and landlords because it possessed the strength, unity and techniques of a militant trade union, supported by a nightly campaign of terror which was no doubt carried out from within its membership, but was not under its official aegis. Its organisation could be suppressed, but the spirit of united resistance which it engendered could only be deflated by substantive concessions. During 1880 it became clear that W E Gladstone's newly-elected Liberal government would tackle the Irish land question on the basis of what was called dual ownership, or the 'three Fs' – fair rent for the tenant as set by a land court, free sale by the departing tenant of improvements he had made to his property, and fixity of tenure. This was likely to satisfy the more moderate elements and so split the united front, without either restructuring Irish land tenure in the way that agrarian radicals wanted, or carrying the national question any further forward. Davitt's report to Devoy, though clearly angled so as to retain the support of a secret revolutionary for an open, semi-constitutional movement, conveys a fair impression of the Land League at its height. Note that 'Nationalist' here is used not in the usual sense but as a code name for the IRB.

Michael Davitt to John Devoy   16 December 1880

It would take me a week to give you anything like an account of immense growth and power of the L.L. It now virtually rules the country ... The income of the League is now about £100 a day. *Nearly all of which comes in from Irish branches.* Our expenditure is enormous as we are sparing no money in the work of organisation, boycotting, relief to evicted people, legal fights with landlords, etc. Land League Courts are being established everywhere in which the affairs of the district are adjudicated. The London Press declares that all the League has got to do now, in order to have the complete government of the country in its hands, is to issue a League currency. You would be astonished to find the class of men who are now joining us inside a movement with which I am connected. There is a danger, however, of this class and the Priests coalescing by and by, and ousting the advanced men or gaining control of the whole thing and turning it against us. I am taking every precaution, however, against this Whig dodge.

The landlords are scaring old Forster [Chief Secretary for Ireland] with stories of an intended Rising, importation of arms, etc., in order to have the League squelched. I am necessitated, therefore, to take a conservative stand in order to stave off coercion, for if the H.C. [Habeas Corpus] is suspended the whole movement would be crushed in a month and universal confusion would reign. These damned petty little outrages are magnified by the Tory organs, copied into the English Press and play the devil with us on outside public opinion. The Government Land Bill is certain to be on the line of the three Fs. This, of course, will not be enough, but it will satisfy a great number inside the League, and be accepted by the Bishops and the Priests almost to a man. I anticipate a serious split in the League when the Government measure comes out ... If we could carry on this Movement for another year without being interfered with we could do almost anything we pleased in the country. The courage of the people is magnificent. *All classes are purchasing Arms openly* ... The Government does not know what to do in the presence of such a state of affairs as we have created, and all our former enemies – Nationalist [IRB] Leaders excepted – are silenced and subdued before the enormous power at our back ... This is something like an outline of the situation at the present moment. All we want is to be left alone for a few months longer by the Government *and the Nationalists* [IRB], and we will have Ireland in such a state of organisation as she never was in before.

W O'Brien & D Ryan (eds) *Devoy's Post Bag*
(1948), ii, 22-24

18 'No Rent': The passive resistance of an entire population

The Land Act of 1881, as expected, embodied the principle of dual ownership. It was accompanied by a Coercion Act to suppress further agitation. Parnell and the League were in a quandary, for there was no doubt that the Land Act, whatever its deficiencies as a radical measure, was likely to bring about substantial rent reductions for many thousands of League supporters. But accepting the act implied a collapse of the Parnellite alliance. The policy was thus devised of 'testing the act', of holding back the mass of tenants while the Land League put forward a small number of selected cases in order to discern the land court's likely attitude. It was a procrastinating policy, likely to collapse with the passage of time if it did not give way earlier in the face of militant ex-Fenians and agrarian radicals on the one side, and tenants anxious to submit their own cases to the court, regardless of politics, on the other. Parnell's tone became more militant during the course of the year, and he was almost certainly relieved by the cabinet's decision to imprison him under the Coercion Act in October 1881. But the 'No Rent Manifesto', which his followers immediately brought forward, was endorsed by him without conviction, and proved more important as a rallying call to a disintegrating nationalist coalition than as a mechanism for disrupting the Land Act.

Fellow countrymen! The hour to try your souls and to redeem your pledges has arrived. The executive of the National Land League, forced to abandon the policy of testing the land act, feels bound to advise the tenant farmers of Ireland from this day forth to pay no rents under any circumstances to their landlords until the government relinquishes the existing system of terrorism and restores the constitutional rights of the people. Do not be daunted by the removal of your leaders. Your fathers abolished tithes by the same method without any leaders at all, and with scarcely a shadow of the magnificent organisation that covers every portion of Ireland today. Do not suffer yourselves to be intimidated by threats of military violence. It is as lawful to refuse to pay rents as it is to receive them. Against the passive resistance of an entire population military power has no weapons. Do not be wheedled into compromise of any sort by the dread of eviction. If you only act together in the spirit to which, within the last two years, you have countless times solemnly pledged your vows, they can no more evict a whole nation than they can imprison them. The funds of the National Land League will be poured out unstintedly for the support of all who may endure eviction in the course of the struggle.

Our exiled brothers in America may be relied upon to contribute, if necessary, as many millions of money as they have contributed thousands to starve out landlordism and bring English tyranny to its knees. You have only to show that you are not unworthy of their boundless sacrifices in your cause. No power on earth except faint-heartedness on your own part can defeat you. Landlordism is already staggering under the blows which you have dealt it amid the applause of the world. One more crowning struggle for your land, your homes, your lives – a struggle in which you have all the memories of your race, all the hopes of your children, all the sacrifices of your imprisoned brothers, all your cravings for rent-enfranchised land, for happy homes and national freedom to inspire you – one more heroic effort to destroy landlordism at the very source and fount of its existence, and the system which was and is the curse of your race and of your existence will have disappeared forever. The world is watching to see whether all your splendid hopes and noble courage will crumble away at the first threat of a cowardly tyranny. You have to choose between throwing yourselves upon the mercy of England and taking your stand by the organisation which has once before proved too strong for English despotism; you have to choose between all powerful unity and impotent disorganisation; between the land for the landlords and the land for the people. We cannot doubt your choice. Every tenant-farmer of Ireland is today the standard-bearer of the flag unfurled at Irishtown, and can bear it to a glorious victory. Stand together in the face of the brutal and cowardly enemies of your race. Pay no rents under any pretext. Stand passively, firmly, fearlessly by while the armies of England may be engaged in their hopeless struggle against a spirit which their weapons cannot touch. Act for yourselves if you are deprived of the counsels of those who have shown you how to act. No power of legalised violence can extort one penny from your purses against your will. If you are evicted, you shall not suffer; the landlord who evicts will be a ruined pauper, and the government which supports him with its bayonets will learn in a single winter how power-less is armed force against the will of a united, determined, and self-reliant nation.

Signed CHARLES S. PARNELL, President, Kilmainham Jail; MICHAEL DAVITT, Hon. Sec., Portland Prison; THOMAS BRENNAN, Hon. Sec., Kilmainham Jail; JOHN DILLON, Head Organiser, Kilmainham Jail; THOMAS SEXTON, Head Organiser, Kilmainham Jail; PATRICK EGAN, Treasurer, Paris.

Reprinted in: Michael Davitt, *The Fall of Feudalism in Ireland* (London, 1904) pp 335-7

19 Parnell and the march of a nation

When Parnell emerged from prison in the spring of 1882 it was under the terms of a 'Kilmainham Treaty' with the government whereby he undertook to cease resistance to the Land Act (which the government in turn agreed to amend in the interests of tenants with long arrears of rent and those with leases) and to cooperate with the Liberals in a broad programme of reform in Ireland. Henceforward his policy was increasingly one of open constitutionalism. If the three-sided alliance of revolutionaries, parliamentarians and agrarians had effectively broken up, it was nonetheless clear that a good proportion of grass-roots attracted initially by the alliance remained adhering to the parliamentarian centre after the final breach. Parnell had got from militant agrarianism the stature to take advantage of the next great development, the Representation of the People Act, 1884. This enfranchised the bulk of the Irish peasantry who, in 1886, swept Parnell at the head of a united, militant home rule party to the centre of the parliamentary stage with 85 out of 103 Irish MPs and one from Liverpool. The election victory of the "86 of 86" had destroyed the Irish Liberal party, the moderate home rulers, and the entire power of Irish Unionism outside Ulster. At Westminster they now constituted a large and cohesive group, with reasonable hopes of winning the balance of power often enough to command the attention of the English parties. An Irish republic might not emerge from an English parliament, but as Parnell explained at Cork on 21 January 1885, the possibility of a halfway house emerging by constitutional means was no longer the remote dream it had been in O'Connell's time.

I go back from the consideration of these questions to the consideration of the great question of National self-government for Ireland. I do not know how this great question will be eventually settled. I do not know whether England will be wise in time and concede to constitutional arguments and methods the restitution of that which was stolen from us towards the close of the last century. It is given to none of us to forecast the future, and just as it is impossible for us to say in what way or by what means the National question may be settled, in what way full justice may be done in Ireland, so it cannot ask for less than restitution of Grattan's Parliament, with its important privileges and wide and far-reaching constitution. We cannot under the British Constitution ask for more than the restitution of Grattan's Parliament, but no man has the right to fix the boundary to the march of a nation. No man has a right to say to his country 'Thus far shalt thou go and no further', and we have never attempted to fix the *ne plus ultra* to the progress of Ireland's nationhood, and we never shall.

The Times, 22 January 1885

20 Gladstone: An Irish motor muscle and imperial patriotism

The first Home Rule Bill was introduced by Liberal prime minister, W E Gladstone (1809-98) on 8 April 1886. But he had already lost the support of the Whig group within his party, and when the full scope of the bill became clear he also lost the backing of Joseph

Chamberlain's radical group. The Bill was defeated on its second reading in the House of Commons by 341 votes to 311 and Gladstone's government resigned. The weakened Liberal party remained in opposition for seventeen of the following twenty years. Gladstone introduced a second Home Rule Bill in 1893, which passed the Commons but was roundly defeated in the Lords by 419 votes to 41. Home rule was no nearer, but the Liberal party's commitment to it after 1886 forged a 'union of hearts' with Parnell and his successors which survived until the first world war. The prolonged association between the two parties produced a modified style of nationalism and a new view of Irish nationality, foreshadowed by Gladstone himself in his speech introducing the 1886 Bill.

We are not called upon to constitute another Co-ordinate Legislature. While I think it is right to modify the Union in some particulars, we are not about to prepare its repeal. A supreme statutory authority of the Imperial Parliament over Great Britain, Scotland, and Ireland, as one United Kingdom, was established by the Act of Union. That supreme statutory authority it is not asked, as far as I am aware, and it is certainly not intended, in the slightest degree to impair.

There are those who say, 'Let us abolish the Castle'; and I think that gentlemen of very high authority, who are strongly opposed to giving Ireland a domestic legislature, have said nevertheless that they think that there might be a general reconstruction of the administrative government in Ireland. Well, sir, I have considered that question much, and what I want to know is this how, without a change in the legislature, without giving to Ireland a domestic legislature, there is to be, or there ever can possibly be, a reconstruction of the Administration ...The fault of the administrative system of Ireland, if it has a fault, is simply this – that its spring and source of action, or, if I can use an anatomical illustration without a blunder, what is called the motor muscle is English and not Irish. Without providing a domestic legislature for Ireland, without having an Irish Parliament, I want to know how you will bring about this wonderful, superhuman, and I believe, in this condition impossible result that your administrative system shall be Irish and not English ... Well, sir, what we seek is the settlement of that question; and we think that we find that settlement in the establishment by the authority of Parliament, of a legislative body sitting in Dublin for the conduct of both legislation and administration under the conditions which may be prescribed by the Act defining Irish, as distinct from Imperial affairs. There is the head and front of our offending ... I cannot conceal the conviction that the voice of Ireland, as a whole, is at this moment clearly and constitutionally spoken. I cannot say it is otherwise when five-sixths of its lawfully chosen representatives are of one mind in this matter. There is a counter voice; and I wish to know what is the claim of those by whom that counter voice is spoken, and how much is the scope and allowance we can give them. Certainly, sir I cannot allow it to be said that a Protestant minority in Ulster, or elsewhere is to rule the question at large for Ireland. I am aware of no constitutional doctrine tolerable on which such a conclusion could be adopted or justified. But I think that the Protestant minority should have its wishes considered to the utmost practicable extent in any form which they may assume ...

We stand face to face with what is termed Irish nationality. Irish nationality vents itself in the demand for local autonomy or separate and complete self-government in Irish, not in Imperial affairs. Is that an evil in itself? Is it a thing that we should view with horror or apprehension? Is it a thing which we ought to reject or accept only with a wry face, or ought we to wait until some painful and sad necessity is incumbent upon the country, like the necessity of 1780 or of 1793? Sir, I hold that it is not, ... I do not believe that local patriotism is an evil. I believe it is stronger in Ireland even than in Scotland. Englishmen are eminently English, Scotchmen are profoundly Scotch, and if I read Irish history aright, misfortune and calamity have wedded her sons to her soil . The Irishman is profoundly Irish, but it does not follow that because his local patriotism is keen he is incapable of Imperial patriotism. There are two modes of presenting the subject. The one is to present what we now recommend as Good, and the other to recommend it as a choice of Evils. Well, sir, I have argued the matter as if it were a choice of evils; I have recognised as facts entitled to attention the jealousies which I do not share or feel ... But in my heart I cherish the hope that this is not merely the choice of the lesser evil, but may prove to be rather a good in itself ...

H C Deb 3rd series, vol 304, cols 1049-83
(8 April 1886)

21 Lord Randolph Churchill: Ulster will fight and Ulster will be right

By the end of 1885 Gladstone had announced his conversion to the home rule cause. The return of Parnell to Westminster with the balance of power in his hands appeared to confirm the shrewdness of Gladstone's vision. This decision was shortly to bring about a realignment of the British party system along pro- and anti-home rule lines. Ambitious maverick politicians on both sides, who is 1884 had been exploring possible compromises to neutralise Parnell and take the Irish issue out of the front line of British politics, quickly retreated behind party lines. In particular the Conservative prime ministerial hopeful, Lord Randolph Churchill (1849-95), whose private political dealings had hinted at a very flexible approach to Irish constitutional matters, decided to 'play the Orange card' and, in a remarkable speech at the Ulster Hall on 22 February 1886 began the alliance between British Conservatives and Ulster Unionists which continued until Edward Heath's government dissolved the Stormont Parliament in 1972.

... All Mr Gladstone's policy ... since 1880 has been a policy of concession to the party of Mr Parnell, to weaken the power of the Loyalists and to strengthen that of the disloyal party ... England has heard of nothing else but the Nationalists or Separatists of Ireland. The attention of Parliament has been concentrated upon their action and the time of Parliament has been monopolised by their proceedings in the struggle that has been going on. The Loyalists have lost much of their parliamentary influence. All the corporations, the municipal bodies, and the local boards of guardians out[side] of Ulster have fallen into the hands of the enemy, and in these bodies the Loyalists have scarcely any longer any representation ...

... Mr Gladstone, inflated by all his previous triumphs over you, and believing ... that the Orange Party is played out, has come to the conclusion that the Loyalists of Ireland, to use a vulgar expression, have not got a kick left in them ... There is a general disbelief in England as to the power of resistance which the Loyalists of Ireland would offer to a policy of repeal ...

... You are, gentlemen I believe, in this great crisis the first line of defence, the second line of defence and the last line of defence. With you it primarily rests whether Ireland shall remain an integral part of this great Empire, sharing in all its glory, partaking of all its strengths, benefiting by all its wealth, and helping to maintain its burdens ... If we cannot hold Ireland why obviously we cannot hold India ...

... The forces which Mr Parnell directs emanate from the basest prejudices of class and sect − forces which are kept together by means of appeals to covetousness and greed, and by terms held out to them of the acquisition of property by plunder, violence and fraud ... [They] ... are brought into effect by the most extraordinary system of organised intimidation which history can record ... There are other forces which I do not say Mr Parnell directly controls or with the exercise of which I do not say he is in any way personally connected. But there are nevertheless forces for the exercise of which he must be content to bear a large responsibility. Those forces are bred by foreign agencies and nourished by foreign gold − forces that act by murder by assassination and by dynamite − forces which terrorise the peasantry ...

... I appeal to the loyal Catholics of Ireland to show which side they are on ... but I say that in these times no practical politician can be content with mere negative support of any kind. He that is not with us is against us (cheers) and I have a right to call on those loyal Catholics whose existence we know of ... to stand forth publicly ... [and] ... to declare in favour of that legislative Union ... If this appeal ... should fall upon deaf ears ... I would not hesitate in such untoward circumstances to confide all my hope in the salvation of the nation and the security of the United Kingdom to the efforts of the Protestants in Ireland (loud cheers) and especially to the efforts of the

Protestants of Ulster (renewed cheering). For nearly 200 years ... your cry has been 'No Surrender' (cheers) ... Now is the time for you to show whether all those ceremonies and forms which are practised in the Orange Lodges are really living forms or only idle and meaningless ceremonies ...

I believe myself very confidently that this storm will blow over (hear, hear), and I think that the vessel of the Union will emerge with her Loyalist crew stronger than before; but it is right and useful that I should add that if the struggle should continue, and if my conclusions should turn out to be wrong, then I am of opinion that the struggle is not likely to remain within the lines of what we are accustomed to look upon as constitutional action. No portentous change such as the repeal of the Union, no change so gigantic, could be accomplished by the mere passing of a law. The history of the United States will teach us a different lesson, and if it should turn out that the Parliament of the United Kingdom was so recreant from all its high duties, and that the British nation was so apostate to its traditions of honour and courage as to hand over the Loyalists of Ireland to the domination of an Assembly in Dublin, which must essentially be to them a foreign and an alien assembly ... I do not hesitate to say ... that in that dark hour there will not be wanting to you those who on all hands in England are willing to cast in their lot with you, and who, whatever the result may be, will share your fortunes and your fate ...

The Times, 23 February 1886

22 Belfast 1886: The battle-lines drawn

The early development of segregated Catholic and Protestant working-class districts in Belfast was greatly intensified by the waves of sectarian rioting which became a regular feature of the city. The one-day clashes associated with 12 July or with election contests which characterised the first half of the nineteenth century gave way to periodic outbursts which remained uncontrolled for weeks on end, beginning in 1857. After a further summer of violence in 1864 the Government moved to disband the undertrained (and almost exclusively Protestant) Town Police force and bring in the all-Ireland Royal Irish Constabulary, which was mixed in religion. But the provision of a more fully professional police force seemed to make little impact on the situation. There were further serious riots in 1872, and in 1886 came the worst outbreak to date, lasting intermittently from May until September, with 32 killed and 371 injured. The occasion was the introduction and prompt defeat of the Liberal government's Home Rule Bill.

... Belfast is a great manufacturing town, which in progress and wealth enjoys a foremost place among the centres of population of the United Kingdom. Its population in 1881, according to the Census returns, was 208,122, and since that time has probably increased to about 230,000. It has an area of 6,805 acres, and a valuation of £604,537 ...

The town is, in its present proportions, of very recent growth; and the result is that the poorer classes, instead of, as in other cities, occupying tenements in large houses, reside mainly in separate quarters, each of which is almost entirely given up to persons of one particular faith, and the boundaries of which are sharply defined. In the district of West Belfast, the great thoroughfare of Shankill Road, with the network of streets running into it, and the side streets connecting those lateral branches, is an almost purely Protestant district; and the parties referred to in the evidence as 'the Shankill mob', are a Protestant mob. The great Catholic quarter is due south of the Shankill district, and consists of the thoroughfare known as the Falls Road, and the streets running south of it; and the parties referred to in the testimony before us as the 'Falls Road mob', are therefore a Catholic mob. Due south of the Falls district is Grosvenor Street; almost entirely inhabited by Protestants, so that the Catholic quarter lies between two Protestant districts. The Shankill Road and Falls Road are both largely inhabited by shopkeepers who supply the wants of the population, and whose houses are sometimes large and comfortable. The streets running off these thoroughfares consist of long rows of cottages of artisans and labourers. The great points of danger to the peace of the town are open spaces in the border land between the two quarters; and two of these spaces – the Brickfields and Springfield – will be found to have been the theatres of some of the worst scenes of the riots.

The great number of working people who dwell in the districts we have described are, at ordinary times, a most peaceable and industrious community. But unfortunately a spirit has grown up amongst these people, which has resulted in that, on three previous occasions within the last thirty years, in 1857, 1864, and 1872, the town was the scene of disturbances and long-continued riots.

[In 1886] ... a main cause of the prolonged continuance of the disturbances was the wild and unreasoning hostility exhibited by large section of the Protestants of Belfast against the police.

It was an expression of the extraordinary belief which so largely prevailed amongst Belfast Protestants – a belief that the late [Liberal] Government of the Queen was packing the town of Belfast with Catholic policemen, carefully selected from certain southern counties, and charged with the duty of shooting down the Protestants. There can be no doubt that this belief was honestly held by large sections of the humbler Protestants in Belfast, and was the secret of the bitter hostility shown against the Royal Irish Constabulary.

We are sorry to add that certain persons having great influence in Belfast, thought proper, at various periods during the riots, to indulge in language, written and spoken, well calculated to maintain excitement at a time when all men of influence should have tried to assuage it. We feel it our duty to draw special attention to a letter of the 4th day of August, 1886, written by Mr De Cobain, Member of Parliament for one of the divisions of the town – a letter the publication of which the Mayor of Belfast most properly brought under the notice of the Government. Another cause of the continuance of the riots was the unhappy sympathy with which, at certain stages, the well-to-do classes of Protestants regarded the proceedings of the rioters. At one stage of the riots it seemed as if the greater part of the population of the Shankill district united against the police. This is the more to be regretted as it was on all sides admitted that no more valuable aid could have been given to the police than that afforded by respectable and influential people of the localities in which the troubles arose.

Some few witnesses appeared to think that it was desirable to organise a kind of vigilance committee consisting of respectable men acting solely in their own localities and among their own co-religionists. Such proposals are more specious than feasible, and the efforts of many of the peacemakers in Belfast during the riots did more harm than good. At the same time we direct attention to the evidence of Mr Combe (of the [engineering] firm of Combe, Barber, and Combe), which shows plainly that in large works it is perfectly possible to make such arrangements as will tend to keep order among the workmen, and to prevent religious difficulties interfering with the earning of a livelihood. We regretted to find that in some other large works no effort was made to check cruelty and intolerance, and that in one, the workmen freely carried away large numbers of iron bolts and nuts, which they and others afterwards used in the riots; nor was any effort made to check such misconduct ...

BPP 1887 XVIII *(Report of the Belfast Riot Commissioners)*, Report, p 4, 16-19

23 *The Galway election 1886: Swallowing O'Shea*

If one resilient strand in the Conservative and Unionist armoury of opposition to home rule was the strength of feeling in Protestant Ulster, a second was the series of attempts – ultimately successful – to weaken the Nationalist party by undermining the reputation of its leader. Parnell was especially vulnerable to such attack because since late 1880 he had been the lover of Katharine O'Shea (1845-1921), with whom he had three children by 1884. She was the wife of Capt W H O'Shea (1840-1905) and, though they were in practice long-estranged, the formalities were preserved to such an extent that O'Shea could later claim in court (credibly rather than truthfully) that he was for many years unaware of his wife's relationship with Parnell. O'Shea was a Dubliner of upper middle-class Catholic background, a high-living adventurer who entered Parliament for Co Clare in 1880. In that year his vote helped to elect Parnell as party leader, but he seems never to have been more than a nominal home ruler.

O'Shea did not adhere to the party's pledge to 'sit, act and vote' with the Irish Party, and in 1885 he sought unsuccessfully to return to Parliament for Liverpool as a Liberal. It is not known precisely when O'Shea became aware of his wife's relationship with Parnell, or how he viewed the situation. Both he and Katharine were heavily dependent on her elderly 'Aunt Ben' for financial support, which made divorce an unattractive means of escape. In February 1886 Parnell, notwithstanding O'Shea's record of disloyalty in the previous parliament, and in the teeth of opposition from his own colleagues, nominated him as the Irish Party candidate at a by-election in Galway City. O'Shea's return to Parliament was short-lived, ending at the dissolution in June 1886, but it was clear that Parnell had mortgaged his political future.

William O'Brien MP to John Dillon MP   Galway, 7 February 1886

...Your feelings and ours about O'Shea are, of course, the same – loathing. So is our feeling about the infamous way in which Parnell has put him forward and slighted the party. The question was, in the special circumstances of the moment, whether we should swallow O'Shea or utterly destroy our movement and party at its brightest moment for a personal reason which we could not even explain. It was a most bitter and scandalous alternative, but it seemed to us an alternative between accepting an odious personality and chaos. We were all thoroughly in favour of terrorising Parnell by every means short of public scandal; but when he had committed himself by the announcement in the *Freeman* and the letter he gave O'Shea, it became a question as to whether, if defeated by members of his own party, it would be possible for him to continue [as] leader.

... We pressed Parnell by all possible means short of open revolt, but his answer was emphatic and he is plainly bound by some influence he cannot resist ... It is a terrible pass but I think we cannot hesitate. Posterity would execrate us for wrecking this movement at such a moment for so miserable a cause.

cited in T W Moody (ed) 'Parnell and the
Galway Election of 1886', in *Irish Historical Studies*
no 35 (March 1955), p 327

24 Parnellism and crime: The Pigott forgeries

After 1886 Parnell's leadership of the Irish party became more spasmodic. He lived mostly with Mrs O'Shea at her home on the outskirts of London and gave no encouragement at all to the new agrarian 'Plan of Campaign' which his lieutenants had developed to force down rents, preferring to press the home rule case entirely through parliamentary links with the Liberal opposition. Early in 1887 the pro-Unionist *Times* newspaper, with discreet help from the Conservative government, began what today would be called a 'dirty tricks campaign' to discredit him through evidence of past association with terrorist movements. A series of articles on 'Parnellism and Crime' culminated in the publication of a facsimile letter bearing his signature. The letter appeared to confirm Parnell's support for the Phoenix Park murders of 1882 in which the new Chief Secretary for Ireland, Lord Frederick Cavendish, and his permanent under secretary T H Burke had been stabbed to death in Dublin by a republican gang. A special parliamentary commission was set up by the Conservative government to examine the allegations, but the case collapsed in 1889 when a Dublin journalist, Richard Pigott (c1828-1889) confessed to the forgeries in the witness box and subsequently committed suicide.

In concluding our series of articles on 'Parnellism and Crime' we intimated that, besides the damning facts which we there recorded, unpublished evidence existed which would bind still closer the links between the 'constitutional' chiefs and the contrivers of murder and outrage. In view of the unblushing denials of Mr Sexton and Mr Healy [Nationalist MPs] on Friday night, we do not think it right to withhold any longer from public knowledge the fact that we possess and have had in our custody for some time documentary evidence which has a most serious bearing on the Parnellite conspiracy, and which, after a most careful and minute scrutiny is, we are satisfied, quite authentic. We produce one document in facsimile today by a process the accuracy of which cannot be impugned, and we invite Mr Parnell to explain how his signature has become attached to such a letter.

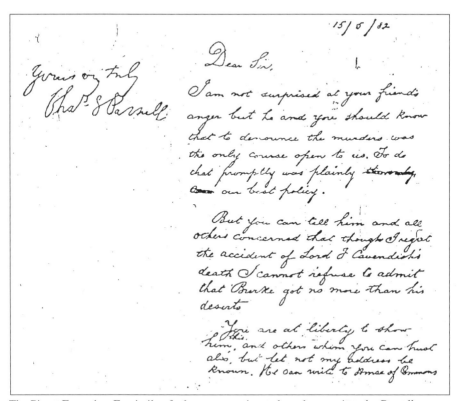

The Pigott Forgeries: Facsimile of a letter purporting to have been written by Parnell, reproduced in *The Times*, 18 April 1887.

It is requisite to point out that the body of the manuscript is apparently not in Mr Parnell's handwriting, but the signature and the 'Yours very truly' unquestionably are so ...

The body of the letter occupies the whole of the first page of an ordinary sheet of stout white notepaper, leaving no room in the same page for the signature, which is placed on the fourth page near the top right hand corner. It was an obvious precaution to sign upon the back instead of upon the second page, so that the half-sheet might if necessary be torn off, and the letter disclaimed.

It is right and necessary to explain that the 'Dear Sir' is believed to be [Patrick] Egan [treasurer of the Land League] and that the letter was addressed to him in order to pacify the wrath of his subordinate instruments in the Phoenix Park murders ...

The Times, 18 April 1887

25 English wolves, Irish bishops, and the fall of Parnell

Parnell's vindication in the matter of *The Times* forgeries was offset within the space of a few months when Capt O'Shea filed for divorce, naming Parnell. Parnell had no defence, and did not offer one. He and Mrs O'Shea were later married. The lodging of O'Shea's suit, after years of apparent complaisance, was inspired by a complex mixture of political and pecuniary motives: Mrs O'Shea had at last inherited her long-awaited fortune on the death of 'Aunt Ben' in 1889, while the divorce suit offered an alternative means of discrediting Parnell following the Pigott debacle.

The immediate political outcome of the divorce verdict was a denunciation by Gladstone, in December 1890, of the continued leadership of the Irish party by a convicted adulterer, and Parnell's subsequent refusal to bow to the majority view of his colleagues and step down. Debate revolved initially around the question of whether an English political leader should be permitted to impinge upon the 'independent opposition' of the Irish party or whether, on the other hand, the cause of home rule should be jeopardised for the sake of one man's career. But when the struggle was carried from Westminster to a bitter series of by-elections in Ireland, the main appeal of the anti-Parnellites was to the Catholic clergy, who endorsed them wholeheartedly. Parnell, meanwhile, appeared to reverse his political direction entirely, turning back once more to the revolutionary tradition for support. How he would have resolved his position was never put to the test, for he died, aged only forty five, in October 1891. These two extracts are from manifestos issued during the North Kilkenny by-election of December 1890 although the first, issued by independent supporters of Parnell, was repudiated by him.

(a) Men of the Hillsides, Gather in your thousands to support the leader of your race, Charles Stewart Parnell MP. What Englishman shall dare to tell you who shall be your chief or what shall be the method of your warfare? We have fought for liberty in defiance of England. We have advanced along the path of freedom in spite of England's fraud and force. In the past we have succeeded because we have trusted ourselves alone. In the future we shall succeed by fighting along the same lines, by defying the English dictation, by acting with the spirit and the resolution of the self-respecting nation. Shall the radicals of England choose your leader? Men of the hillsides, will you, the countrymen of Grattan and the volunteers of O'Connell, Davis and Wolfe Tone, of gallant Father Murphy, priest and patriot, who fought and bled for the independence of our country; will you, men of the hillsides, inspired by the glorious memories of the past, will you abandon your chief? Will you give him up to the Saxon wolves who howl for his destruction or will you rally round him as your fathers rallied round the men of 98, and shout with a thousand united voices, 'No Surrender'. Hurrah for Charles Stewart Parnell, the leader of an independent Irish party, and down with the faction which would make Irish people the servants of a foreign power.

The Times, 18 December 1890

(b) Mr Parnell speaks as if he were an injured man, but the facts cannot be forgotten. Mr Parnell is responsible, and he alone, for the present deplorable situation. He pledged himself, again and again, to repel the charge against him. His pledges were accepted in good faith. When the time for speaking came, he remained silent. The pledges were broken. The charge was not repelled. Upon these facts a strong opinion was formed by multitudes of Englishmen, true friends of the liberty of Ireland. Mr Parnell does not hesitate to denounce them as 'English wolves'. But the fact remains that the 'English wolves' and the Irish bishops express the same opinion about him, and he cannot mend the matter by calling nicknames ...

The Times, 11 December 1890

26 Butter on Nationalist principles

It was widely held by 'non-political' observers and by many Unionists at the end of the nineteenth century that the root of the continuing 'Irish problem' lay in inefficient agriculture. One such agricultural reformer was Sir Horace Plunkett (1854-1932), younger son of an Anglo-Irish nobleman, who emerged in Irish public life during the 1890s with a movement for agricultural co-operation. Plunkett at first sought the backing of Nationalist politicians for his 'non-political movement', but rather queered his pitch in that quarter when he fought and won the South County Dublin constituency as an independent Unionist (1892-1900). But the Unionist government took up his ideas, and in 1900 he became vice-president and working head of the new Department of Agriculture and Technical Instruction. Although immediately losing his parliamentary seat he continued to hold what Nationalists argued was a political appointment until 1907, when the Liberal government responded to Irish party pressure to dismiss him. He remained a middle-of-the-road conciliationist, no matter where the road wandered, and in 1917 reappeared at the centre of the stage as an advocate of dominion home rule. In this extract he quotes a story originally told by his deputy in the Irish Agricultural Organisation Society.

It was hard and thankless work. There was the apathy of the people and the active opposition of the Press and the politicians. It would be hard to say now whether the abuse of the Conservative *Cork Constitution* or that of the Nationalist *Eagle*, of Skibbereen, was the louder ... Once when I thought I had planted a Creamery within the precincts of the town of Rathkeale [Co. Limerick], my co-operative apple cart was upset by a local solicitor who, having elicited the fact that our movement recognised neither political nor religious differences – that the Unionist-Protestant cow was as dear to us as her Nationalist-Catholic sister – gravely informed me that our programme would not suit Rathkeale. 'Rathkeale', said he, pompously, 'is a Nationalist town – Nationalist to the backbone – and every pound of butter made in this Creamery must be made on Nationalist principles, or it shan't be made at all'. This sentiment was applauded loudly, and the proceedings terminated.

H Plunkett, *Ireland in the New Century*
(John Murray, London, 1904) pp 190-1

27 *Agrarianism again: The United Irish League*

The Parnellite split continued throughout the 1890s. In face of continued Unionist government in Britain and a clear loss of Liberal enthusiasm for the home rule issue after Gladstone's retirement in 1894, constitutional nationalism seemed to be a declining force. But although the bad rural conditions of the 1880s had been eased considerably by controlled rents and continued emigration, there remained large areas of the country where the problem was more complicated. In the far west the barren coastline was quite unable to support its relatively dense population in acceptable conditions, and a government board had been set up in 1891 to stimulate farming, fishing, and other occupations in these 'congested districts'. In the eastern area of Connaught and parts of Munster the problem differed again in that many landlords, faced with the application of the new land laws to permanent tenancies, let most of their best land on 'eleven months' leases to large graziers, whose 'ranches' were typically surrounded by small and much poorer tenanted holdings.

It was against this background that a disillusioned anti-Parnellite MP, William O'Brien (1852-1928) founded the United Irish League in 1898. In later years the League was to become a rather sleepy constituency organisation for the parliamentary party, but from 1898 to 1902, and more sporadically from 1907 to 1909, it was a formidable force on the land. It also provided a platform for the reunification in 1900 of the Irish Parliamentary Party, under the chairmanship of John Redmond (1856-1918). George Wyndham (1863-1913), who served as Chief Secretary for Ireland from 1900 to 1905, described the situation to a colleague soon after taking office.

(a) The Very Rev Canon Greally, who was greeted with loud and prolonged cheers, said he had great pleasure in proposing the following resolutions:

1. That we the Nationalists of West Mayo in monster meeting assembled to celebrate with reverence and pride the memories of Ireland's glorious struggle for liberty in 1798, and we trust that in the centenary year our countrymen will do honour to the memory of the United Irishmen by sinking personal and sectional differences and uniting in one solid mass to organise a series of demonstrations ... and we hereby pledge ourselves to take immediate action for the formation of United Irish clubs on a basis that will secure the fullest representation of every section of Irish Nationalists and their elected representatives, party and local. (Cheers)

2. That the population of large districts of the Westport Union are already reduced to the direst condition of destitution and starvation, and have absolutely no means of their own of averting a widespread famine for the next three months. That we condemn in the strongest terms the tardy and cruelly made 'relief proposals' made by the Government, which proposals throw all the responsibility and a great part of the pecuniary burthen of relief on the unfortunate rate-payers, the majority of whom are themselves crushed with merciless rack-renters, debts and rates, and we appeal to the public opinion of the world and of our exiled countrymen against this barbarous neglect of the Government to afford adequate relief out of the millions unjustly wrung by England out of this impoverished country. (Cheers)

3. The most effective means of preventing the frequent cries of distress and famine in this so-called congested district would be the break-up of the large grazing ranches with which the district is cursed, and the partition of them amongst the small landholders, who were driven into the bogs and mountains to make room for the sheep and bullocks of English and Scotch adventurers and Irish grabbers. (Cheers) ...

6. That for the purpose of carrying out the resolutions of this meeting an organisation be hereby established, to be called the West Mayo United Irish League, open to all sections of Irish Nationalists and consisting of parish branches to be governed by a central committee meeting from time to time in Westport, and composed of the clergy of all the parishes of West Mayo, all Nationalist town commissioners and poor law guardians and six representatives of each parish to be elected by the parish branches ...

Connaught Telegraph, 29 January 1898

(b) George Wyndham to A J Balfour   26 November 1900

The *United Irish League* started two and more years ago by O'Brien in Mayo, has spread over the country. Redmond discouraged it; Healy stabbed it, the Priests fought it at the election. It won 'hands down'. Redmond acquiesces. The Bishop of Raphoe, Father O'Hara, and a few more of the abler Priests, are sailing with it in the hope of getting a hand on the tiller. The so-called 'National Convention' to meet whilst our December Parliament is sitting will be composed of delegates from the League and will – see Dillon's speech at Tullamore of yesterday – construct a Parliamentary Party to the exclusion of Healy and his remnant ...

Agrarian Agitation. The League began by an attack upon 'graziers'. Thanks to T.W. Russell [Ulster Liberal Unionist MP, later Liberal home ruler] they are now doubling this policy with 'Compulsory Land Purchase'. All the 103 Irish members with the exception of Col. Saunderson 'sans phrase' and McCartney [both Irish Unionists] with a minimum of hedging, have committed themselves to that policy. The only material difference between the Unionists and Nationalists is that the former wish to give a fair, the latter an unfair, price to the Landlord.

All, friends and foes, are strangely cut off from British sentiment. They believe that in spite of War taxation and Imperial politics, Ireland is going to bathe once more in the limelight. The Nationalist party, armed with a mandate from the Convention and assisted by Russell, mean, if they can, to imitate Parnell's Parliamentary tactics.

> J W Mackail & Guy Wyndham, *The Life and Letters*
> *of George Wyndham* (1925), ii, 409-11

28 The Land Act of 1903: The entire soil of Ireland for our people

After 1886 it was clear that the Unionist party in Great Britain had lost all flexibility on the question of Irish self-government. Confronted nonetheless with the responsibility of governing Ireland for most of the following twenty years, it implemented or sought to implement a series of measures – in the areas of land tenure, agricultural self-help, rural labourers' housing, university education and local government – which historians, perhaps discerning a more coherent plan than ever really existed, have characterised as 'killing home rule with kindness'. George Wyndham, the paternalistic idealist entrusted by the Unionists with developing what proved to be the last phase of that policy, came to grief in 1904-5 when his attempts to ease Protestants, landlords and 'moderates' back into Irish politics by means of a negotiated scheme for very limited devolution were stifled by opposition from the Unionist side. But earlier Wyndham had ensured his reputation as the instigator of nation-wide peasant proprietorship in Ireland through the Land Act of 1903, which made the credit facilities of the state, plus an attractive bonus, available to facilitate the sale of entire estates to the tenants on the basis of voluntary sale. He has built on the initiative of a little-known Galway landowner, Capt John Shawe-Taylor, to achieve the initial consensus which brought his measure to fruition. The Nationalists could not reject such a measure, but they were divided in their response. The aftermath brought about a final rift between Parnell's leading lieutenants. William O'Brien effectively withdrew from the party after 1904 to advocate a policy of 'conference, conciliation and consent' with the landlord class for political as well as economic grievances, while party leader Redmond was gradually won over to the view of John Dillon (1851-1927) and the mainstream of the party, that the Act would saddle tenants with repayment obligations which they would regret, would perpetuate the problem of the grass ranches, and did nothing to strengthen the power of the Congested Districts Board or assist the evicted tenants, 'the wounded soldiers of the land war'. But, as the following extracts make clear, Dillon's objections were as much political as economic.

(a) Letter to Irish newspapers from Captain John Shawe-Taylor, 3 Sept. 1902

For the last two hundred years the land war in this country has raged fiercely and continuously, bearing in its train stagnation of trade, paralysis of commercial business and enterprise, and producing hatred and bitterness between the various sections and classes of the community. Today the United Irish League is confronted by the Irish Land Trust, and we see both combinations eager and ready to renew the unending conflict. I do not believe there is an Irishman, whatever his political feeling, creed or position, who does not yearn to see a true settlement of the present chaotic, disastrous and ruinous struggle. In the best interests, therefore, of Ireland and my countrymen I beg most earnestly to invite the Duke of Abercorn, Mr John Redmond MP, Lord Barrymore, Colonel Saunderson MP, the Lord Mayor of Dublin, the O'Conor Don, Mr William O'Brien MP and Mr T.W.Russell MP, to a conference to be held in Dublin within one month from this date. An honest, simple and practical suggestion will be submitted, and I am confident that a settlement on terms alike satisfactory to landlords and tenants will be arrived at.

D Gwynn, *The Life of John Redmond* (Dublin, 1932), p 99

(b) We had won the property in the entire soil of Ireland for our people by a mortgage of $68\frac{1}{2}$ years to pay from 20 percent to 40 percent less than their existing rents, they having been hitherto mortgaged, not for $68\frac{1}{2}$ years but for all time to pay from 20 percent to 40 percent more, not as freeholders, but as tenants whose obligations had to be settled by a lawsuit, renewable every 15 years!

W O'Brien, *An Olive Branch in Ireland* (London, 1910), p 257

(c) [Dillon] spoke last night in support of the bill, but he tells me that but for loyalty to his party he should be inclined to oppose it in committee and vote against it on the third reading. His view is that it is useless to try to get the landlord class on the side of nationalism, that they would always betray it when the pinch came, that the land trouble is a weapon in nationalist hands, and that to settle it finally would be to risk home rule, which otherwise must come. For this reason he was opposed to the Conference with the landlords, and was opposed now in principle to the bill. He should, however, of course support it, since it had been decided to do so, for the one thing in Ireland was union in the parliamentary party.

W S Blunt, *My Diaries*, 5 May 1903
(London, 1932), p 468

(d) George Wyndham to Moreton Frewen   14 November 1903

I am disappointed and chagrined by recent events. Nor can I take the sanguine view that the Land Act will fulfil the objects of the Land Conference if it is to be assailed daily by the *Freeman*, Davitt and Dillon. My power of usefulness to Ireland is already diminished and may be destroyed. I have convinced my colleagues, a majority of our supporters in the House, and a still larger majority in the large towns of England, that it was right in itself to foster Union among Irishmen, and to obliterate the vestiges of ancient feuds without troubling ourselves about the ultimate effect of social reconciliation on Ireland's attitude towards the 'Home Rule' versus 'Union' controversy. And if this is set back, you cannot deal with the 'University Question' or the 'Labourers' question if so large and beneficent a measure as the Land Act is to be used only to divide classes more sharply ... Unless those who care for Ireland can show that the Conference and the Land Act have produced social reconciliation, I cannot get a hearing for using *Imperial* credit and *Irish* savings in accordance with the views of a United Ireland ...

If, however, I had a united Irish Party, with leaders not subject to repudiation, prepared to cooperate, to a certain extent with Irish landlords, scholars and business men, I could get Irish savings for Irish purposes and equivalent grants whenever England helps herself too freely out of the common Exchequer. My point is that I get beaten in detail if I am rebuffed by jeering allusions to Irish reconciliation. I am nearly tired out ...

J W Mackail & Guy Wyndham, *The Life and Letters
of George Wyndham* (1925), ii, pp 472

29 James Bryce: When they have the land

Gladstone had made the cause of Irish home rule something of a crusade for a generation of rank-and-file Liberals. But many others, especially the younger ones who had grown up in a party twice wrecked on the issue, were less enthusiastic. Liberal sentiment in the post-Gladstone era was less anti-home rule as such than based on a feeling that the Irish question ought no longer to be the burning question of the hour, that it stood between the new Liberalism and a major programme of social reform in Britain, and that any attempt to re-introduce it implied a head-on collision with the Unionist-dominated House of Lords. Apart from a radical minority who saw it as an issue inextricably linked with the overblown power of the upper house, many Liberals were coming implicitly to share the Unionist analysis - that political nationalism might wither away when exposed to a modicum of prosperity and widespread reform on all material fronts. This was certainly the view of James Bryce (1838-1921), who became Liberal Chief Secretary in December 1905. His correspondent Dicey was a fellow constitutionalist and a Unionist propagandist, so that Bryce may have taken a certain academic delight in emphasising and exaggerating any covert home rule tendency in the recent Unionist administrations.

James Bryce M. P. to A. V. Dicey   3 February 1905

You are right in thinking that a policy tending towards wider self-government must be pursued by a Liberal government. But then it will be pursued, to judge from the past, by a Tory government also. The last ten years have under the Tories done more than a Liberal government with a bare majority could have done in that direction. No Liberal government could, perhaps would, have given the land to the tenants; probably could not have given the local government scheme. Both measures bring home rule nearer in two ways – they give more power to the masses and they lessen the dangers feared in 1886 and 1893. The forces of nature seem to me to be working for Home Rule; and it will come about under one English party just as much as another *if*, an important *if*, the Irish continue to press as strongly for it. That is perhaps not so certain. When they have the land, much of the steam will be out of the boiler.

[Joseph] Chamberlain would of course give them anything they asked in return for support for him. He has tacitly made offers, but they don't trust him ... a succession of Chamberlains would be far more dangerous to England than the Irish are.

That Home Rule will come in our time seems unlikely. But under our democratic government a resolute section is pretty sure to get sooner or later whatever does not conflict with the direct interests or direct passions of the English masses. So I expect it to come, if the Irish go on pressing as they have done since O'Connell.

NLI: Bryce Papers, MS 110-11

Chapter 3
Nationalism old and new

30 The Parnellite split continues: 'All a question of jealousy and hates'

Parnell died in October 1891, but the 'Parnell split' continued until January 1900, with two distinct parties in Parliament and two faltering organisations in the country – the Parnellite Irish National League and the anti-Parnellite Irish National Federation. Bitter memories of 1890-91, and apparent lack of any new galvanising force comparable to the Land League agitation of 1879, helped to prolong the split quite pointlessly. Another reason for its continuation, however, was the development of what became an even more bitter division within the anti-Parnellite camp between the followers of John Dillon and William O'Brien on the one hand, and the followers of Tim Healy (1855-1931) on the other. Healy, a distinguished barrister but a difficult colleague, offered a conservative, constituency-based nationalism which was attractive to many priests and also endeared him to his kinsman William Martin Murphy (owner of the *Irish Independent*) and to the Cardinal Archbishop of Armagh. By 1900 his family-based 'Bantry Band' was isolated within the parliamentary party, and he was later forced to seek sanctuary in a bizarre alliance with the anti-clerical William O'Brien. But Healy had been the most vitriolic opponent of Parnell in the split, and was a formidable force in the anti-Parnellite Party until at least 1896, when John Dillon took over the leadership from its ageing figurehead, the London-based literary figure Justin McCarthy (1830-1912).

(a) T.M.Healy MP to Maurice Healy MP   13, 20 January 1893

... Undoubtedly Dillon and O'Brien have made a permanent fissure in the Party, which ran sweetly and smoothly until they were released from jail ...

In consequence of ... the certainty that there will be a bounder [i.e. Dillonite] ticket for the committee of the Party, I think it has become absolutely necessary for us in self-preservation to take measures of precaution ... I am convinced that unless we can strengthen ourselves on the committee, we shall be completely crushed by a combination against us which is resolute and unscrupulous and relentless ... Of course it is a dreadful thing to have this Open Sesame, but it is just as little use weeping over it as it is regarding Parnellism. They will knife us if we don't prevent them ... They will dance a war-dance over my carcass at every opportunity. I am therefore going to take the field against them openly if necessary, and quietly in any case, to spare myself the alternative of being trampled upon ... I greatly fear that the net result of the valuable assistance of Messrs Dillon and O'Brien will be to create a third party in the country, unless the disease is immediately and vigorously taken in hand.

Healy Papers, cited in F Callanan, *T M Healy*
(Cork: University Press, 1996), pp 418-19

(b) Justin McCarthy to Mrs Campbell Praed   10 June 1893

We have fallen into hopeless disunion in our party. While we were trying to fight the enemy we have a mutiny in our own ship. [Thomas] Sexton has hopelessly given in his resignation and resolves to withdraw from public life ...It is all a conflict of jealousies and hates, and the national cause is forgotten. And we are fighting this difficult battle with a narrow majority and with Gladstone's declining years – and we are frankly telling our opponents that we are not able, even at such a crisis, to govern ourselves and our rancours and our tempers! I am well nigh sick of it all ... I am sorry for [Edward] Blake [Irish-Canadian Member of the Irish Party] ... who gave up his home and his well-earned ease to come and fight this hopeless battle – which is to be lost by our fault! He says he feels broken-hearted – and his conviction is that the present [home rule] bill is lost. I am not quite so un-hopeful – but I feel terribly depressed.

J McCarthy & C Praed, *Our Book of Memories:
Letters of Justin McCarthy to Mrs Campbell Praed*
(London: Chatto & Windus, 1912), pp 362

31 Irishmen and Boers

The long years of Unionist government at Westminster after 1895 offered Nationalist MPs, divided or not, very little opportunity for patronage or influence. Considerable Unionist efforts went into social and economic reform in Ireland, but always with the intention of deflating Nationalist politicians rather than of helping them to strengthen their positions. The one issue which enabled Nationalists to cut a dash and demonstrate militancy was the Anglo-Boer War of 1899-1902. Many British Liberals supported the war, so that Nationalists were able to achieve a good measure of prominence, or notoriety, alongside radical Liberals in the minority pro-Boer camp. A small Irish Brigade fought in South Africa on the Boer side. Nationalist MPs did not aspire to this level of commitment, but passionate anti-imperialists like John Dillon became adroit at linking the Irish and Boer causes.

Predominant race! That is what you are fighting for – to put the Dutch under your feet in South Africa; but allow me to tell you you will never succeed. It is an infamous object; the conscience of humanity will be against you in this struggle, and although for a time you may beat down these people by overwhelming numbers, you are but creating for yourselves, as a result of this war, far away in the southern seas, 7000 miles away from your shores, another Ireland, which will be infinitely more difficult to hold down than the Ireland which is so close ... These people will rise and rise again, and my conviction is that even if you conquer the Transvaal the ultimate result will be the loss of South Africa to England.

H C Deb 4th series,
vol 78, cols 654-662

32 John Dillon: No faith in the doctrine of conciliation

We saw earlier (doc 28) that the Land Act of 1903, the centre-piece of Tory reform in Ireland, was initially welcomed by many senior Nationalist politicians, but that a growing number of them became wary once it became clear that there existed a broader political agenda on the part of those 'moderate landlords' and their associates who has brought it forward. A small number of Nationalists, led by William O'Brien, did commit themselves to the new 'conference and conciliation' policy, so to that extent the conciliationists' strategy did create a split within Nationalism. The split was contained and ultimately defused, however, when the leading opponent of conciliation, John Dillon, was able to win party chairman John Redmond and the mainstream of the movement to his side. The main thrust of the Dillonite case was strongly materialist – not only was conciliation a hopeless policy he argued, but the operation of the Land Act itself would pay landlords more than their estates were worth, while tenants would be saddled with a lifetime of excessive payments. This did not prove to be true, and in those parts of Ireland where farm holdings were predominantly of viable size, purchase went ahead rapidly. But in political terms Dillon's point of view won the day. He first nailed his colours to the mast in a speech in his East Mayo constituency, at Swinford, in August 1903.

We hear a great deal about conciliation. To the amazement of some of us old campaigners, we hear Irish landlords talking of conciliation, and of intention to go into conferences with the leaders of the Irish Party. That is the new feature, and some men are asked to believe it is due to what the Methodists describe as a new birth or infusion of grace into the landlord party. I don't believe a word of it, I believe the origin and source of it was the fact that the landlords of Ireland were behind the scenes, and they knew that the whole policy of coercion was going to topple about their ears ... When the landlords talk of conciliation, what do they want? They want 25 years' purchase of their land ... for my part ... I am so far sceptical that I have no faith in the doctrine of conciliation.

Freeman's Journal, 26 August 1903

33 Sir Antony MacDonnell: 'I was not concerned with party politics'

The intellectual force behind the conciliation policy was not the group of reforming landlords led by the Earl of Dunraven (1841-1926), who participated in the Land Conference of 1902 and who established the Irish Reform Association in 1904, but the head of the Irish civil service, the Under Secretary at Dublin Castle, Sir Antony MacDonnell (1844-1925). He was from a well-off Catholic family in Co Galway, and his brother was a Nationalist MP. MacDonnell had retired from the Indian civil service in 1902, and was asked by the Conservative government to apply his experience to Ireland in a rather unorthodox way. His 'middle way', once it became public, proved unacceptable to Conservative backbench opinion, and justified John Dillon's scepticism. It was not MacDonnell however, but his political master George Wyndham who was obliged to resign in March 1905. Although MacDonnell's experience was no happier under the succeeding Liberal regime, he survived in Dublin Castle until 1908, and retired to the House of Lords.

(a) Memorandum by Sir Anthony MacDonnell enclosed in a letter to George Wyndham   10 Feb 1905

1. An effort will, I understand, be made in Parliament to censure me for having helped Lord Dunraven in preparing his Devolution Scheme. The attack on me will, it is suggested to me, be directed to showing:
   (a) That I exceeded my functions in giving Lord Dunraven my assistance;
   (b) That I failed to inform my official superiors of what I was doing;
   (c) That generally my participation in such a scheme was inconsistent with my duty to the present Government.
All these propositions are incorrect, as I proceed to show.

2. I did not take office in Ireland as an ordinary Under-Secretary. Before accepting the offer made to me of this office, I inquired into the system of Irish Government; and my acceptance of the Under-Secretaryship was conditional on opportunities being given to me to devise reforms. The conditions under which I accepted this office are stated in the following extract from a letter dated 22 September 1902, which I wrote to Mr Wyndham with reference to the offer of the appointment:

" ... I am an Irishman, a Roman Catholic and a Liberal in politics; I have strong Irish sympathies; I do not see eye to eye with you on all matters of Irish administration, and I think there is no likelihood of good coming from such a regime of coercion as *The Times* has recently outlined. On the other hand ... I find there is a substantial measure of agreement between us. Moreover, I should be glad to do some service to Ireland. Therefore, it seems to me the situation goes beyond the sphere of mere party politics ..."

4. It is therefore clear that when Mr Wyndham asked for, and when I promised, my assistance in the Government of Ireland, we both understood that my functions were to be a good deal wider than those ordinarily appertaining to the Under-Secretary ...

5. Acting on this conception of my duties, I have from the very outset taken the initiative in matters beyond the sphere of the Under-Secretary's ordinary duties, and have carried on negotiations of a political nature. If examples are wanted, I point to Lord Dunraven's Land Conference, the Land Purchase Bill, and the University negotiations ...

6. In this "Devolution" I acted in the same way and spirit. Before I took office I had been impressed with the want of efficiency resulting from the uncontrolled and divergent action of the numerous Irish "Boards". But when I had gained experience (from within) on the working of the Irish Government I clearly saw that the root of Irish maladministration lay in the financial arrangements between the two countries.

10. In the beginning of 1904 a conversation took place between Mr Wyndham, Lord Dunraven and myself on Irish politics. Lord Dunraven was particularly interested in the creation of a moderate Irish Party, of which he had hopes from the temperament of a section of Irish Unionists and of the Nationalist wing which drew its inspiration from Mr William O'Brien ...

16. I was much surprised and disappointed when I saw Mr Wyndham's letter to *The Times* [date] condemning the "Devolution Scheme" ...

17. I am now told that Lord Dunraven's scheme appeared inopportunely from the Party point of view. I was not concerned with party politics. My concern lay in the improvement of the Irish Administration, and in the reconciliation of the Irish people to it. ...I was not concerned with the distinctions between Liberal and Unionist. The Devolution scheme was not a party move ... .

J W Mackail & Guy Wyndham, *The Life and Letters of George Wyndham* (1925), ii, 783-88

(b) F.H.Crawford to Lord Ranfurly   Belfast, 14 December 1906

...There is a rumour ... that Mr A.J.Balfour would be asked during the spring or early summer, to come over here to a monster demonstration to be held as a protest against Home Rule ... I write to let you know the feeling in the north of Ireland towards Mr Balfour ... At one time all Unionists in the north of Ireland trusted Mr Balfour completely. When he allowed out the Dynamitards, the Orange working man was suspicious, when he started his Catholic University campaign, all the Unionists here distrusted him and when he was a party to the appointment of Sir Antony MacDonnell every true Unionist here thought him a traitor ...

Since the MacDonnell incident we have lost a lot of staunch Unionist workmen in Belfast. They consider themselves betrayed by their leader Mr Balfour and have gone in for the labour and socialist programme. This is what we have to combat locally. The old Unionist enthusiasm is dead among the masses here ...

P Buckland, *Irish Unionism, 1885-1923:*
a Documentary History (Belfast: HMSO 1973), pp 202-03

34   Sir Henry Campbell-Bannerman: Take it any way you can get it

Long before the autumn of 1905 it was clear that Balfour's Unionist government was in trouble, bitterly split by the free trade versus tariff reform debate and by rivalry amongst the party's leadership. For the Nationalist leaders, enthusiasm for the prospect of a Liberal government was tempered only by anxiety that the retreat from the home rule commitment favoured for some time by the former prime minister Lord Rosebery (1849-1929) and the Liberal Imperialist wing of the Liberal party would be forced upon the party leader, Sir Henry Campbell-Bannerman (1836-1908) by Rosebery's followers. In the event the Conservatives resigned office in December 1905 and the Liberals were returned with an enormous overall majority in January 1906 on the basis of a commitment to devolving administrative powers to Ireland short of legislative home rule. The Nationalists had had to press hard for such an outcome. Their most influential weapon was their influence over the Irish vote in British cities, which might otherwise have regarded the Conservatives as more convincing defenders of Catholic schools – in a speech at Sunderland, Co Durham in November 1905 Redmond told Irishmen 'that the interests of their country and the interests of their creed were identical'. This rapprochement with the post-Gladstonian Liberals required careful negotiation.

(a) John Dillon to John Redmond   2 November 1905

... if the Liberals quarrel with us after the election, we shall have it in our power to make their position an impossible one. And unless absolutely driven to it by the conduct of Asquith and Rosebery I do not think we should do or say anything calculated to make a sweeping defeat of the Unionist party and the formation of a strong Liberal government impossible.

I am in favour of your seeing CB [Campbell-Bannerman], if possible before he speaks. And the line I suggest you urge upon him is this ... that ... no remedy will be found fully effective [for the reform of Irish government] except an elected legislative body and executive responsible to it. But that having laid down these principles he must declare that all questions of priority of any measures of reform, of time, opportunity or possibility are questions for after the election and that he absolutely decline to give any pledges whatever on these matters.

If CB follows this line and sticks to it – all will go well. But you ought to draw his attention to the language in his speech on Tuff's resolution – in which he said that 'home rule was not now before the country' and warn him of the enormous mischief done by such language. And the very great difficulty it caused us.

NLI: Redmond Papers, MS 15182

(b) Campbell-Bannerman at Stirling   23 November 1905

If I were asked for advice – which is not likely, perhaps – by an ardent Irish Nationalist I would say "Your desire is, as mine is, to see the effective management of Irish affairs in the hands of a representative Irish Parliament. If I were you I would take it any way I can get, and if an installment of representative control was offered to you, or any administrative improvements, I would advise you thankfully to accept it, provided it was consistent with and led up to the larger policy". I think that would be good advice. But I lay stress on the proviso – it must be consistent with and lead up to the larger policy. To secure good administration is one thing, and a good thing in itself, but good government can never be a substitute for government by the people themselves.

In the immediate future, whatever be the result of a general election, the time of Parliament will probably be mainly occupied by certain great questions – social questions for the most part – which call for treatment, and on which opinion among us is more than ripe ... Undoubtedly they will take time. I trust that the opportunity of making a great advance on this question of Irish government will not be long delayed; and when that opportunity comes my firm and honest belief is that a greater measure of agreement than hitherto as to the ultimate solution will be found possible, and that a keener appreciation will be felt of the benefits which will flow to the entire community of British people throughout the world if Ireland, far from being disaffected, disheartened, impoverished and disunited, takes her place, a strong, harmonious, and contented portion of the Empire.

The Times, 24 November 1905

35   Augustine Birrell: the failure of the Irish Council Bill, 1907

MacDonnell's devolution scheme, which has caused the downfall of George Wyndham under the previous government, was dusted down and brought forward again in the spring of 1907, in accordance with Campbell-Bannerman's Stirling pledge. Through 1906 MacDonnell and his political chief James Bryce developed it privately as a small non-legislative assembly, elected indirectly from the membership of county councils, to oversee and co-ordinate the main Irish boards. When the Nationalist leaders were briefed about the scheme they were furious. Bryce was packed off to be British Ambassador in Washington in January 1907, and was replaced by Augustine Birrell (1850-1933), who expanded the scheme quite considerably. The Irish Council Bill was introduced into the House of Commons on 7 May 1907. It received a non-committal reception from Redmond and Dillon, who wanted to accept it if they could. But Irish public opinion proved to be bitterly disappointed by it, Dillon was removed from the crisis by the sudden death of his young wife, and Redmond took the safest way out by calling for the rejection of the bill at a National Convention on 21 May. The Liberal government allowed the measure to lapse.

Augustine Birrell to James Bryce   17 June 1907

My life has been one long controversy – and perhaps my main antagonist has been our excellent friend and 'colleague' (woe's me!) Sir A.M.[MacDonnell], late of Bengal. We looked at the same problem from opposite ends. I may have attached too much importance to the House of Commons. He ignored it entirely, and with the obstinacy of 10,000 mules could only be drawn back with oaths and violence from each position that he assumed. He is such a good fellow that we never quarrelled, but anything more irritating and exhausting I could never have imagined – I daresay he still believes that if we had brought in a snug little advisory Anglo-Indian parlour council of 50 members nominated by the county councils, it would now be very nearly the law of the land. Whereas every member of the House of Commons knows that such a bill would never have been read a *first time*. Sir A.M. still believes that the *moderates* in Ireland who drink tea in the Phoenix

Park are capable of compelling the Nationalists in the House to accept 'moderate' measures. No bigger delusion has ever got hold of a man, not even an Anglo-Indian. However, that is over now.

As to the National Convention I have had various accounts of it. Our good friend Barry O'Brien was in the back of the crowd – he thinks highly of it and thinks a great wave of national sentiment, displacing money and educational control and the little baser things, passed over it, and compelled the rejection of the bill. Others think that if a chance of deliberation had been given and the measure explained – two-thirds of the delegates would have recommended *amendments* in Committee. Some see the priests in the rejection. Others deny that they had much to do with it – I feel sure they had a good deal, but *how* much who can say?

Our present relations with the Irish Party are a little strained ...

Bodleian Library, Oxford: James Bryce Papers, MS 19

36 University education for Catholics: Catholic and Protestant views

Trinity College, the sole constituent college of the ancient University of Dublin, had long been resented by majority nationalist opinion as an Anglo-Irish Episcopalian institution which monopolised higher education in Ireland. In 1879 an examining body, 'The Royal University' was created, awarding degrees and endowing fellowships at five small colleges (including a Jesuit foundation in Dublin). But most of the Royal's graduates were in fact private students, unattached to any of the five colleges, and by the end of the century such a concept of university education was very much at variance with prevailing trends in Britain and elsewhere. Successive British governments as well as Nationalist politicians were anxious to come to terms with the problem, but repeatedly found themselves at an *impasse* – the Catholic church in Ireland, without whose support any move would have been pointless, wanted an institution where a prevailing Catholic atmosphere could be ensured and maintained, whereas the weight of backbench parliamentary opinion in Britain was against any such endowment. Efforts by successive Unionist governments to tackle the problem, in 1898 and 1904, petered out.

Nonconformist church pressure tended to influence the Liberal party in the same inflexible direction as the Ulster contingent led the British Unionists. It was therefore with some foreboding that the new Liberal government in 1906 set out to find a mutually acceptable solution. The Irish party, which began by suspecting incorrectly that the government intended only a foredoomed attempt to 'make Trinity College acceptable to Catholics', was prepared to consider a number of other options, notably the creation of a separate but equal college in the University of Dublin, or alternatively an entirely new federal university, embracing existing colleges at Cork and Galway, and centred on a major new college in Dublin. Irish government and much educated Catholic lay opinion tended to favour the former solution, involving more prestige and the hope of less segregation, but the Irish party bowed to clerical opinion and in 1908 the National University of Ireland and its constituent University College, Dublin, came into being. The following examples of rather extreme views, from opposite sides of the ethnic divide, indicate why a solution had taken so long to achieve.

(a) An anonymous Catholic writer, 1874

> Now, it is a plain fact that by giving Catholic youth a higher education you open a new and large avenue, by which the godless spirit of the times may gain admittance. And unless they be furnished with fully sufficient moral and intellectual protection, you expose them to imminent danger, not merely of holding the Faith with less simplicity and heartiness (though this would be bad enough), but of wilfully admitting a fully deliberate doubt as to its truth – or, in other words, of actual apostasy. It is this which makes the whole subject so anxious, and which makes one a little impatient with common-places about marching with the times, and aiming at progress, and growing in largeness of thought. We are very far from meaning that ignorance is the Catholic youth's best preservative against intellectual danger, but it is a very powerful one, nevertheless, and those who deny this are but inventing a theory in the very teeth of manifest facts. A Catholic destitute of intellectual tastes, whether in a higher or a lower rank, may, probably enough, be tempted to idleness, frivolity, gambling, sensuality; but in none but the very rarest cases will he be tempted to that which (in the Catholic view) is an immeasurably greater calamity than any of these, or all put together, viz. deliberate doubt on the truth of his religion. It is simply undeniable, we say, that the absence of higher education is a powerful preservative against apostasy, and those who watch over souls will reasonably refuse to bear part in withdrawing that preservative, until they are satisfied that some other very sufficient substitute is provided. It is the work of higher education, as such, to cultivate and enlarge the mind; but it is the work of Catholic higher education as such, so to cultivate and enlarge the mind as to guard against the danger that such cultivation do immeasurably more harm than good. Now, the Church's interest is not in higher education, as such, but in Catholic higher education ...

> *Dublin Review*, vol. xxii new series
> (January-April 1874), p 192

(b) Vice-Provost Barlow of Trinity College, Dublin, 1906

> I am very far from agreeing with some who hold that inasmuch as the ratio in Ireland of Catholics to Protestants is at least three to one, we

should have three times as many Catholics as Protestants at Trinity College. These persons quite ignore the fact that the great Catholic majority consists of poor and ignorant peasants, and I think that to facilitate the education of a poor and perhaps stupid youth by paying his college fees ... is but a cruel kindness. I would gladly see a clever boy helped through his course ... but a stupid or even mediocre youth, turned by charitable assistance into a profession would very likely starve, and if he did not emigrate might become a discontented and possibly dangerous member of society, instead of remaining a useful agriculturist as, but for misplaced charity, he might have been. This plan of turning universities into gigantic charity schools, as has been done by Mr Carnegie, may be successful in Scotland, but would certainly not suit the atmosphere of Ireland.

BPP 1907 XLI *(Royal Commission on Trinity College,*
Dublin and the University of Dublin)
Final Report, Appendix, p 38

37 The Ancient Order of Hibernians: Debasing the national ideal?

After the implementation of the 1903 Land Act it became increasingly difficult for the Nationalist organisation – the United Irish League – to sustain the fiction that its supporters in rural Ireland shared a common material interest in the land question regardless of whether they were tenants or landless men, satisfied purchasers or 'congests' with uneconomic holdings. In the larger towns and cities the UIL inspired even less enthusiasm, faced with vestigial Parnellism and with new challenges from the labour movement and cultural nationalism. The Belfast Nationalist leader Joe Devlin (1871-1934) had a particular ability to appeal to urban minorities of Irish Nationalists who lived outside the heartlands – whether in Belfast, Glasgow or further afield. After entering Parliament in 1902 he became a full-time fund-raiser and organiser. Although General Secretary of the UIL, 1905-20, he also took control of the main Irish wing (the Board Of Erin) of the predominantly American-based benefit society, Ancient Order of Hibernians, and was its National President, 1905-34. The leadership of the American AOH was much courted by both parliamentary and revolutionary Irish nationalists and, most of the time, tried to steer a middle course. But seeing the movement's potential in Ireland itself, Devlin used the Board of Erin as a personal machine to bolster the faltering UIL after 1905. This proved an effective strategy, at least until 1914, but the Catholic exclusivity and the Masonic-style secrecy were negative aspects of the Order which opponents of the UIL and the Irish Parliamentary Party – Catholic and Protestant, Unionist and Nationalist – constantly sought to exploit.

(a) Joe Devlin to John Redmond   Boston, USA   24 May 1903

...The Directory of the [Ancient Order of] Hibernians have issued a flabby approval of our movement and that marks a very considerable advance, because we have had practically to cope with the opposition of the AOH as well as that of the Clan [Clan na Gael, the leading Irish-American republican lobby]. Our friends in the AOH are at least free now to give us their active co-operation and support in the future. Up to this, unless in a few instances, they have been afraid to openly identify themselves with the [United Irish] League.

NLI: Redmond Papers
MS 15181

(b) Bishop Patrick O'Donnell of Raphoe to Mgr Michael O'Riordan, Rector of the Irish College, Rome   13 December 1909

... About the AOH I know a good deal, and I am very glad of the view you take. It is greatly to the credit of the Board of Erin that it pulled so many men out of secret societies and formed them into an organisation with Irish Catholic principles. Because of the antecedents of some of the men it was difficult enough to secure 'the toleration' of the bishops as a body. In giving it they made a reservation about 'no chaplain'. I always said I'd understood this as 'no national chaplain'. Here we have county and divisional chaplains. The poor fellows are anxious to have their priests with them. With the priests all goes straight ... They are proud at approaching Communion in a body. Generally the sashes are laid aside as they approach the altar rails. But they'd greatly like to wear them.

In country districts there is not much room for them as a Benefit Society, and they take from the strength of the U.I. League. Yet all the same, on the grounds of legitimate human liberty all round, I have been on their side from the start ...

Archives of the Irish College, Rome:
O'Riordan Papers f 101

(c) ...There had of late years [c 1905] crept into the north of Ireland a seceding wing (calling itself the 'Board of Erin') of the great American Ancient Order of Hibernians, a genuine benefit society which had distinguished itself by many works of charity and benevolence. The seceding Board of Erin never offered any public explanation of the objects of their establishment in Ireland. Their work was carried on in secret, under an obligation equivalent to an oath, not to reveal their secrets and passwords; and nobody was admitted to membership who was not a Catholic, frequenting the Catholic sacraments. Such a body would have been entirely harmless, if confined to the legitimate sphere of a friendly society; but suddenly and secretly established in control of the entire visible Nationalist organisation, the effect in Ulster was that of a brand flourished in a powder-magazine. The transformation was effected by a stealthy process, without any consultation with or consent of the [Irish Parliamentary] Party, the [United Irish] League or the country ... .The paid secretary of the United Irish League (Mr Joseph Devlin of Belfast, who now for the first time came into prominence) became the National President of the Board of Erin ... The public organisation [ie the United Irish League] gradually ceased to exist save as a respectable means of collecting funds and passing resolutions ...

The Board of Erin Hibernians, who became thenceforth the real dispensers of all power and offices and titles, from 1906 to 1916, had every demerit that could inflame sectarian passion in Ulster ... [This] debased the National Ideal from the aim of Wolfe Tone – which was 'to unite the whole people of Ireland.' ... – to the level of a Catholic Orangeism in green paint, deformed by the same vices of monopoly and intolerance which had made Protestant Orangeism a national scourge. The results were catastrophic ...

William O'Brien, *The Irish Revolution and How it Came About* (1923), pp 30-31

38 'The muscular power and manly bearing of our Gaelic ancestors'

With the exception of Joe Devlin, the leadership of the Irish Parliamentary Party never felt the need to look much further than the land question and the loyalty of the Catholic clergy to provide steam for its boiler and illustration that Irish administration would make Ireland a prosperous and loyal state within the Empire, where English administration has so patently failed. The party leadership remained very much in the hands of men who had learnt their nationalism as Parnell's lieutenants in the Land League, and who showed little interest in alternative bases for Irish national consciousness. In particular the party failed, with minor exceptions, to associate itself in the public mind with either the Gaelic Athletic Association or the Gaelic League. The GAA was founded in October 1884 at a meeting at Thurles, Co Tipperary, to foster an interest in Gaelic football and other 'national' games, and to exclude from participation in them all members of the armed forces and RIC.

Michael Davitt to Michael Cusack   30 October 1884

Sorry I cannot attend the meeting which you announce for Thurles on Saturday. In any effort that may be made to revive a natural taste for games and pastimes, such as once developed the muscular power and manly bearing of our Gaelic ancestors, I shall be most happy to lend a hand. Why should we not have our athletic festivals like other peoples – I mean on a national scale?

In this, as in so many other matters, we ought to cut ourselves adrift from English rules and patronage, and prevent the killing of those Celtic sports which have been threatened with the same fate, by the encroachment of Saxon custom, as that which menaces our nationality under alien rule. Why not make an effort for the revival of the Taltine games? A grand National Festival could be organised to come off at some historic spot, at which prizes could be awarded for merit, not only in the various athletic spo'ts peculiar to the Celtic people (and in this expression I could include the Scotch, Welsh and Manx), but in music, poetry, oratory, and other kindred accomplishments. To throw the prizes open to the Celtic race throughout the world, and give a couple of years in which to organise the first grand national competition, would, I am confident, ensure a great success. There are, of course, many other reasons why the physique of our people is not developing as it ought to be, but there is no doubt that one reason for the degenerate gait and bearing of most of our young men at home is to be found in the absence of such games and pastimes as formerly gave to Irishmen the reputation of a soldier-like and self-reliant race.

Cork Examiner 3 November 1884, cited in
A Mitchell & P Ó Snodaigh (eds), *Irish Political Documents, 1869-1916* (Dublin: Irish Academic Press, 1989), p 61

39   Douglas Hyde: The hideousness of an artistic race

The Gaelic League was founded in 1893 by Eoin MacNeill (1867-1945), Dr Douglas Hyde and others, to stimulate a revival of the Irish language. Hyde (1860-1949) was a Protestant, the son of a Church of Ireland rector in Connaught, who later became the first President of Ireland, 1938-45. He always maintained that his movement was non-political, and staved off a radical nationalist revision of its constitution until 1915. But although his personal commitment to Irish culture was strongly positive the movement, especially at the popular level, did define Irish nationality and Irish problems in contradistinction to the values and influence attributed to England. This feature is clearly apparent in Hyde's own seminal lecture, 'The necessity for de-anglicizing Ireland'.

If we take a bird's-eye view of our island to-day, and compare it with what it used to be, we must be struck by the extraordinary fact that the nation which was once, as every one admits, one of the most classically learned and cultured nations in Europe, is now one of the least so; how one of the most reading and literary peoples has become one of the least studious and most un-literary, and how the present art products of one of the quickest, most sensitive, and most artistic races on earth are now only distinguished for their hideousness.

I shall endeavour to show that this failure of the Irish people in recent times has been largely brought about by the race diverging during this century from the right path, and ceasing to be Irish without becoming English.

It is a fact, and we must face it as a fact, that although they adopt English habits and copy England in every way, the great bulk of Irishmen and Irishwomen over the whole world are known to be filled with a dull, ever-abiding animosity against her, and – right or wrong – to grieve when she prospers, and joy when she is hurt ... I believe it is our Gaelic past which, though the Irish race does not recognise it just at present, is really at the bottom of the Irish heart, and prevents us becoming citizens of the empire, as, I think, can be easily proved ...

Let us suppose for a moment – which is impossible – that there were to arise a series of Cromwells in England for the space of one hundred years, able administrators of the empire, careful rulers of Ireland, developing to the utmost our national resources, whilst they unremittingly stamped out every spark of national feeling, making Ireland a land of wealth and factories, whilst they extinguished every thought and every idea that was Irish, and left us, at last, after a hundred years of good government, fat, wealthy, and populous, but with all our characteristics gone, with every external that at present differentiates us from the English lost or dropped.

How many Irishmen are there who would purchase material prosperity at such a price? It is exactly such a question as this and the answer to it that shows the difference between the English and Irish race. Nine Englishmen out of ten would jump to make the exchange, and I as firmly believe that nine Irishmen out of ten would indignantly refuse it.

And yet this awful idea of complete anglicization, which I have put here before you in all its crudity is, and has been, making silent inroads upon us for nearly a century ...

What we must endeavour to never forget is this, that the Ireland of today is the descendant of the Ireland of the seventh century; then the school of Europe and the torch of learning. It is true that Northmen made some minor settlements in it in the ninth and tenth centuries, it is true that the Normans made extensive settlements during the succeeding centuries, but none of these broke the continuity of the social life of the island. Dane and Norman drawn to the kindly Irish breast issued forth in a generation or two fully Irishised, and more Hibernian than the Hibernians themselves and even after the Cromwellian plantation the children of numbers of the English soldiers who settled in the south and midlands, were after forty years' residence, and after marrying Irish wives, turned into good Irishmen and unable to speak a word of English, while several Gaelic poets of the last century have, like Father English, the most unmistakably English names. In two points only was the continuity of the Irishism of Ireland damaged. First, in the north east of Ulster, where the Gaelic race was expelled and the land planted with aliens, whom our dear mother Erin, assimilative as she is, has hitherto found it difficult to absorb and in the ownership of the land, eight-ninths of which belongs to people many of whom have always lived, or live, abroad, and not half of whom Ireland can be said to have assimilated.

D Hyde, *The Revival of Irish Literature and Other Addresses* (London: T Fisher Unwin, 1894), pp 126-7

40 D P Moran: We are all Palemen now

D P Moran (1871-1936) was probably the most gifted Irish journalist of his generation. Always an independent figure, he nonetheless voiced more clearly than anyone else the developing 'Irish-Ireland' ethos which the Irish party failed to capture. His thinking, though clearly influenced by Hyde, was more overtly nationalist, and sometimes crudely so, as in the first extract below, but probably none the less influential for that. In the second extract he argues that every nationalist movement in modern Irish history had failed in its task of resisting English encroachment. The basis of nationality in a generalised hostility to English influence is very clear.

(a) It takes an Englishman to get the most out of English literature, as it takes a Frenchman to get the most out of French literature. A literature steeped in the history, traditions, and genius of one nation, is at the best only an imperfect tutor to the people of another nation; in fact, the common half educated people of another nation will have none of it. The Irish nation has this century, been brought up on English literature. Of course it never really kindled their minds or imaginations; they were driven to look at literature as a thing not understandable and above them – a position, I need scarcely say, not making for the development of self-respect or intellectual self-dependence. In most cases when they left school they ceased to read anything but the newspapers. Of course there are many exceptions to this generalisation. If an Irishman received a higher English education and lost touch with Irish aspirations, he practically became an Englishman, and many people with less advantages, by force of exceptional ability, got their heads above the entanglements around them and breathed something like free air. But I am talking of the common run of men who make up a nation, and not of the few exceptions. Tell me of any ordinary man in Dublin, Cork or elsewhere, who professes an appreciation for the best products of English literature, and I will have no hesitation in informing you that he is an intellectual snob, mostly composed of affectation.

D P Moran, 'The Battle of Two Civilisations', Originally published in *The New Ireland Review*, Reprinted in *The Philosophy of Irish Ireland* (Dublin: James Duffy & Co Ltd, 1905), p 101

(b) No one wants to fall out with [Thomas] Davis's comprehensive idea of the Irish people as a composite race drawn from various sources, and professing any creed they like, nor would an attempt to rake up racial prejudices be tolerated by anyone. We are proud of Grattan, Flood, Tone, Emmet, and all the rest who dreamt and worked for an independent country, even though they had no conception of an Irish nation; but it is necessary that they should be put in their place, and that place is not on the top as the only beacon lights to succeeding generations. The foundation of Ireland is the Gael, and the Gael must be the element that absorbs. On no other basis can an Irish nation be reared that would not topple over by force of the very ridicule that it would beget. However, since the glories of 1782 the process has been reversed, and we are all Palemen now.

The movement of 1782 placed the Pale at the head of Ireland for the first time in history, and ever since the Pale has retained that place. The '98 and '48 movements, the Fenians and the Parnellite agitation, were Pale movements in their essence, even when they were most fiercely rebellious. In many respects they were tinkering movements, for, while they were making a loud noise the great canker was left unheeded. The passions and excitements of those days distracted all men's attention from one long monotonous series of fateful sounds. No one heeded the dull incessant sap, sap, of English ideas, ideals and manners – mostly of the worst English kind too – that were all the time rotting the only possible foundation for the Ireland that the people were vaguely, incoherently seeking after ...

The great present result of our conquest by the Pale, and of the failure of subsequent partly national movements – whose success would probably have long since put Pale influence into its proper subordinate place – is that Irishmen are now in competition with Englishmen in every sphere of social and intellectual activity, in a competition where England has fixed the marks, the subjects, and has had the sole making of the rules of the game.

> D P Moran, 'The Pale and the Gael', *The New
> Ireland Review*, reprinted in *The Philosophy of Irish Ireland*
> (Dublin: James Duffy & Co Ltd, 1905) pp 37-47

41 'Old Ireland is name of the Shan Van Vocht'

The Shan Van Vocht (the Poor Old Woman) was a literary and political monthly magazine edited by two young women from prosperous suburban Belfast, Alice Milligan (1866-1953) and Anna Johnston (1866-1902). Anna was a Catholic, whose father Robert was a veteran Fenian leader, but Alice's background was Ulster Protestant. Operated from the office of Robert Johnston's timber yard off York Street, Belfast between 1896 and 1899, the magazine was distinctive in a number of ways. Its editorship was female, its base was Belfast, and it was the first strong literary voice in the movement which linked cultural nationalism to revolutionary politics – when *The Shan Van Vocht* closed in 1899 it passed over its subscription list to Arthur Griffith's Dublin paper *The United Irishman* (later to become *Sinn Fèin*).

For some time now we have realised the necessity of bringing *The Shan Van Vocht* more into touch with the times we live in. We chronicle the events of historic '98, from month to month, and have published a history of the last era of Irish revolution; we will do all in our power to honour the memory of Ireland's illustrious dead, but except in our reports of the Literary, Gaelic and Amnesty Societies, we have scarcely alluded to the events passing in the world. We were prompted to preserve this silence, partly from a desire to stand entirely aloof from the fray of party politics which, for some years back, has so bitterly divided the people of Ireland ... but the country as a whole has happily abandoned any intense partisan interest in the suicidal civil war, the combatants have laid down their arms and the young men, and boys growing into men, see no necessity why they should dispute as to who is to take the lead in the British House of Commons; perhaps they have realised that there is nothing to be gained or lost there, and that they themselves are of more importance to Ireland, and more powerful to advance her than any of the MPs ...

It is time that someone should speak out boldly to break through the conspiracy of silence into which the Dublin press seems to have entered with regard to the progress of the national cause outside the narrow fighting ring of Irish politics. We are not at liberty to preach revolution, but there is no restraint put upon our reporting the doings of revolutionists, insurgents, conspirators in Matabeleland, Johannesburg, Cuba, Canada and elsewhere ... Our space is limited, but every inch of it is devoted to the interests of Ireland's nationhood, and those who support us would have nothing to do with us had we any lower aim. In a few pages we can monthly compress a record of a very incident which is of permanent importance to 'the cause', and which will give our readers a right understanding of the events of the day as they affect the destiny of Ireland ...

The Shan Van Vocht, vol 1, 1896, p 178

42 John Dillon: Friends and foes of the Gaelic revival

Although much of the early work of the Gaelic League was in the study and revival of Irish literature, its most vigorous and politically significant activity was in the field of language agitation. Much of this consisted of contests and 'test cases' with petty bureaucracy, but the League's most distinguished operation was its successful campaign to establish Irish as a compulsory matriculation requirement for entry into the new National University. The deputy leader of the Home Rule party, John Dillon (1851–1927) very much a Victorian and a liberal on issues of this nature, delivered a strong attack on compulsion to the National Convention in February 1909, but the University senate bowed to the League's pressure.

... After all, it is our own university. The constitution is such that the will of the people must in the long run prevail in its government. If it fails, the shame and discredit of its failure will not rest on the British government, but on the Irish people (applause). 'Blow the university to fragments if Irish is not immediately made compulsory', says one controversialist. 'Burn it down' says another.

A delegate – Right (hear, hear).

Mr Dillon – Right, says my friend here ... We must at least wait for the university before we can blow it up or burn it down. And I would ask you again why didn't you blow up or burn down the Royal University?

A delegate – It was not national.

Mr Dillon – And is it to be contended by my friend that we are to tolerate every institution except a national institution (applause) which is your own, and which in the long run you can do what you like with? It is the first time since the Union ... that the British government has to meet us fairly on the question of higher education; and is it wise, does it not tend to discredit our country, that now when for the first time a British government has met us fairly and given us an institution which we can control ourselves, that we should select that opportunity to fall upon each other with fury for a detail? ('Not a detail'). Not a detail? You may think there is a great deal involved in the detail, but it is a detail. ('No, no') I do not attach importance to the point, but I ask does it not tend to discredit our country that after all these hundred years during which primary education and university education in our country has been enslaved, and our language and the literature of our country has been trampled underfoot, that when the British government for the first time gives us the opportunity of modelling our own university we should select this opportunity of failing upon each other with fury over this question ...

It has been said and repeated that this is a fight between the friends and foes of the Gaelic revival ('Right' and 'No, no') ... To my own knowledge many of those most strongly opposed to making Irish compulsory for matriculation in the new university are just as keen friends of the language and of the Gaelic movement as the most violent of the advocates of compulsory Irish. The question truly stated is not an issue between friends and foes of the Gaelic revival. It is a question of educational method.

Weekly Freeman's Journal, 20 February 1909

43 The Leader: Nationalism in a Catholic atmosphere

D P Moran's most powerful weapon was *The Leader*, a weekly newspaper which he founded in 1900 and edited for a generation. In essence the paper took up the thinking of the Gaelic League and Irish-Ireland movement generally, simplified the issues and disseminated them far more widely. In later years *The Leader* took an active part in the destruction of the Irish Parliamentary Party. But during this early period its role was rather in helping to create an atmosphere in which a different style of nationalism might thrive. In particular Moran's journalism played a key part in linking the 'Catholic' and 'Gaelic' concepts of Irish nationality, and in winning widespread support amongst the younger clergy for Irish-Ireland. Unrelenting opposition to 'Bung' [his nickname for the licensed trade] and its influence on the public life of nationalist Ireland, for which he tended to blame the Irish Parliamentary Party, was another cornerstone of Moran's journalism.

(a) ... I cannot call to mind any case in which a policeman got a testimonial [a cash gift from local people upon leaving his post] for discharging his duty strictly, fairly and fully. In any case ... that I know of, the man who got it was a "damned good fellow" ... Since being a "damned good fellow" entitles a man to a purse of sovereigns, let us see what are the qualities that go to make him.

"Well, in the first place he is ten years in the town and what harm did he ever do? Many a time he could have summoned me for Sunday work [ie opening] and other things, and did not pretend to see me ... I say it would be a shame to let him go away without a testimonial", says Bung No.1.

"Many a time he could have caught myself and you too, Johnny, but he never gave us any trouble, and I agree with Tom there, that it would be a mean thing to let him go now ... without a testimonial", says Bung No.2.

Others, not Bungs – but frequenters of their drunkeries – agree that something should be done to show their respect for the man. They remember gratefully how many 'chances' they got, what a decent fellow he was ... I do not know how those things are done in other countries, but this is how they are done in our 'green' country.

The Leader, 11 November 1905

(b) It has been hinted to us that it is our opinion that no one but a Catholic can be an Irishman. We never said so, nor do we think so ... We are prepared to be perfectly frank with our sympathisers who think we are 'too Catholic'. We have great admiration and respect for Thomas Davis, but his 'Tolerance' scheme did not work ... When we look out on Ireland we see that those who believe, or may be immediately induced to believe, in

Ireland a nation are, as a matter of fact, Catholics. When we look back on history we find also, as a matter of fact, that those who stood during the last three hundred years for Ireland as an Irish entity were mainly Catholics, and that those who sought to corrupt them and trample on them were mainly non-Catholics ...

Such being the facts, the only thinkable solution of the Irish national problem is that one side gets on top and absorbs the other until we have one nation, or that each develops independently. As we are for Ireland, we are in the existing circumstances on the side of Catholic development; and we see plainly that any genuine non-Catholic Irish nationalist must become reconciled to Catholic development or throw in his lot with the other side ... If a non-Catholic nationalist Irishman does not wish to live in a with Catholic atmosphere let him turn Orangeman ...

The Leader, 27 July 1901

(c) Douglas Hyde to Lady Gregory   7 January 1901

... The fact is that we cannot turn our back on the Davis ideal of every person in Ireland being an Irishman, no matter what their blood and politics, for the moment we cease to profess that, we land ourselves in an intolerable position. It is equally true, thought, that the Gaelic League and *The Leader* aim at stimulating the old peasant, Papist aboriginal population, and we care very little about the others, though I would not let this be seen as Moran has done.

Gregory MS, Berg Collection (New York Public Library), cited in L P Curtis Jnr, *Anglo-Saxons and Celts*, p 147 (Conference on British Studies, University of Bridgeport, Conn. New York University Press, 1968)

44 'Hungary never once sent a parliamentary party to Vienna'

Another Dublin journalist of Moran's generation, Arthur Griffith (1870-1922), shared the same 'Irish-Ireland' ethos, but linked it directly to a separatist political position in a way that Moran did not. Griffith was a non-violent separatist who founded the first Sinn Féin Party in 1905, based on ideas of passive resistance and parallel institutions. These ideas later played an important role, though secondary to physical force, in the War of Independence. Another of Griffith's imaginative ideas was to draw a potential parallel between Ireland's relationship with Britain and Hungary's relationship to Austria, independent under the Habsburg crown.

...You may be old enough yourself to remember when Hungary fell [in 1848] and 'Freedom shrieked aloud' – when Kossuth [Hungarian nationalist leader] was a fugitive, with the bloodhounds of Austria on his track, when the Austrian dragoon was the law from Budapest to the Carpathians, when day after day Hungarian patriots were shot or hanged like dogs by the victorious soldiers of Francis Joseph ... Therefore, when you look around today and see Hungary freer and stronger and more prosperous than Austria, when you know that if Hungary declares itself a republic tomorrow – which she intends to do when the sad old man who reigns in Vienna dies – Austria would not fight, because she could not – you may well rub your eyes, reflecting that Hungary never once sent a Parliamentary Party to Vienna to 'fight on the floor of the House' for home rule, never once admitted the right of Austria to rule over her, never once pretended to be 'loyal' to the power that had smitten her, never once held monster indignation meetings and resolutioned, and fired strong adjectives – and yet notwithstanding, forced Austria to her knees and wrung from her unwilling hands the free constitution which has made Hungary the power she is today ...

> *United Irishman*, 2 January 1904, repr. in A Mitchell &
> P Ó Snodaigh (eds) *Irish Political Documents, 1869-1916*
> (Dublin: Irish Academic Press, 1989)

45 *A new moving spirit in the country?*

Disappointments in nationalist Ireland over the Irish Council Bill, the low priority granted to Irish national concerns by the Liberal government, and the apparent inability of the ageing Irish Party to respond to new, predominantly cultural forces, came together between 1907 and 1909 to create anxiety in the minds of Irish Party leaders. This was rapidly dispelled by the excitement of the years following 1910, which propelled nationalist parliamentarians back into the forefront of events, but it was a warning for the future which came only too true after 1914.

(a) Land Commissioner W F Bailey to James Bryce   14 June 1907

> Those who have been a generation in Irish politics say that they never remember a time when things were so difficult to forecast. I see distinct signs of a new group in Irish politics – of a new moving spirit in the country. A younger generation is coming up and no-one can yet tell what the outcome will be ...

> Bodleian Library, Oxford: James Bryce Papers, MS 19

(b) Alfred Webb [Irish Party Trustee] to John Redmond   26 June 1906

I am greatly impressed with the character of the support being given to the Gaelic League – Dr Hyde – and the Sinn Féin movement, as compared with the character of the support we are receiving. The cream of the youth and spirit of the country are being gathered into these movements ...Who are being left to us in the country? The bishops, who with a few honourable exceptions will leave us to our fate when they have gained their point ... the farmers and the labourers, most of them as have not yet got the best of what they want. And when they get it they appear inclined, like the County Wexford – the county really with the most material commonsense grit in Ireland, to draw away ... and we have the rag-tag and bobtail. Suppose [Joe] Devlin were returning from the USA tomorrow night – imagine the character of the reception he would meet here compared to that accorded to Dr Hyde ...We cannot always be content to go on fighting for home rule through the assistance mainly of persons who are only using us for their own purposes and ends, and who care little for the desires burning in our hearts ...

NLI, Dublin:
Redmond Papers

Chapter 4

Unionism old and new

46 Providence smiles on Belfast?

Early nineteenth-century Belfast was still a small linen-trading town. The sectarian conflicts of rural Armagh and some other places only gradually began to make an impact on urban centres. In 1815 the town's Protestant elite gave generous support to the Catholic community when St Patrick's Church was opened. The town was beginning to grow rapidly however, as both Catholics and Protestants entered in large numbers to work in the new mills and factories. On 12 July 1813 the first recorded sectarian riot in the town took place (see a, below). Soon Sandy Row and the Pound Loney (from which grew the Lower Falls) developed as Protestant and Catholic neighbourhoods. In the 1830s and 1840s, 12 July and election days came to be characterised by sectarian rioting, accentuated somewhat by the brief appearance of Daniel O'Connell in Belfast in 1841. In 1857 rioting became a very much more formidable activity, virtually uncontrolled by the authorities for months on end. One causal factor identified by the Riots Commissioners of Inquiry in 1857 was a sermon delivered to the Sandy Row Orangemen by the Rector of Christchurch, Dr Thomas Drew, on 12 July (see b, below; also Document 11, above). This further passage from his sermon illustrates both the outspoken anti-Catholic sensationalism of his appeal and his commitment to international liberal and progressive causes. This conjunction of views was the main content of political Protestantism in Ulster at that time. With the Union unchallenged, and political nationalism scarcely articulated, Unionism as a political programme was yet to emerge.

(a) Mr Dunn, on the part of the prosecution, in rising to address the court in the present case [said], it excites no small degree of regret in my mind, that I am this day called upon to state to the court occurrences of a most disgraceful nature, which have recently occurred in Belfast. Such an event is the more to be regretted because the town of Belfast appears to have been favoured in a peculiar degree by the smiles of Providence: it has hitherto stood distinguished by the improved state of its civilisation and manners, and by the intelligence, the industry and the wealth of its inhabitants; yet in this town, amidst a people so well-informed were the streets stained with the blood of its inhabitants. This, while our fleets and armies are waging war abroad to protect us from foreign foes, to preserve this favoured land in peace and tranquillity, we must counterfeit a war at home, we must bring it home to ourselves, we must riot in its horrors and exhibit scenes of slaughter in our streets.

... Sorry I am to observe that, from a mistaken zeal, from too eager a desire of making a conspicuous display of extra loyalty, by distinguishing themselves by peculiar signs and badges, certain societies have presumed to arrogate to themselves a title to exclusive loyalty. Such societies, whatsoever be the name by which they call themselves, whatsoever be their professions, tend to disturb the public peace, by exciting an irritation in the public feelings; and I must say that those who devise, and those who set themselves at the head of such associations, are in the eyes of God and justice answerable for whatever consequences result therefrom. If magistrates have given encouragement to such associations, they have deviated from their duty: they hold from the King an authority to keep peace, not to propagate dissension.

The melancholy effects of this system are best illustrated by the facts which are now to undergo the investigation of the law. It will appear that on 12 July last a number of these societies departed from Belfast and proceeded in military array to Lisburn, each led by a master, with colours flying, and a man called a Tyler, bearing a drawn sword. Here they were met by other societies; here also they were greeted by some persons of distinction in the country. After remaining here some time, they returned to Belfast, and about 7 o'clock came to the Linen-Hall, where it was thought they would have dispersed; however, some of the lodges returned through Donegall Place. At the Bank Buildings Morgan, one of the prisoners, stepped out from among his fellows and, advancing into the crowd who were assembled there to see the procession pass by, struck one of them, an inoffensive servant, a man of no party, and nearly knocked him down. This unprovoked assault produced an affray. They then proceeded through Hercules Street [then a narrow, Catholic street, comprised mainly of butchers' premises, now Royal Avenue] to the house of a publican called Thompson, in North Street. Here a number of persons, partly collected from curiosity, partly excited by the previous provocation pressed upon them, and stones were thrown by both parties. The Orangemen, on finding themselves likely to be overpowered, went into Thompson's house, apparently as a place of refuge, but in the twinkling of an eye reappeared with arms which had been handed to them by persons in the inside, ready primed and loaded, and immediately commenced a cool and deadly fire ...

Gentlemen of the Jury, you have a high and arduous task to perform; your verdict is to decide a question of the greatest public moment; it is to determine whether peace and tranquillity are to be restored to your once happy town, or whether its inhabitants are to be still exposed to the wanton outrages of an infuriated assembly ...

Trial of the Belfast Orangemen
(Belfast: Joseph Smyth, 1813), pp 4-7

(b) *Rev Dr Thomas Drew*: The Sermon on the Mount is an everlasting rebuke to all intolerance, and all legislative and ecclesiastical cruelty. Of old time, lords of high degree with their own hands, strained, on the rack, the delicate limbs of Protestant women; prelates dabbled in the gore of helpless victims; and the cells of the Pope's prisons were paved with calcined bones of men and cemented with gore and human hair. Would that such atrocities were no longer formidable What has been done may be repeated, and, at this hour, the world had its record of existing wrong. Austria crushes the throbbing hearts of Italy. France basely upholds the Pontiff's detested throne; and America has not yet regarded the cry of millions she calls 'chattels' and not men. This sad anomaly cannot forever last ... The Word of God makes all plain; puts to eternal shame the practice of persecutors; and stigmatises, with enduring reprobation, the arrogant pretenses of popes, and the outrageous dogmata of their bloodstained religion ...

... At no period were the resources of Rome more available. All that literature and the fine arts; all that painting, sculpture and music can do, are employed in her service. The strangest result of all this fascination is, that men of intelligence and learning, who have drunk of her cup, are men so intoxicated by its poison, as to endorse and uphold the most fantastic and incredible inventions, lies and practices of the Romish sect ... It is painful to see how false views of the real state of Ireland are still maintained by wily statesmen, and by persons from whom better things might reasonably be expected. By reason of a falsified census, the numbers of the Protestants were set down vastly below their amount. In many instances, treacherous census takers actually returned no Protestants, and counted those who are really Protestants as Romanists!

... The faint-hearted clergy of the past century have to answer, to some extent, for the race of semi-infidel legislators and pro-Popery legislators which abound. It is not to be credited, if preachers had really been scriptural (and to be really Scriptural they must be really Protestant) preachers, that their flocks, especially the young, would have grown up in such deplorable deficiency of Protestant feeling and conduct ... Our princes want prelates like Latimer and Ridley to stand at their sides. Italy wants another Savonarola; Scotland another Knox; and England another Wicliff!

BPP 1857-8 XXIV
(Report on Riots in Belfast, 1857),
Evidence, pp 248-52

47 Triumph of the Romish mobs, 1857

The Irish census took no account of religion until 1861. But we may be fairly certain that Belfast in 1800 was a predominantly Protestant town, numbering only about 2,000 Catholics (10 per cent) in its population. But the large-scale urban migration which followed was for half a century disproportionately Catholic, for Catholics occupied the least secure position in Ulster's rural economy. The famine, we may be certain, accentuated this trend, so that by 1861 the Catholic proportion of the population reached its registered peak at 34 per cent (41,000). The proportion in the early 1850s may have been even higher. But with the onset of an era of major riots in 1857, Ulster Catholic migrants tended increasingly to choose Britain or America as their destination in preference to the Orange citadel of Belfast. The immediate cause of the 1857 disturbances was an outbreak of evangelical Protestant street-preaching in the town, most notably on the Custom House Steps (see also Document 55). To Catholics such preaching seemed less the exercise of a religious right than an abuse of free speech. In origin, at least, the movement was part of a revival movement which extended far beyond Ireland. But to many people in Belfast the issue came to be seen as a struggle for mastery in the city, as the Protestant daily newspaper (a, below) discerned clearly when the magistrates intervened to cancel one such event. Its Catholic counterpart predictably took a different view (b, below).

Faced with the disapproval of the magistracy and the incontrovertible fact that street-preaching was in practice likely to be followed by serious rioting, the Church of Ireland Mission, led by Rev William McIlwaine, called a halt to its 1857 programme. But a young Presbyterian clergyman, Hugh 'Roaring' Hanna (1824-92), though opposed by his own Belfast Presbytery, came forward to take up the challenge (see c, below). He would, he said in his 'First Letter to the Protestants of Belfast', uphold the right to preach in the open. Hanna later became a prominent public figure in Belfast, as a commissioner for national education and a leading opponent of home rule. The 1857 troubles were something of a stepping-stone in his career. His decision to proceed with his service on the Custom House Steps on 6 September, leading as it did to the inevitable rioting, made him an important witness before the subsequent riots commission. His evidence under cross-examination by Alexander O'Rorke, counsel for the Catholics, gives some impression of his brash and irrepressible style (see d, below).

(a) The Romish mobs have triumphed in our town. They have succeeded in accomplishing what no Protestant in Belfast ever supposed he should live to see realised. The preaching of the Gospel in our streets to the destitute, ragged poor is put down. Belfast ranks now with Kilkenny, or Cork, or Limerick. In these Romish cities, where priests are regnant, and their mobs omnipotent, and the authorities bow to their behests, no Protestant minister dare lift his voice in the streets or highways, to proclaim the peaceful message of the Cross – he would be stoned or murdered. We write what everybody knows to be fact. It is one of the dark features of the Romish South that there is no religious liberty tolerated there by the priesthood; and the mobs, under their complete influence and domination, obey their fiats, and resist with the violence of fiends, every public effort to make known to the benighted masses the blessed tidings of salvation.

But no one ever supposed that it should be thus in Protestant Belfast. Hitherto fullest liberty has been given to our ministers to carry out their benignant purposes of doing good. They have preached in the streets – in all parts of the town – without let or hindrance. The Romanists interfered not. Hitherto they had a deep policy to carry out. They were without influence in this town – they were poor – they feigned great gratitude for the foolishly bestowed, and ill-requited benefactions of so-called liberal Protestants. We remember their solitary chapel near the precincts of Smithfield. When Donegall-street chapel was built, lasting gratitude was expressed to the generous Protestants who had aided Dr Crolly [former parish priest] in the erection of that edifice. Dr Crolly was one of our most eloquent lip-advocates of toleration, forbearance, good-will among Christian brethren. And many of our townsmen were deceived. They began to think Romanism a changed, mild, humble, harmless system.

Look at the daring, intolerant, and triumphant attitude and operations of the system now? We do not think lightly of the Papal mob-law domination. We have the worst fears because of it. Is our town henceforward to be degraded by the reproach that a Protestant minister shall not dare to preach in its streets? Are our magistrats to rebuke ministers of God for obeying their divine Master's command, 'to go into the streets and highways', to discharge the functions of their office?

... A mighty Romish movement is now in operation in this town to assimilate it to the degraded Popish towns of the South and West of Ireland ... Our object is not to inflame Protestant against Papist. We advocate the right of the poor and of the outcasts to have the Gospel preached to them on the streets.

Belfast Newsletter, 5 September 1857

(b) Every unprejudiced person – every man of common sense – knows that street-preaching is not got up for the purpose of enlightening Protestants 'who sit in darkness'. That is not the object of the raving system. Its real object and aim is to insult the feelings of Catholics and deride their faith; to show that here, in the midst of a population of 50,000 Catholics, there is a tyrannical, rampant, and 'dominant' faction, struggling for mastery over those who do not agree with them either religiously or politically. That faction must be at their old work of division, disunion, and religious hate ... The exercise of a public or private right when it becomes obnoxious to the community and results in violence, has no longer the character of right; it then becomes a wrong; and it is the duty of those entrusted with the administration of the law to act with determination and vigour, and put down this hateful system, which in defiance of judicial remonstrance, promises us a reign of confusion, terror, and, possibly, bloodshed. We warn the authorities in time, and thus have done our duty.

Belfast Morning News, 5 September 1857

(c) *Letter of Rev Hugh Hanna to the Protestants of Belfast*

MEN AND BRETHREN, – Your blood-bought and cherished 'RIGHTS' have been imperilled by the audacious and savage outrages of a Romish mob. The well-meant but foolish leniency of an easy-natured magistracy, vainly hoping to disarm resentment by conciliation, has hastened and aggravated the present crisis ... *Your ministers have a legal right to preach in the open air.* No man can honestly deny that. You have also a right to listen to them. Let them choose *convenient* places for their services. When you assemble around, leave so much of the thoroughfare unoccupied that such as do not choose to listen may pass by. Call that clearance the 'Pope's pad'. No man has any right to interrupt the services ...

(d) *Cross Examination before the Riots Commissioners of Rev Hugh Hanna:*

Mr O'Rorke – *You have the character of being a controversialist?* – I do not know that I have that character, but some people are kind enough to say that I was rather a smart hand at it.
Well, certainly you do not want for a trumpeter – you can blow your own trumpet? – To be sure.
You have preached very often on controversial subjects? – Yes.
And you have advertised these sermons? – Some of them.
What were the subjects of these sermons? – The various subjects that are litigated between the two churches; and I think I have logically overturned, among other things, the Pope's supremacy; and if you wish for something more specific, I will go on and tell you what further damage I have done your church.
What further damage have you done my church? – I intended it.
Do you think you have moved one stone out of it? – I think I have.
You have not removed the roof off it yet? – The covering is very scanty.
You do not like coverings at all? You like open air better? – Yes.
At the risk of a shindy? – Let the people who precipitate the shindies take the consequences.
You are just in the Presbyterian Church what Mr McIlwaine is in his church? – I just wish to be a faithful minister, a useful man, and a loyal citizen.
Do you not wish to be simply what Mr McIlwaine is? – I have no particular

anxiety to be what Mr McIlwaine is. Mr McIlwaine is only an incumbent. I would never be satisfied till I realised the top of my ambition. I would not be satisfied with his ecclesiastically humble position. If I were in the Episcopalian Church, I would not be satisfied till I was Archbishop of Canterbury.

About how far are you off the head of your own church? — Oh! I am a considerable distance off; but I am climbing as fast as I can.

And you want to climb by notoriety? — I want to climb by honest endeavour.

Honest endeavour, on Sundays, to create riots? — No; that is not part of my policy or principle either.

You take the Regium Donum?[1] — I do. I am only sorry that it is not more than twice as much.

BPP 1857-58 XXVI *(Report on Riots in Belfast, 1857)*, Evidence pp 169, 252-3

48 William Johnston of Ballykilbeg

Although it was religious affiliation that delineated the two communities in Ulster, and although outbursts of religious enthusiasm on either side might serve to bring the communities into sporadic conflict, Christian rhetoric alone could not easily sustain a regular political movement, particularly on the Protestant side where church attendance was lower and where the diversity of denominations posed an organisational problem. The Orange Order had been officially dissolved by its Grand Lodge in 1836, but the grass-roots refused to die and indeed flourished as strongly in the new working-class districts of Belfast as they had done in rural Armagh. One of the Order's most active spokesmen from about 1860 onwards was William Johnston (1829-1902), a small landowner from Ballykilbeg, Co Down. He won attention, imprisonment, and a political career at Westminster, in that order, following an Orange march which he led from Newtownards to Bangor in 1868 in defiance of the Party Processions Act, a measure through which British governments sought unsuccessfully to stifle political excitement in Ireland, by banning all Orange and other contentious processions between 1850 and 1872. Following the wide extension of the franchise implemented by the Second Reform Act, Johnston stood as an independent in the Belfast parliamentary election of 1868, entering Westminster at the expense of an official Conservative. His victory, and his endorsement as Conservative candidate at future elections, mark the establishment of a formal link between the Ulster Conservatives and the popular Protestantism of the Orange Order. In this extract, from an early speech to the Grand Orange Lodge of Belfast, Johnston expounds the basic political justification for Orangeism.

Such a demonstration as this is a glorious thing. Would to God there were more of them all over the length and breadth of Ireland. (Hear, hear). We

1 The *Regium Donum* (Royal Bounty) was a grant made from public funds to Presbyterian ministers in Ireland. Initiated by William III in 1690 in return for Irish Presbyterian support against James II, it was discontinued in 1869 when the Church of Ireland was disestablished.

should not then be told that Orangeism was a thing of the past, that the Orange Institution was not in existence, that the thing had passed away, and that only a man here and man there was engaged in maintaining Orangeism. We should then be able to point to our glorious demonstrations, and say – Are these the men that are not in existence? Such a glorious demonstration as we can show here tonight is a proof that, under God, Orangeism shall never be extinguished in Ireland. (Loud cheers). There are some who dread demonstrations. There are some who tell us we should confine ourselves to our monthly meetings in our lodge rooms. We are forbidden by the law of the land to go forth in procession on the 12th July ... Are we not then, to show our force in any way? Are we to hide ourselves in holes and corners for fear of giving offence to our fastidious fellow countrymen? God forbid it. If they believed that we were extinguished, if that belief could be entertained by those who hate us, we would see re-enacted in this country those deeds of blood which stained the hills and alleys in bygone days ... The Orange Institution is a religio-political institution ... But Popery is something more than a religious system; it is a political system also. It is a religio-political system for the enslavement of the body and soul of man, and it cannot be met by any mere religious system, or by any mere political system. It must be opposed by such a combination as the Orange Society, based upon religion, and carrying our religion into the politics of the day. We must carry our religion into the politics of the day. We must tell our representatives in Parliament that they must support Protestantism in their politics as well as go down on their knees before God on the Sabbath Day. (Cheers).

Belfast Newsletter, 15 May 1861

49 United against Home Rule, 1886

The Fenian movement of the 1860s required no political opposition from Unionists, though its violent excesses of course provided them with a welcome propaganda weapon. The gradual emergence of parliamentary nationalism from the mid-1870s came to be of much more serious concern, especially once it achieved its interim objective of converting one of the main British political parties to home rule, at the end of 1885. The forces of upper class Conservatism and plebeian Orangeism came together with the great majority of Protestant Liberals in Ireland to establish Irish Unionism as a formal political organisation, both at Westminster and in Ireland. An important stage in this process was the coming together of the Conservatives and erstwhile Liberals of Ulster in a joint meeting in the Ulster Hall to oppose Gladstone's first Home Rule Bill.

The feeling in Belfast against Mr Gladstone's scheme grows in intensity. Public bodies and private individuals are making every effort to have their view proclaimed, and Liberals and Conservatives seem to have buried their old animosities in the face of what they believe to be a common danger.

Today the Belfast Presbytery, at its monthly meeting, passed a resolution condemnatory of the measure, and tonight a great meeting of merchants, traders, and general rate-payers convened by the Mayor, in response to a requisition signed by Conservatives and Liberals, was held in the Ulster Hall. The Hall was crowded by the leading citizens and not by those who ordinarily form the rank and file of local popular demonstrations. The chair was taken by the Mayor, Sir Edward Harland [shipbuilder and subsequently Unionist MP], who on entering the Hall was most enthusiastically received, the grand organ striking up the National Anthem and the entire audience rising to their feet and cheering for some minutes.

The first resolution was proposed by Mr W.G.Ewart, Conservative [linen manufacturer], and was as follows: 'That we, the merchants, traders and other rate-payers of the town of Belfast, assembled in this public meeting, composed of both political parties, declare our unchangeable loyalty to the Queen and to the Constitution of this country, that we fully recognise the incalculable advantages which Ireland derives from the Union with Great Britain, and earnestly appeal to the people of England and Scotland to aid us in preserving the present connection between the two countries'. Mr Ewart dwelt at some length upon the evils home rule would bring upon Ireland and Irish credit, and said that after a short trial of an Irish Parliament the country north and south would be one in decay. Those represented at the meeting had expended millions in building up and creating property in Ulster, but not one-tenth of those millions would have been invested if they had not been confident that the Act of Union would not be repealed ... Mr Adam Duffin LlD, Liberal, seconded the resolution. The next resolution was moved by Mr Finlay McCance JP, Liberal ...

The Times, 14 April 1886

50   1892: *The mischievous and unchristian policy of Home Rule*

The 1886 Home Rule Bill was defeated in the House of Commons by Liberal Unionist defections from Gladstone's party. When Gladstone brought forward his second bill, in 1893, a Commons majority was assured, but the Conservative and Unionist majority in the House of Lords still proved an effective barrier to legislation. Irish Unionists however, especially in Ulster, left nothing to chance. Prior to the general election of 1892, while the Conservatives were still in power, a group of Ulster Liberal Unionists who were in touch with Joseph Chamberlain developed the idea of holding a massive anti-home rule convention in Belfast. After meetings with Ulster Conservative leaders, consultations with Unionist MPs at Westminster through Thomas Sinclair and Rev R R Kane, Rector of Christchurch, and a series of nominating meetings throughout the Protestant communities of Ulster, the Great Convention met on 17 June 1892 – under what was then still a non-partisan Irish-language slogan *Erin go Bragh*. The agreed emphasis was to be on dignity, moderation, non-violence and, above all, size. 12,000 delegates were assembled, and as the Ulster Hall was too small the Convention took place in an enormous temporary building erected in an undeveloped corner of Belfast's Botanic Gardens. The Liberal-Presbyterian paper *The Northern Whig* was as enthusiastic about the event as the Orange and Conservative press. (See Volume 1, illustration No 10.)

(a) The delegates, as each contingent passed up the pavilion amid the hearty cheers of the citizens, would have formed a curious study to anyone whose acquaintance with Ulster politics and Ulster politicians had suddenly arrested, say, ten years ago. Here were men, marching shoulder to shoulder, wearing the same spirit, who a few years ago would have been as opposite as the poles in their opinions on political questions, especially on the eve of a general election.

Here were the old tenant-righters of the sixties ... Here were the sturdy reformers of Antrim ... here again were the Unitarians of Down, always progressive in their politics ... And here were the old-fashioned Tories of the counties ... Then there were the modern Conservatives ... And then the Orangemen, more directly regardful, as far as rank and file of them were concerned, of religious than of political distinctions ... All these various elements – Whig, Liberal, Radical, Presbyterian, Episcopalian, Unitarian and Methodist ... united as one man. Anyone who knows the sturdiness and firmness of each of these sects and parties in their old-time political opinions and beliefs can readily understand that it required a powerful motive indeed to make them sink all differences of class and creed and hold themselves together in a 'band', the homogeneity of which nothing now can shake.

Northern Whig, 18 June 1892

(b) *Thomas Sinclair, Liberal Unionist:* A conviction of common duty in the presence of a common danger has healed divisions that formerly embittered many of our social relationships, and has united in common defence of their common birthright as British citizens men who through all their previous lives had never stood on the same platform. We are here Radicals and Tories, Presbyterians and Episcopalians, Orangemen and Roman Catholics, landowners and land occupiers, masters and men, but with threatened disaster at our gates we speak and act as one man.

(c) *John Dunville, Liberal Unionist:* Gentlemen, I trust that the separatists will note the fact that there are here today hundreds of Unionists who, like myself, are representatives of families that for years supported the Liberal party, and who in the past were strongly opposed to the Orange party; but we see here today one united party – Conservatives, Orangemen, and Liberals – all equally unanimous in our determination to resist this mischievous and unchristian policy of home rule...

(d) *Rev R R Kane, Belfast Grand Master of the Orange Order:* We appeal from this platform to the common sense of Englishmen, Scotchmen and Welshmen, our brothers in the great and glorious confederacy of the United Kingdom; and we ask them what claim for ascendancy is involved in the claim to remain subject to the self-same Parliament to which they themselves are subject, the Parliament which has seen fit to take from us any ascendancy we ever had [ie Disestablishment of the Church of Ireland, 1869], the Parliament which has seen fit to remove every disability under which our fellow-countrymen ever laboured, the Parliament which more than any other legislative assembly in the world has been steadily and rapidly progressing in its consideration for popular rights and which is filled with a passionate resolve to do justice to every class and creed.

(e) *Sir William Ewart, Conservative:* The maintenance of our industries and the employment of our people depend upon our general and mercantile credit being maintained at its present high standard. They depend upon the accumulated capital being safe from attack, and on outside capital continuing to flow in for investment, on freedom from excessive local taxation, which would assuredly be the only resort of a lavish and unpractical Government.

> G Lucy, *The Great Convention: the Ulster Unionist Convention of 1892*
> (Lurgan: Ulster Society, 1995), pp 17, 27–30

51 The Irish Loyal and Patriotic Union: The true interests of Ireland

With the abolition of the property qualification for county electors in 1885, most male householders who were small farmers or labourers had their first opportunity to vote in a general election. At the same time, twenty-two of the smallest borough constituencies in Ireland were abolished, which also weakened landlord influence. The overall number of Irish seats in the House of Commons remained at 103, incidentally leaving Ireland heavily over-represented at Westminster. In an attempt to salvage something from the impending electoral disaster which faced them in the south, pro-Union activists developed a number of cross-party groupings: one, the Loyal Irish Union, was too predominantly Tory and soon foundered, but the Ulster Loyalist Union in the north (for a while) and the Irish Loyal and Patriotic Union in the other three provinces were more effective in bring about genuine electoral collaboration between Liberals and Conservatives, running anti–home rule candidates in 54 seats in the 1885 general election. The two parties nonetheless lost more than half of their Irish seats, including all their non-Ulster seats except for Dublin University, with the Liberals securing no seats at all. The ILPU, which had its headquarters in Dublin, was too landlord-dominated to be attractive to Ulster businessmen or farmers, and gradually transferred its main efforts from fighting hopeless elections in the south to lobbying for the Unionist cause in Britain. But in 1885 it sponsored many candidates and produced 286,000 election pamphlets. Such was the political climate in southern Ireland, however, that much of the ILPU's work was carried out in semi-secrecy, with the names of sponsors and many leading members not being published. The organisation itself, though founded discreetly in May 1885, was not announced until October. In 1891 the ILPU changed its name to the Irish Unionist Alliance, still a Dublin-based body, which continued to be the main grass-roots organisation for Unionists until the formation of the Ulster Unionist Council in 1905 (see Doc 57).

(a) An Association has been in existence since 1 May 1885, under the name of 'The Irish Loyal and Patriotic Union', the object of which is to uphold the true interests of Ireland by affording to those Irishmen of all creeds and political opinions, who believe that their country can best prosper as part of the imperial system, an opportunity of uniting in an organised opposition to the efforts being made by the party led by Mr Parnell to sever the legislative connection between Ireland and Great Britain; and of thus asserting and maintaining by their votes the integrity of the Empire, the general supremacy of the united parliament and, not least, the social freedom of the individual, of which in the opinion of the Association, these are essential bulwarks and guarantees.

The Association is entirely unsectarian in its character, and is composed of members of both great political parties in the state. It will support indifferently those candidates – whether Liberal or Conservative – who, while standing on the principles of the Association, will be likely to be most acceptable to the electors in each constituency. While expecting from them a firm adhesion to the mainlines of the existing Constitution, it would be desirable that they should approach, in a fair and candid spirit, the consideration on their merits of any proposals for the reform of Irish institutions or the promotion of Irish industries that may be submitted to the imperial legislature ...

The operation of the Association will be confined to the three southern provinces – Leinster, Munster and Connaught – and its endeavour will be to put it in the power of every voter in these provinces to record his vote at the coming election for a candidate pledged to oppose every proposal aimed at the severance of the parliamentary and imperial connection.

In these provinces there are seventy constituencies, and it is intended to oppose the election of 'separatist' candidates in each of these, in so far as may be found practicable, and to such an extent as the funds of the Association will permit ...

Irish Times, 16 October 1885

(b) In order:

(1) to continue, extend and render more efficient the work initiated and carried on since May 1885, by the Irish Loyal and Patriotic Union,

2) to further consolidate the several Unionist Associations existing in Ireland, and

(3) to establish cordial relations with the Unionist Associations that have since been formed in England and Scotland,

It is desirable to alter the name, and in some respects the Constitution, of the Irish Loyal and Patriotic Union ... The Association shall in future be known as the Irish Unionist Alliance ...

Belfast: PRONI D989A/1/4, cited in
P Buckland, *Irish Unionism 1885-1923:*
a Documentary History (Belfast: HMSO 1973) p 125

52 Unionism in rural Ulster: Landlords' men and tenants' men

Once Liberals and Conservatives, Presbyterians and Episcopalians, found common cause in opposition to Gladstonian home rule, the way was almost entirely cleared for Unionism to emerge as an effective pan-Protestant movement. But in Ulster, unlike in the rest of Ireland, the land question remained for a while a serious threat to this unity. In most of Ulster the farming class, the very class which was at the forefront of agrarian and nationalist agitation in Catholic Ireland, was predominantly Protestant, though frequently differentiated from the Episcopalian landlords by its own Presbyterianism. During the early 1880s many Ulster Protestant farmers held views on the land question not dissimilar from those of Nationalists. Some Liberal Unionist politicians, most notably T W Russell (see Doc 54), continued to allow agrarian concerns to determine their overall political outlook, but from 1886 onwards the 'threat' of home rule proved powerful enough to sweep most Protestant farmers into the Unionist fold for most of the time. This landlord-tenant alliance was not easy to construct or maintain, as this post-election exchange between Richard Dane (1852-1903) and Hugh de Fellenberg Montgomery (1844-1924) illustrates. Dane, a barrister and later a county court judge, was Unionist MP for North Fermanagh, 1892-98, and espoused the tenants' point of view; Montgomery, of Blessingbourne, Fivemiletown, who held estates of more than 12,000 acres in south Tyrone and Fermanagh, was an influential and moderate figure behind the scenes of Unionism for more than forty years.

(a) R M Dane to H de F Montgomery   Enniskillen, 11 June 1892

> I wish to place upon record my appreciation of the patriotic and unselfish stand you made in support of the Unionist cause at the election just won. The course adopted by yourself ... and other landowners in this division having regard to my pledges in support of compulsory sale and purchase considerably minimised the great difficulties I had to contend with.
>
> I have written the Duke of Abercorn and Lord Erne pointing out (as I did some months ago to Mr Balfour) that this question must be tackled in Ulster and that all fair-minded landowners should meet and confer as to some liberal and fair course of united action – if something is not done the judicial rents will not be paid and we shall have an agitation amongst the best and most honest farmers in Ulster – I am sure you will accept my word for it that I voice the views of the best of the farmers in this matter, who feel that they have not so far touched any of the benefits of land purchase. I would like to see this question settled, and that by the Unionist Party.

(b) H de F Montgomery to R M Dane   12 July 1892

> I had no hesitation or difficulty in giving you, as the Unionist candidate, any little help or support I could, though I disapproved of your advocacy of compulsory purchase. On former occasions, when a candidate whom many tenants regarded as a "landlords' man" was up [for election] we exhorted them to put aside selfish class views and vote for him, for the sake of the Union and our common rights and liberties, civil and religious. We were bound, when the Unionist candidate was a "tenants' man", to practise what we preached, and we have done so.
>
> As to the question of "land purchase", I have been an advocate of a large extension of occupying ownership for many years, and am prepared to renew the efforts I made, in conjunction with the Irish Landowners Committee, when Mr Balfour's measures were under discussion, to mould the law so as to make it easier for landlords to sell at a price that will bring relief to tenants and for tenants to offer a price that will be fair to landlords; but to *compulsory* sale or purchase I remain uncompromisingly opposed, holding that it is in principle, grossly unjust to landlords; that in

practice it is totally impossible to carry out, no Land Commission being capable of fixing a fair price; that it is part of the propaganda of the Land League conspiracy for undermining British rule, by ruining and expelling the gentry, and that Protestant tenants, in adopting the demand, are cutting a rod for their own backs as – the principle once admitted – there is nothing to prevent a Radical [ie Liberal] government applying it to any body of Protestant occupiers that a Popish or Fenian majority wish removed out of any part of Ireland to make room for "men of their own".

Belfast: PRONI D627/428/182 & 189,
cited in P Buckland, *Irish Unionism 1885-1923:*
a Documentary History (Belfast: HMSO 1973) pp 196-7

53 Debating the Second Home Rule Bill: An extraordinary spectacle

The second Home Rule Bill passed through the House of Commons in 1893, as the 1886 Bill had not. It was soon heavily defeated in the House of Lords, and a struggling Liberal Government did not press the matter further. But the apostasy of Joseph Chamberlain (1836-1914) from the Liberal cause in 1886 had not been forgotten – as a Liberal Unionist he served in Conservative cabinets, 1895-1903 – and these animosities provoked a pitched battle on the floor of the House of Commons during the debates on the second Home Rule Bill. Both the main protagonists – the Ulster Unionist leader, Orangeman and Cavan landowner Col Edward Saunderson (1837-1906) and the Nationalist member and Cork labour organiser Eugene Crean (1856-1939) – were renowned for their pugnacious irascibility.

MR CHAMBERLAIN: ... We have come, at all events, to the last scene in what I think I may call the discreditable farce (loud opposition cheers) to which the Government have reduced the proceedings of the mother of parliaments (cheers), and it is to us not the least matter of regret that this position should have been reached by the action of one whom we are all ready to recognise as one of the greatest of parliamentary figures ... I say that this bill has been changed in its most vital features, and yet it has been found perfect by hon. members behind the treasury bench. The prime minister says 'black' and they say 'it is good'; the prime minister calls 'white' and they say 'it is better' (loud laughter). It is always the voice of a god (loud cheers). Never since the time of Herod has there been such slavish adulation (Ministerial cries of 'progress' and Nationalist cries of 'Judas').

MR JOHNSTON and MR GIBBS rose simultaneously and tried to address the Chairman, but could not make themselves heard in the din that prevailed.

MR CHAMBERLAIN ... sat down, it being 10 p.m., the hour for the application of the closure.

THE CHAIRMAN [Deputy Speaker] put the question, but his voice could not be heard owing to the cries that arose from all parts of the Chamber. In the general uproar the cries of 'Judas' and 'Gag' could be distinguished. An extraordinary and probably unparalleled scene in the history of the House of Commons followed ...

MR V. GIBBS: ... I wish to call attention to a point of order. I heard the hon. member for the Scotland division of Liverpool [T P O'Connor, Irish Nationalist] call out 'Judas' when the right hon. member of West Birmingham [Chamberlain] was speaking ...

The Chair, however, did not take any further notice of the incident. Meanwhile Gladstonians and Nationalists were leaving their seats to take part in the division. An effort was made by some of the more active Conservative members to keep the Opposition benches from being cleared ...

... Meanwhile the floor was completely crowded with members, some showing traces of amusement, others showing great excitement. Mr Gladstone remained seated opposite the box on the front treasury bench during all this time, evidently waiting until the House was sufficiently clear to enter the division lobbies ... At this juncture also Lord Randolph Churchill was seen trying to get the Conservatives to leave the House and enter the division lobbies; but his efforts were not responded to. At this time Mr Logan [Liberal] was observed to cross the floor of the House and say something to Mr [Edward] Carson [Irish Unionist], which was apparently warmly resented .... . In an instant the House appeared to resolve itself into a general fight ... Members clambered over benches and crowded pell-mell among the Conservatives and the Nationalists. Mr Timothy Healy [Nationalist] was seen to be fighting with Mr Gibson Bowles [Conservative] on the second bench, while a really serious fisticuff encounter was in progress between the Nationalists and the Conservatives ... The House at this time presented an extraordinary spectacle. Hisses were loud and vehement; there was a seething, struggling mass of members between the floor and the back Nationalist bench below the gangway. Col. Saunderson was hitting straight from the shoulder, and members were falling here and there in the crush. The back bench was broken in the struggle ... and the Prime Minister [Gladstone] evidently extremely pained at what he saw in progress before his eyes, was standing a mute spectator ... Opposite to him stood Sir E. Ashmead-Bartlett [Conservative], labouring under great excitement, and shouting from time to time at the Prime Minister, 'This is your doing' ...

[Later] THE SPEAKER: ... It appears that a point of order did arise before the House was cleared for a division ... It seems to me ... that the originating cause of the disturbance was some opprobrious expression alleged to have been used ... I am quite sure that if any hon. member who did use those words in the heat of the moment and in the irritation perhaps of circumstances (cheers) will simply state to the House that he regrets having used them, perhaps the House will think that it will be my duty to take no further notice of the incident (cheers) ...

MR T. P. O'CONNOR: ... Two of my hon. friends, one an English member and the other an Irish member, have been physically assaulted (Nationalist cheers). Mr Speaker, if in any way whatsoever any observation of mine may have contributed to bring about that most regrettable state of affairs, I most humbly apologise (Cheers, and Opposition cries of 'withdraw').

COL. SAUNDERSON [Irish Unionist, North Armagh]: ... I regret, Sir, to feel it my duty to call attention to a circumstance which occurred after the event which we have just been considering. A sudden charge was made by a number of hon. members below the gangway [Nationalist benches] on to the seat on which I was sitting. I rose in my place, not desiring to be run over (laughter) by the charge, and the hon. member for the Ossory division [Eugene Crean, Nationalist], without provocation at all, struck me a violent blow on the side of the head (Nationalist cries of 'no' and Opposition cheers) ... When I turned round he was about to repeat it ...

MR. CONDON [East Tipperary, Nationalist]: ... I am compelled, in the interests of fair play and truth ... [to state that] ... When I came into the House after recording my vote, the first thing I saw was the hon. member for North Armagh striking my hon. friend (Mr Crean) a blow in the face and attempting to strike him a second time, when two or three of his friends above the gangway prevented him from doing so ...

The Times, 28 July 1893

54 *T W Russell: Ireland has changed, and I have changed with it*

T W Russell (1841-1920) was a Presbyterian Scot who settled in Ireland through marriage. Entering public life as a temperance advocate he quickly became a militant and stubborn advocate of land reform on behalf of Ulster tenant farmers, being returned as Liberal Unionist MP for South Tyrone in 1886. He was less willing to compromise with the landlord interest than other Liberal Unionists (see Doc 52), and though he became a junior minister in the Conservative Government of 1895, he was dismissed in 1900 after he called for compulsory land purchase. This extract, from a parliamentary speech in 1901, illustrates the ideas which prompted his gradual political move to the other side of Irish politics. During 1902-4 he supported Independent Unionist candidates, known as 'Russellites', at Ulster by-elections, running in opposition to official Unionist candidates on a platform of land reform. In 1906 he was opposed in South Tyrone by an official Unionist, but retained the seat as a Liberal Unionist, thanks to the absence of a Nationalist candidate. In 1907 he joined the Liberal Party, thereby espousing home rule, and became once more a junior minister. Although forced to switch from the South Tyrone to the North Tyrone seat in 1911, he remained a minister in Liberal Governments until 1918, but his chequered career did not really represent any major change in Ulster voting behaviour – until 1900 his seat in Parliament was based on the support of Tyrone Protestants and Unionists; from 1906 he was sustained instead by the votes of Tyrone Catholics and Nationalists.

MR T.W. RUSSELL (Tyrone South, Liberal Unionist): All those members who remember the relations between myself and the Party opposite during the ten years of bitter strife and conflict that took place between 1886 and 1895 will doubtless feel surprised that I should rise to second an Amendment to the Address proposed by the hon. and learned gentleman opposite [John Redmond, Nationalist] ...

... I notice that some of my friends have taken the trouble to go scavenging in the dust-bin of my old speeches, and have published for the edification of the House five or six speeches that I have made at different times during the last fifteen years to my constituents in South Tyrone. I am one of the few Ulster members who ever take the trouble to speak to their constituents, and I think it would give anyone a great deal of trouble to find five or six speeches even in fifteen years from any other Ulster member that would bear publication. I am here tonight, if you like, a convert. Ireland has changed, and I have changed with it, and it will do nobody any good to bring up speeches of the past in which I have not spoken so much against this as I have endeavoured to hold the people back and to get them not to press it urgently.

I desire to place before the House a clear record of what has precipitated this question, and made it the dominant issue in Irish politics. My conviction at the moment is that the real reason is the utter and irretrievable breakdown of the present system of dual ownership in the land which was legalised by the Act of 1881, due to the maladministration of the Land Court ...

There are four things which have brought this question irresistibly to the front in Ireland – first, the treatment by the Courts of appeals on value; secondly, the treatment by the Courts of tenants' improvements; thirdly, the conspiracy among landlords and land agents in Ulster absolutely to destroy the Ulster custom under which the Ulster tenant is being robbed of his property every day; and fourthly, the very success of the Purchase Act itself ... necessitates the House facing this question ...

My position with regard to the question of the Land Purchase Acts is that, with the exception of the administration, those Acts have been an unqualified success. The people who bought are satisfied, and the landlords who sold are satisfied, and peace has taken the place of turbulence in the districts where these Acts have been applied ... But, while that is true, there is one result which will certainly cause great difficulty ... You will not get a man to pay 20 shillings to a landlord for a thing that another man only pays the State 10 shillings for ... The purchaser in many cases has been a turbulent tenant to whom the landlord was willing to and anxious to sell, in order to get rid of the trouble and annoyance; but to the honest tenant who steadily pays his rent the landlord has no inducement to sell ... Such a system as that cannot be allowed to continue. The very success of land purchase invites progress ...

I may be asked what right has the House to apply the principle of compulsion to Irish land any more than to any other form of property. My answer is that there is an enormous difference between the English and the Irish landowner. The English landowner is a real owner of property, and lets to a tenant a fully-equipped going concern; he gets rent, but gives much of that rent back to the property. The Irish landlord is only a part-owner. The tenant provides the plant, the labour, the capital to work the farm; the landlord draws the rent, but he gives nothing back. The Irish landlord has never in the history of the land question done much for the land, but since 1881 he has done nothing at all, and his real position at this moment is that of a sleeping partner in this business. He draws money out of the partnership that it cannot afford. He is really a rent-charger and nothing else ... We simply stand alone in maintaining this antiquated system ...

My hon. and learned friend [John Redmond] proceeds with this motion perhaps from a standpoint different from mine. He thinks that this scheme will make Ireland independent and her people better Nationalists. I do not object. I think that by this we should not only buy out the fee simple of Irish land, but we should also buy out the fee simple of Irish disaffection; we should end the Irish trouble (Nationalist cries of dissent). We should end 80 percent of the Irish trouble in achieving this great object. That is the reason I am here tonight. During the last few months I have touched the heart of Ulster. I know how in every hamlet and townland of Ulster the pulse of the Irish tenant is beating on this question ... I second this amendment tonight with all my heart and with all my soul. I see a new Ireland rising up that will stand together for great public needs and great public purposes. Those gentlemen opposite may remain Nationalists and I shall continue a Unionist, but that will not prevent me standing behind them in all their constitutional endeavours for the benefit of Ireland.

H C Deb 4th series, vol 89,
cols 728-746 (21 Feb 1901)

55 Tom Sloan: The first real representative of Orangemen?

Yet another challenge to orthodox Unionism in Ulster, and one which was to prove a more enduring one throughout Belfast's twentieth-century history, was that supplied by 'popular Protestantism' – ie urban working class Unionism underpinned by a militant evangelical Protestantism and a distrust of both the 'Protestantism' and the 'loyalty' of the Protestant middle and upper classes, the 'fur coat brigade'. During the nineteenth century those who could command the support of subscribers to such sentiments – such as Rev Hugh Hanna and William Johnston of Ballykilbeg (Docs 47 and 48) – tended to deliver it to mainstream Conservatism and Unionism. After 1900 this did not always happen, and 'Independent Unionism' emerged from time to time as a distinct political force. The earliest parliamentary practitioner was Tom Sloan (1870-1941), a cementer in Harland & Wolff's shipyard, who was a temperance advocate and leading figure in the Belfast Protestant Association. Sloan had strong support in Sandy Row, holding the South Belfast parliamentary seat in opposition to official Unionism, 1902-10. The Belfast Nationalist Joe Devlin, himself a recent by-election victor and new MP, sought to give Sloan a warm welcome to Westminster.

MR [JOSEPH] DEVLIN [Nationalist, Kilkenny North] moved the adjournment of the House for the purpose of discussing a definite matter of urgent public importance – viz. 'the riotous proceedings on Sunday last at the Custom House Steps in Belfast, and the neglect and refusal of the Government to take steps to prohibit the holding of such meetings on Government property in that city' .... On Sunday last a scene of indescribable disorder and tumult took place on the Custom House Steps in Belfast. The House had heard of the Custom House Steps before. It was the arena in which the bigots and supporters of the present Government were engaged on Sunday after Sunday in using the most ribald and blasphemous language, not only about the Catholics and the Catholic Church, but against that portion of the Protestant Church whose ritual did not suit their aesthetic tastes. He might mention to the House that the Protestant Association of Belfast had been broken up into two parties – the Sloanites and Trewites. The Sloanites were represented by the hon. member for South Belfast and the Trewites would later on be represented in that House, when Mr Trew took the place of the hon. member for North Belfast [Sir J H Haslett[2]].

There were two leaders in the camp. There was the hon. member for South Belfast [Tom Sloan], and there was Mr A. Trew, and the latter gentleman thought he was entitled to occupy the place now occupied by the hon. member for South Belfast. The hon. member for South Belfast, taking advantage of Mr Trew's absence in one of His Majesty's prisons, entered into the arena and, in the words of the hon. member for North Armagh [Col.

2 At the by-election following Haslett's death in 1905, the Unionist candidate held the seat by a narrow majority of 474 against a pro-British Labour candidate, William Walker (see Doc 60). Trew had meanwhile disappeared from view.

Saunderson, leader of the Irish Unionists] 'climbed on the back of Mr Trew into Parliament, and then kicked Mr Trew from under him'. The be-all and end-all of the purposes for which the organisation [the Belfast Protestant Association] was carried on to the detriment of the public order and the peace of the city was the collection [of money] ... The Chief Secretary for Ireland declined to assent to the railing in of the Steps so that such meetings should be no longer possible ...

The hon. member for South Belfast has been returned against the official candidate of the Tory Party. He threatened that after the next general election he would come back with three other members to support him, and instead of the philosophic calm and great experience of the right hon. gentleman the Member for West Belfast [H O Arnold Foster, Liberal Unionist], the hon. member would bring back one of the gentlemen who had added so many choice phrases to their political vocabulary ...

MR SLOAN [Independent Unionist, Belfast South]: ... He has been in the habit of going to the Custom House Steps for a good number of years, but he had seen more disorderliness and rowdyism in the House of Commons during the past week than he had ever seen on the Custom House Steps. There was an old adage 'Begin at Jerusalem'. He would suggest to the Government, if they were to begin at all, it would be to the credit of the House and to the safety of Members of the Government that they should commence by railing in the Nationalist benches ...

... He did not associate himself with any particular language which had been used at the Custom House Steps. He had quite enough do to be responsible for what his own tongue said. He would like to point out, however, that there had never been any of the individuals who had figured as speakers on the platform at the Custom House Steps sent to gaol for boycotting or intimidation, for the simple reason that all loyal subjects of His Majesty King Edward VII did not believe in that sort of work ... If it were imagined that any such attack made on him would in any way debar him from doing his duty as a loyal subject and as a Protestant, those concerned in such an attack were labouring under a great mistake. The coupling of his name with others in the use of language which he deplored as much as any man was not only an injustice to him, but was ungentlemanly on the part of those who made the charges ... If the Irish Nationalists did not pursue a different course from what he had seen in the House of Commons during the past week, it seemed to him that the Irish Chief Secretary would have to build them an asylum ...

MR [Jeremiah] MACVEAGH [South Down, Nationalist]: ... The hon. member for South Belfast, in his entertaining speech, had contended that the

Motion was intended as an attack upon him. Nothing was further from the thoughts of the Nationalist members. They were delighted to see the hon. member elected for South Belfast, because they recognised in him the first real representative the Orangemen of Ulster had ever had in the House of Commons. There were several Ulster representatives, some of them posing as Orangemen, but the House had never had the real article before. He was afraid, however, that the hon. member's constituents would be somewhat disappointed at the character of their representative's maiden speech, as they really believed that the first time the hon. member got up in the House of Commons it would be to impeach the Pope, or to submit a Motion ordering all the Jesuits in the country to be brought to the bar of the House. He did, however, sincerely congratulate Mr Speaker on the speech to which they had just listened, because the hon. member announced on the Custom House Steps in Belfast that if he did not catch the Speaker's eye he would kick up a row, that if he did not get what he wanted he would make himself a nuisance, and that while he did not want to be dragged out of the House of Commons, he would be if necessary.

MR SLOAN: I was not aware that there were so many nuisances in the House when I said that.

H C Deb 4th series, vol 113,
cols 687-700 (23 October 1902)

56 The Magheramorne Manifesto: Room for a patriotic party?

For opposing (and defeating) the Unionist candidate in 1902 Sloan was ejected from the Orange Order. He had been supported in his by-election campaign by Lindsay Crawford (1868-1945), an evangelical Dublin-based idealist, and in 1903 they founded the Independent Orange Order. Crawford, though a militant opponent of Catholicism, was an Irish patriot. Between 1902 and 1908 he made strenuous efforts to carve out a middle ground in Irish politics based on the unusual combination of evangelical Protestantism, support for labour militancy in Belfast, and conciliatory politics. The high point of Crawford's brief career in Irish public life was a manifesto which he persuaded the leadership of the Independent Orange Order to sign, and which was announced at their demonstration at Magheramorne, near Larne, Co Antrim, on 13 July 1905. He and Sloan were improbable bedfellows, and Sloan never really recovered from signing the Manifesto, notwithstanding his later half-retraction of support for it. Once the labour militancy of Belfast was dissipated following the 1907 strike, and as home rule returned to the parliamentary agenda, Unionism reasserted itself: Sloan was heavily defeated by an official Unionist in the general election of January 1910, and left public life. Crawford emigrated to Canada a few months later, from where he later became a prominent supporter of the Irish revolution and the Free State Government.

To All Irishmen whose country stands first in their affection, from The Independent Orangemen of Ireland.

... [The Independent Orange Order stands] once more on the banks of the Boyne, not as victors in the fight nor to applaud the noble deeds of our ancestors ... but to ... hold out the right hand of fellowship to those who, while worshipping at other shrines, are yet our countrymen - bone of our bone and flesh of our flesh ...

... [Dublin] Castle government stands self-condemned. All parties are agreed as to the necessity for sweeping reforms in the government and administration of Ireland. Bureaucratic government, it is everywhere recognised, must be superseded by the rule of the people. It only remains to determine on what lines reform is to proceed, and what part Irishmen are to play in bringing it about. On the willingness and ability of Irishmen to cooperate in carrying out reasonable reforms in their own country will rest their claim to a more extended form of self government. We do not hide from ourselves the dangers that have to be faced in the further extension of the elective principle in the government of Ireland, but the principle having been already conceded by the Unionists, under the [1898] Local Government Act, cannot now be seriously disputed, and must proceed to its logical conclusion. Government by the people for the people is a democratic principle, limited only in its application by the ability of the people to govern ...

... Surely the facts suggest to the Nationalists and the Unionists alike the unwisdom of perpetuating a suicidal strife, in which both parties are ever sacrificed to the demands of clericalism and to the exigencies of English parties. We do not trust either of the English parties on any of the questions that divided Ireland, and we are satisfied that both Liberals and Tories will continue in the future, as they have done in the past, to play off Irish Protestants and Nationalists against each other, to the prejudice of our country. This being so, we consider it high time that Irish Protestants should consider their position as Irish citizens and their attitude towards their Roman Catholic countrymen, and that the latter should choose once for all between nationality and sectarianism. In an Ireland in which Protestant and Roman Catholic stand sullen and discontented it is not too much to hope that they will reconsider their positions and, in their common trials, unite on a common basis of nationality. The higher claims of our distracted country have been too long neglected in the strife of party and of creed. The man who cannot rise above the trammels of party and of sect on a national issue is a foe to nationality and to human freedom. There is room in Ireland for a patriotic party, with a sound constructive policy such as we have outlined – a party that will devote itself to the task of freeing the country from the domination of impractical creeds and organised tyrannies, and to secure the urgent and legitimate redress of many grievances. We foresee a time in Irish history when thoughtful men on both sides will come to realise that the Irish question is not made up of Union and Repeal; that not in acts of parliament nor in their repeal lies the hope and salvation of our country, so much as in the mutual inclination of Irish hearts and minds along the common plane of nationality that binds the people together in ... the material interests of our native land, and the increased wealth and happiness of her people.

Belfast Newsletter, 14 July 1905

57 The Ulster Unionist Council: 'Turn the other provinces into "Ulsters" '

The Ulster Unionist Council came into formal public existence on 3 March 1905, following a preliminary meeting on 2 December 1904. Older interpretations attribute this new move primarily to Unionist alarm at the British Conservatives' flirtation with devolution (see Doc 33). In fact it was little more than coincidence that the devolution issue came to public attention at the same time as the UUC launch. Far more important was a concern in the constituencies over the remoteness from Unionist opinion of the Party's MPs and lack of any formal mechanism for influence or dialogue. The three electoral threats facing the Party, from the Independent Orange Order, the agrarian Russellites and the emerging British-affiliated Labour movement, alarmed sitting MPs far more than the devolution incident, and appeared to underline the need for such a dialogue.

The Ulster Unionist Council itself was a body of at least 200 members, one half of whom were constituency representatives, the remainder of places being divided equally between Orange Order representatives and nominated Unionist notables. An executive council of 66 was responsible for the day-to-day operation of the movement: its membership reflected the preponderance of linen magnates and other big businessmen and lawyers in the movement, with the landed gentry as an important but subsidiary element in the leadership. Certainly UUC reorganisation helped to make the party a more modern and efficient force, although from 1910 the prominence of the home rule issue put an end to independent Unionist and Labour challenges, so that the issue of constituency control over MPs was never really put to the test. The most important outcomes of the UUC's emergence were the more effective binding together of Belfast Unionism with the movement in the Ulster counties, and a confirmation of the separate status of Ulster Unionism as the Dublin-based, landlord-led Irish Unionist Alliance further reduced its role in the North. The first extract (a) is the founding resolution of the Council, from its preliminary meeting on 2 December 1904. The second (b), from a special report presented to the UUC's annual meeting on 30 January 1911, articulates in detail Ulster Unionism's growing perception of its regional distinctiveness and, with hindsight, can be seen as the beginnings of a partitionist outlook.

(a) [It is resolved] that an Ulster Unionist Council be formed, and that its objects shall be to form an Ulster Union for bringing into line all local

Unionist associations in the province of Ulster, with a view to a consistent and continuous political action; to act as a further connecting link between Ulster Unionists and their parliamentary representatives; to settle in consultation with them the parliamentary policy, and to be the medium of expressing Ulster Unionist opinion as current events from time to time require; and generally to advance and defend the interests of Ulster Unionism in the Unionist Party.

Belfast: PRONI D 1327/7/6A, cited in
P Buckland, *Irish Unionism 1885-1923:
a Documentary History* (Belfast: HMSO 1973) p 204

(b) ... Ulster Unionists rest their case upon what they believe to be the impregnable foundation of the right to have their equal championship in the United Kingdom maintained unimpaired. They have built up their industries and brought Ulster to its present prosperous condition under the protection of the Imperial Parliament and rely on that protection being continued. Any policy which deprives them of this safeguard they would regard as a criminal betrayal of their birthright. This position they are prepared to maintain at all hazard. Among recent attacks upon the Ulster position one is contained in a manifesto intended for perusal in England and Scotland, issued by the Nationalist leader Mr John Redmond, and in this document he declares that 'There is no Ulster question'. In support of this strange doctrine he lays stress on the admitted fact that the Protestant – which, with very few exceptions, means the Unionist – population of Ulster is only 55.9 percent of the whole. Ulster Unionists have never put forward the absurd contention that their province as a whole is overwhelmingly Protestant. But they do claim that in the Ulster six counties in which, or in large sections of which, there are to be found loyalty to the throne, industrial enterprise, commercial prosperity, independent religious and political opinion, enthusiasm for social reform, and contribution of the best talent within their borders to the various public services of the United Kingdom and of the Empire – in these counties the proportion of Unionists to Nationalists in the population is within a small fraction of as two is to one. Again, if we take the rateable valuation of these six counties as compared with that of the other three, which are preponderantly Nationalist, the ratio is practically as five and one-half to one – a condition which illustrates the important fact that where there is prosperity in Ulster it is associated with Unionist life and work ...

... Ulster and the loyal minority in Ireland are determined that no local majority in Ireland shall bear rule over them. At the same time they will continue their efforts to promote the good of Ulster and of all Ireland, relying on the continued protection and equal justice of the Imperial Parliament, through whose wise and beneficial legislation, under Unionist governments, Ulster and the whole country have recently attained to a record degree of prosperity. Until Mr Redmond and his colleagues turn the other provinces of Ireland into 'Ulsters' the Ulster question will, with ever-increasing force, continue to confront them. But should they decide to conform Leinster, Munster and Connaught to the Ulster ideal of industry and self-help, the Irish question will be at an end and Irishmen, north and south, will be found permanently united in their loyalty to the principle of ONE FLAG, ONE CROWN, ONE PARLIAMENT.

Belfast: PRONI D972/17/1912, cited in
P Buckland, *Irish Unionism 1885-1923:*
a Documentary History (Belfast: HMSO 1973) pp 15-17

58 Walter Long: The dark shadow of Home Rule

Edward Saunderson (see Doc 53) led the Irish Unionist Parliamentary group from its inception in 1886 until his death in 1906. An effective leader in the home rule bill debates of 1886 and 1893, he was less successful in combating the challenges to mainstream Unionism which gathered force after 1900. His successor, Walter Long (1854-1924) was an Englishman, a Wiltshire landowner who had links to the Anglo-Irish gentry through both his mother and his wife. For most of his parliamentary career Long represented English constituencies, but he was briefly Chief Secretary for Ireland in 1905, when his presence reassured Conservatives and Unionists that the Party was not about to take up devolution. He was therefore able, upon losing his English seat in 1906, to return to Parliament for South County Dublin, the only Unionist territorial seat outside Ulster. Long's substantial cabinet experience, landlord background and die-hard style made him the obvious successor to Saunderson. He became chair of the Unionist parliamentary group in October 1906 and chair of the Irish Unionist Alliance. His election as chair of the Ulster Unionist Council in January 1907 enabled him to hold together the two wings of Unionism, as anxiety grew in Unionist Ireland over the return of home rule to the Liberal Government's agenda. Long directed all his efforts towards making home rule and its potential 'threat to the Empire' the central issue in British as well as Irish politics. He remained a strong supporter of Irish Unionism after he returned to an English constituency in January 1910 and handed on the leadership of Irish Unionism to Sir Edward Carson. In 1919 he chaired the cabinet committee which formulated the Government of Ireland Bill (Doc 146). This extract is from his address to the Ulster Unionist Council meeting at Belfast during the election campaign of January 1910.

Mr Long ... said that once again there had been thrown across the path of Ireland that dark shadow of home rule which, if it was, by the cowardice of members of Parliament, to be turned into reality meant the destruction as he believed of the prosperity of Ireland and of the happiness of her people (Hear, hear). Four years ago the Government, the party who were then seeking office, declared that home rule was to be no part of their programme. They now told them that home rule was to be a leading plank in their programme. They were bound to try and find a reason for that extraordinary change, and he thought it could be found in the fact that at the last general election they [the Liberals] believed that home rule might injure their cause in England, whereas now they thought that possibly they might gain a few votes in Parliament and out of it by adopting the cause of home rule. So far as Great Britain was concerned the situation was unchanged; so far as Ireland was concerned the situation was changed, but in a direction which pointed in the opposite way to home rule. The Unionist Party in Ireland was united, confident and strong (cheers) ... Home rule for Ireland would mean the loss of individual liberty, the absolute insecurity of property, and the negation of everything they cared for affecting the welfare of the country ... They had read in the press recently about the Nationalist conventions to select candidates, and how the police had to be called in to preserve order. Did anyone out of Bedlam suggest that the police should be handed over to the control of the Nationalists? The Unionists of Ireland were as determined as ever to oppose home rule ...

The Times, 5 January 1910

Chapter 5
Labour rise and fall

59 Karl Marx: Crippled by the disunion with the Irish

Karl Marx (1818-83) and his collaborator Friedrich Engels (1820-95) attached considerable importance to the problem of Ireland's relationship with Britain, and both wrote extensively about it. Their interest was stimulated, and largely driven, by what was for them the most visible and pressing part of that problem - the large number of workers and paupers of Irish birth or descent living in British cities in the generation following the Great Famine. In some cities this amounted to a quarter or more of the workforce. Although many Irish migrants flourished in Britain, and the great majority integrated and steadily improved their circumstances, anti-Irish feeling remained a powerfully divisive social and political force within the working classes until the end of the nineteenth century.

It was this concern, rooted in the circumstances of the working classes in Britain, which shaped Marx's analysis of the problem in Ireland itself. The rural background of most of the migrants led him to link the Irish land question to the national question almost ten years before Parnell and Davitt forged their alliance between the home rule movement and the Land League.

I have become more and more convinced – and the only question is to bring this conviction home to the English working class – that it can never do anything decisive here in England until it separates its policy with regard to Ireland in the most definite way from the policy of the ruling classes, until it not only makes common cause with the Irish, but actually takes the initiative in dissolving the union established in 1801 and replacing it by a free federal relationship. And, indeed, this must be done, not as a matter of sympathy with Ireland, but as a demand made in the interests of the English proletariat. If not, the English people will remain tied to the leading strings of the ruling classes, because it must join with them in a common front against Ireland. Every one of its movements in England itself is crippled by the disunion with the Irish, who form a very important section of the working class in England. *The primary condition* of emancipation here – the overthrow of the English landed oligarchy – remains impossible because its position here cannot be stormed so long as it maintains its strongly entrenched outposts in Ireland. But, there, once affairs are in the hands of the Irish people itself, once it is made its own legislator and ruler, once it becomes autonomous, the abolition of the landed aristocracy (to a large extent the *same persons* as the

English landlords) will be infinitely easier than here, because in Ireland it is not merely a simple economic question, but at the same time a *national* question, since the landlords there are not like those in England, the traditional dignitaries and representatives, but are the hated oppressors of a nation. And not only does England's internal social development remain crippled by her present relation with Ireland, her foreign policy, and particularly her policy with regard to Russia and America, suffers the same fate.

Letter to Dr L Kugelmann, 29 November 1869,
in K Marx & F Engels, *Selected Correspondence,*
1846-95 (New York, 1942)

60 James Connolly v William Walker: Internationalism or imperialism?

Marx had less to say about the ethno-sectarian division within the urban working classes of Ireland itself. James Connolly (1868-1916), was the first major writer to develop a Marxist analysis of urban industrial relations in Ireland. Born of Irish Catholic parents in Edinburgh, Connolly settled in Ireland during the 1890s. In a massive body of writing, mainly pamphleteering, he developed what remains the most cogent statement of Irish republican socialism. His early attempt at activism, the formation of the Irish Socialist Republican Party in Dublin in 1896, made little impact, and in 1903 he emigrated with his family to the USA. He returned in 1910 to lead the newly-formed Socialist Party of Ireland, and found employment as Belfast organiser of the Irish Transport & General Workers' Union. In 1914 he moved back to Dublin as the Union's general secretary. In January 1916 he agreed to a late alliance with the Irish Volunteer leaders, and was executed for his part in the Easter Rising.

William Walker (1871-1918) was a Belfast Protestant, a shipyard carpenter who became a trade union official. With the support of the British-based Independent Labour Party he fought three parliamentary elections in the North Belfast constituency, 1905-7, coming tantalisingly close to success on two occasions. He sought to lead Ulster Protestant workers away from Conservative Unionism, and regarded himself and his colleagues as an integral part of the British Labour movement. His emphasis on the 'internationalism' of the Labour movement, when applied to Ireland, denied Connolly's view of Britain's relationship with Ireland as exploitative and imperialist. In 1911 the two men debated their positions at length in the columns of *Forward*, the Glasgow-based labour journal. In this controversy it would probably be fair to say that Walker's statement of the Labour unionist case was rather less accomplished than Connolly's advocacy of the republican socialist position. Walker's followers also lost the practical side of the debate in 1912 when the Irish Trades Union Congress, after several attempts, produced a majority in favour of establishing a separate Irish Labour Party. In Belfast, however, four of the five Labour party branches remained affiliated to the British-based Independent Labour Party.

(a) James Connolly

There are in Ireland today two forms of Socialist organisations – the Independent Labour Party and the Socialist Party of Ireland. The former is strongest in the North, the latter strongest in the South, although it has a active branch in Belfast ... The SPI ... is so convinced of the need for unity among Socialists in Ireland that it is ready at any time to have a joint convention with the ILP ... It believes that these questions which divide Socialists are not serious enough to warrant separate organisations in the one country, but can well be debated within one organisation ... What, then, keeps the two organisations divided? Laying aside all questions of personality, personal ambitions and personal jealousies as being accidental and inessential, it may be truthfully asserted that the one point of divergence is that the ILP in Belfast believes that the Socialist movement in Ireland must perforce remain a dues-paying, organic part of the British Socialist movement, or else forfeit its title to be considered a part of International Socialism, whereas the Socialist Party of Ireland maintains that the relations between Socialism in Ireland and in Great Britain should be based upon comradeship and mutual assistance and not upon dues-paying, should be fraternal and not organic, and should operate by exchange of literature and speakers rather than by attempts to treat as one two peoples of whom one has for 700 years nurtured an unending martyrdom rather than admit the unity or surrender its national identity. The SPI considers itself the only international party in Ireland, since its conception of internationalism is that of a free federation of free peoples, whereas that of the Belfast branches of the ILP seems scarcely distinguishable from imperialism ...

... The only real dividing issue, apart from personal elements, is the question of recognising Ireland as entitled to self-government. Any Irish socialist who recognises Ireland's right to self-government should logically embody his political activities in a form of organisation based upon the principle of Irish self-government ... I pointed out that the trade union movement in Ireland was considering the advisability of establishing a Labour Party, and that the same elements which keep the Belfast ILP from recognising officially the right of Ireland to self-government had acted and voted last year in the Irish TUC against a proposal to establish a Labour Party in Ireland ...

Forward, 27 May & 10 June 1911

(b) William Walker

... I affirm that it has now become *impossible* in Belfast to have a religious riot, and this is due to the good work done by that much despised body, the ILP.

I hold no brief for Belfast, but past bigotry aside, we have moved faster towards municipal socialism, leaving not merely the other cities of Ireland behind, but giving the lead to many cities in England and Scotland. We collectively own and control our gas works, water works, harbour works, markets, tramways, electricity, museums, art galleries, etc ... and our works' department do an enormous amount of 'timed' and 'contract' work within the municipality ...

... The SPI wants the trade unions in Ireland to cease to contribute dues to an amalgamated union ... That the Co-operative movement should cease its financial connection, that the great Friendly Society branches in Ireland should divorce themselves (financially) from their brethren across the channel and that, having done so, we should raise aloft the flag of Internationalism and declare that we, and we alone, are the only true socialists and internationalists! Bunkum, friend Connolly; you are obsessed with an antipathy to Belfast and the black north, and under your obsession you advocate reactionary doctrines alien to any brand of socialism I have ever heard of ...

... The ILP have enabled the Irish in Belfast to unite, James Connolly (Catholic) can – thanks to the spadework of the ILP – come to Belfast and speak to audiences mainly Protestant, and be patiently heard, and it is curious that our comrade never came to Belfast until he was confident that the ILP had won a tolerant hearing for all classes ...

I am an internationalist because the same grievances which afflict the German and the Englishman afflict me. I speak the same tongue as the Englishman; I study the same literature; I am oppressed by the same financial power; and, to me, only a combined and united attack, without geographical consideration, can assure to Ireland an equal measure of social advancement as that which the larger and more advanced democracy of Great Britain are pressing for.

Forward, 3 June & 8 July 1911

61 James Connolly: Plebeian conquerors and conquered

Though occupying a respected place in the canon of international Marxist thought, and arguing for a united Catholic and Protestant working class, Connolly's work was not always entirely free from the nostalgia and race-thinking of the Gaelic movement.

(a) The seventeenth, eighteenth and nineteenth centuries were, indeed, the Via Dolorous of the Irish race. In them the Irish Gael sank out of sight, and in his place the middle-class politicians, capitalists and ecclesiastics laboured to produce a hybrid and, Irishman, assimilating a foreign social system, a foreign speech, and a foreign character. In the effort to assimilate the first two the Irish were unhappily too successful, so successful that today the majority of the Irish do not know that their fathers ever knew another system of ownership, and the Irish Irelanders are painfully grappling with their mother tongue with the hesitating accent of a foreigner. Fortunately the Irish character has proven too difficult to press into respectable foreign moulds, and the recoil of that character from the deadly embrace of capitalist to English conventionalism, as it has already led to a revaluation of the speech of the Gael, will in all probability also lead to a re-study and appreciation of the social system under which the Gael reached the highest point of civilisation and culture in Europe.

James Connolly, *Labour in Irish History* (1910), pp 5-6

(b) The underlying idea of this work is that the Labour Movement of Ireland must set itself the Re-Conquest of Ireland as its final aim, that the re-conquest involves taking possession of the entire country, all its power of wealth-production and all its natural resources, and organising these on a co-operative basis for the good of all. To demonstrate that this and this alone would be a reconquest, the attempt is made to explain what the Conquest of Ireland was, how it affected the Catholic natives and the Protestant settlers, how the former were subjected and despoiled by open force, and how the latter were despoiled by fraud, and when they protested were also subjected by force, and how out of this common spoliation and subjection there arises to-day the necessity of common action to reverse the Conquest, in order that the present population, descendants alike of the plebeian Conquerors and the Conquered plebeians, may enjoy in common fraternity and good-will that economic security and liberty for which their ancestors fought, or thought they fought.

James Connolly, *The Re-Conquest of Ireland* (1915), p 1

62 *William McMullen: With James Connolly in Belfast*

The appeal of republican socialism in Belfast has been restricted mainly to the Catholic population of the city. But in the years immediately prior to the First World War many of the first generation of Belfast's socialist activists, although predominantly Protestants, were attracted by Connolly's analysis. One of the most prominent of these was William McMullen (1888-1984), a shipwright and trade union official of strict Presbyterian and Unionist background who began his political career as a Labour member of the NI Parliament and ended it as a senator in the Irish Republic.

I first met James Connolly in the year 1910 on one of his visits to Belfast to engage in socialist propaganda, soon after his return from America. I was at that time a member of the Independent Labour Party, which had many branches in the City of Belfast, and was actively engaged in Socialist propaganda work. I knew little of James Connolly and his work at this stage, as we were nurtured on the British brand of Socialist propaganda, and all the literature we read, as well as all our speakers, were imported from Great Britain.

I had been introduced to the 'faith' by some of my friends, who like myself worked in Messrs. Harland & Wolff's shipyard, and although my mind, like most teenagers at the time, was concentrated on sport to the exclusion of almost every other consideration, I was induced to take home and read Robert Blatchford's *Merry England* and *Britain for the British*, and I was kept judiciously supplied with pamphlets on various aspects of the Socialist movement until I became quite interested in the subject, and shortly afterwards did not object to the description of Socialist being applied to myself, although at the time, in the circumstances and particularly in the environment this was quite a momentous decision to make. I soon became a frequent attender at Socialist meetings and found myself taking the chair – as we described it – at street corner meetings, and introducing the speaker to the audience, which invariably was not large in those days if one excluded periods of stress or the Sunday afternoon meetings at the Custom House Steps, where a large crowd was attracted by the variety of oratorical fare offered, from the vending of quack medicine to the robust oratory of some of the political-cum-religious orators. There was at this stage a very active Socialist movement in Great Britain, and as our school of Socialist thought had no nationalist tradition, and was not conscious of, and even if it had been would have been contemptuous of, a Socialist movement in any other part of this country. We did not give any thought to much, save the conversion of as many of our fellow workers as possible to the Socialist creed – and often marvelled at their obtuseness in not embracing it – and regarded ourselves as part of a vast International Socialist movement, which one day would emancipate the toiling masses from the thraldom of wage slavery ...

It is quite true I had heard James Connolly and his works discussed ... I had conceived of him ... as being a tall, commanding, and as the advance notices said of him, a silver-tongued orator. I found him, however, to be the opposite of my mental picture: short, squat, unpretentious, with a distinctive, even if ... a slightly raucous brogue ... I recall that the subject matter of his speech, and his method of delivery, were different from what we had been used to – there were no highly imaginative flights of flamboyant oratory. The appeal was not to the emotions but to the head. Calm, clear, incisive analysis of his subject, interlarded with frequent references to Irish history, and a restrained eloquence calculated to carry conviction ...

My mind was, accordingly, attuned to his message a year later in 1911, when he came North to settle in Belfast, and later became District organiser of the ITGWU ... His permanent advent to our city meant that we had two main political Socialist organisations where one had mainly held sway, i.e. the Socialist Party of Ireland and the British organisation, the Independent Labour Party of which I was a member, and of which James Keir Hardie MP was one of its leading figures. Connolly's organisation was Marxist and nationalist in outlook, while the Independent Labour Party was reformist and pseudo-internationalist ... Perhaps it is pertinent to mention here that in the main in those days, the members of the Socialist movement in the city were Protestants, as the Catholics were in the main followers of the Irish Parliamentary Party and their local parliamentary representative – Joe Devlin, MP for West Belfast, who was credited with having Labour sympathies ... Connolly was of course...striving unremittingly to get the entire movement of the city to leave the Independent Labour Party and join the Socialist Party of Ireland. This was a much more difficult matter than Connolly, realist as he was, appeared to apprehend. In those times it was difficult enough for one to break with Unionist family tradition and embrace Socialism, but much more difficult to follow the hook, line and sinker of Irish Republicanism as well. A number there were who did it and paid the inevitable price some twelve months later, during the fierce sectarian troubles which broke out in the Belfast shipyards when practically every known Socialist found it impossible to continue at work ...

... the following year (1912) an attempt was made to secure the unity of the Socialist movement in Ireland ... The main decision ... was to found a new organisation, with the same principles as the Socialist Party of Ireland, but to name it the Independent Labour Party of Ireland. A short time after our return to Belfast, I was chosen as chairman of the Belfast branch of the party, with a room in Upper Donegall Street for business purposes, while we used the room above Danny McDevitt's tailoring premises in Rosemary Street, known as the 'Bounders College' for our propaganda meetings during the winter. Our forum during the summer was at the lamp in Library Street where, on occasion, we drew large crowds ... For a period after William Walker's defection from the movement we had a joint committee, operating between ourselves and the ILP, to conduct propaganda in the city ...

W McMullen, *With James Connolly in Belfast*
(published by the author, 1951), pp 3-26

63 Jim Larkin's nationalist plot, 1907

The most prominent – and flamboyant – figure in the Irish Labour movement before the First World War was not Connolly but the Liverpool-born 'strike organiser' Jim Larkin (1876-1947). (See Volume 1, illustration 16.) At the turn of the century the Labour movement had been a small affair based on craft unions. Its main strength lay among Belfast Protestants, and for that reason it took little interest in nationalist politics. But when Larkin arrived in Belfast in 1907 to organise unskilled workers on behalf of the English-based National Union of Dock Labourers, he found that much of his potential support inevitably lay in the Catholic section of the city. The strike and agitation which he organised cut across, for a brief period, the usual sectarian lines of conflict. The private response of Fred Crawford, a small businessman who later achieved public fame as the leading gun-runner for the Ulster Volunteer Force, 1911-14, is a good illustration of Belfast sectarian thinking.

F. H. Crawford to Major R.W. Doyne   20 August 1907

I am thankful to say our strike troubles are over for the present. It was simply a political move on the part of a section of the Nationalists to discredit Belfast ...

What a blessing all the rioting took place in the Catholic quarter of the city. This branded the whole thing as a Nationalist movement. Larkin the leader is the grandson of Larkin the Manchester martyr.[1]

The whole strike was a big political plot to ruin Belfast trade. The Nationalists are sick of people pointing out to them the Prosperity of Belfast and Protestant Ulster, they want to ruin us and this is one move in that direction. The serious part of the business is that they have duped a lot of Protestants, who call themselves Independent Orangeman, and a few demagogues who love to hear their own voice ...

PRONI: Crawford Letter-book, D1700/10/1/1, pp 148-9

64 Jim Larkin's English invasion, 1913

Larkin's career as Irish organiser for the NUDL ended suddenly in 1908 with the withdrawal of support by an executive alarmed at the outflow of English funds to Ireland. By then he had moved his base to Dublin, and his prompt response was to convert the branches he had initiated into the basis for a new Irish Transport and General Workers Union. Although the emphasis remained on the organisation and recognition of trade

1 Larkin's grandfather was in fact still alive in Liverpool ten years after three Fenians named Allen, Larkin and O'Brien had been executed for the murder of a policeman in Manchester in 1867.

unionism among the dockers, carters and other labourers of Dublin, Cork and the smaller Irish ports, it was inevitable, especially after the 1910 general elections brought home rule back to the forefront of politics, that the ITGWU should come to terms with nationalism. The focus of concern was that Labour's potential strength in urban areas would be given good political representation in the arrangements for distribution of seats in the Home Rule parliament, and that partition should not be allowed to separate industrial Belfast from the rest of Ireland. But more important to Larkin's career was the great strike and lockout which dominated Dublin throughout the winter of 1913-14. The living conditions and wage rates in the city were deplorable by the standard of other United Kingdom cities of the time, but Larkin's ambitious policy of confrontation and general strike was based on too slender a financial base, and failed to win steady support from English unions. The strike, which had set nationalist workers against nationalist employers, ended in lockout and defeat for the men. Larkin's policy aroused the opposition of all strands of nationalism except for the radical wing of the revived IRB, and was openly denounced by the Catholic church. The *Irish Catholic* weekly, endorsed by the Cardinal Archbishop of Armagh as 'a clever exponent of Catholic views and a fearless vindicator of Catholic interests', published a series of editorials on Larkinism, one under the heading 'Satanism and Socialism'.

We earnestly trust that our workers will display a more keen capacity in the future than they appear to have done in the past for discerning where and to what extent their confidence should be bestowed. A palpable attempt has been made within the last few days, to win them over to the ranks of the Labour-Socialist party of England, wherein they would soon be taught to forget their Nationality and to rank Home Rule on the same level as the Eight Hour Day. Everyone knows there is a design afoot to wrest the parliamentary representation of one of the Dublin divisions from the Irish party and bestow it on the secretary of the Transport Union, as if there were no decent native representative of industry available who would worthily defend the interests of his class as well as of his nation. We know what Labour-Socialism has done in France – how it has poisoned patriotism in the minds of those who have yielded to its seductions, how it has striven to make the profession of arms hateful in the eyes of a gallant people, how it has scoffed at the valorous legends of the most glorious army in the world and sought to teach the conscript that he should forsake the sabre for the Socialists' gutter-broom, how it laughs at the ties of frontier and of race, and would make the Frank the bondsman of the Teuton if thereby could be purchased a craven and ignoble peace. We refuse to believe that our brethren among the workers of Ireland will ever allow English Labour-Socialists to degrade them to such a level as this, but it is highly time they were on their guard against sophistry, and realised that the most sacred Right of all at stake today is the Right of Ireland to the support of all her children in the defence and vindication of her national and industrial independence. Our motherland has had enough, and more than enough, of English garrisons!

The Irish Catholic, 13 September 1913

65 Jim Larkin's stagey trick

Larkin was opposed almost as bitterly by Nationalist newspapers as by the ecclesiastical press. The Belfast daily, the *Irish News*, gave his policies and his actions no encouragement, while seeking nonetheless to capitalise on the harsh response of the Dublin police. But the dramatic character of this incident gives some indication of how Larkin was able to retain the adulation of the Dublin masses notwithstanding press opposition and his reckless leadership.

Mr James Larkin's exploit this afternoon was smartly conceived, so ingeniously devised that no-one credits Mr Larkin with inventing it. But it was, after all, a trivial, tawdry, undignified and stagey trick. Having hidden himself from the police for a period of twenty-four hours, Mr Larkin donned a false beard and frock coat, and presented himself at the Imperial Hotel out of a taxicab in the early morning. This hotel is the property of a company presided over by Mr William Martin Murphy, the chairman of the Dublin Tramway Company. At about 1.30 p.m. Mr Larkin, disguised by a beard and dressed in a frock coat, thrust himself through a window on to the parapet or balcony over the street, and shouted some words to a moving crowd of sightseers. Then he ran back through the open window into the arms of the police. But a sympathiser outside had signalised the occasion by throwing a stone through a window, and this act apparently gave the police authorities an excuse for ordering a baton charge.

It was a brutal and thoroughly disgusting performance. A thousand people, most of whom had come out of churches in the vicinity, may have been idly parading between Nelson's Pillar and Sir John Grey's statue. Of the thousand not more than twenty could have been properly described as 'Larkinites', and not more than 100 of the 1000 knew what was about when between three and four hundred men armed with batons rushed at the signal from all sides into the street ... knocking down young and old, men and women, indiscriminately ... I never saw a more causeless attack on a crowd of people ...

Irish News, 1 September 1913

66 Jim Larkin's villainous scandal

One of the many errors of political judgement made by the ITGWU strike leadership was its decision to permit well-meaning English socialists to arrange for about three hundred children of unemployed Dublin workers to be evacuated to various centres in England where they would be cared for by English workers until the strike was over. Such a curious lapse by a republican trade union presented conservative nationalists with a public relations opportunity which the press exploited to the full, its dismissive use of the term 'cosmopolitan' and its repetition of foreign names adding a wider xenophobia to the predictable anti-English spirit. The evacuation scheme was hastily aborted.

A VILLAINOUS SCANDAL

Early yesterday morning fifty little Dublin children were driven into the public baths at Tara Street, there to be washed before being consigned, like lambs to the slaughter, to English addresses selected by an Englishwoman of the Socialist-Suffragette variety named Mrs Montefiore; and the woman appears to have had as esquire an English Syndicalist named Weigall, who seems to be connected with a 'League' of some kind formed to exploit a Syndicalist sheet written by an Irish anti-clerical crank ...

Dublin is a tortured city, and the pressure of hideous want following upon months of destructive strife has, no doubt, disheartened and, to some extent, demoralised some of its poor people; but it is almost impossible to believe that even in the direst extremity to which they can be reduced, Irish Catholic fathers and mothers are willingly handing over the bodies and souls of their little children to the Montefiores, the Weigalls and the nameless crew behind them who have planned this vile and sinister campaign. The 'law', it seems has been 'put in motion'; and not a moment too soon with regard to the matter. Dublin's priests and people cannot be expected to watch the quays and the railways stations hour after hour, by day and by night, in order to outmanoeuvre the Montefiores and Weigalls, and their equally unscrupulous and infamous 'aiders and abettors' – amongst whom the persons responsible for the control of Liberty Hall [ie Larkin and the ITGWU leadership] must evidently be reckoned. The first 'batch' of Irish Catholic children marked out for exportation yesterday were, happily, rescued – thanks to the vigilance and courage of a few priests and the determination displayed by the people when they realised the hideousness and horror of the situation brought about by the 'cosmopolitan' devisors of the scheme ...

... It is now about 268 years ago since Irish Catholic children were 'deported' in large numbers. Oliver Cromwell was the noble-hearted and sympathetic Englishman who put that splendid scheme into practical operation ...

It is an outrageous, dastardly and criminal business; but perhaps the most exasperating and galling thing about it ... is the supreme and unmitigated contempt with which ... the Montefiores and the Weigalls ... must regard the men and women of ... Dublin, with whose children it is sought to play these pranks and who are not, quite evidently, credited with the possession of elementary self-respect.

Irish News, 23 October 1913

67 William O'Brien: The Irish Citizen Army

Perhaps the most significant outcome of the Dublin industrial troubles of 1913-14 was the formation of the Irish Citizen Army – a paramilitary wing of the labour movement which, although small, symbolised and helped to strengthen the bonds between socialism and republicanism which were to draw Connolly and his followers into the 1916 Rising. Here its origins are recounted by William O'Brien of Dublin (1881-1968, not to be confused with the Cork-based Nationalist of the same name). O'Brien was an early member of the ITGWU who, in the years after 1916, imparted a more cautious, non-political ethos to the union, from which he later succeeded in excluding Larkin altogether,

Captain James R. White DSO, who had retired from the British Army, was carrying on a campaign in the north of Ireland, of which he was a native, with a view to inducing Protestants to be reconciled to home rule. Early in November 1913 Capt. White came to Dublin and spoke at a meeting in University College, Dublin. On the following night he volunteered to speak at a strikers' meeting in Beresford Place and did so ... .

After the meeting James Connolly, who was in charge at Liberty Hall at the time in the absence of James Larkin, spoke to him and gave him an account of the activities of the police since the commencement of the dispute, which rather changed the Captain's views on the subject. In the course of the conversation with Connolly he mentioned that the fact that the crowd ran from the police was owing to their not being trained or drilled, and he volunteered to drill them himself. Connolly accepted this offer and said they should be drilled into a Labour army. Connolly gave it the name of the Citizen Army. Now the name Citizen Army was first introduced in the early 1880s in Great Britain. When the Social Democratic Federation was formed it was one of the items on their platform; but it is as well to recognise that their conception of the Citizen Army was an alternative to the standing army of the state. That is where the title came from.

As a result a statement was made by Connolly on 13 November [1913], the day of James Larkin's release from Mountjoy prison. Following that Capt. White drilled a number of the strikers up to the end of the strike, which took place towards the end of January 1914. After that the Citizen Army faded away – for the time being at least – once the strikers got back to work.

... on Sunday 29 March [1914] ... I ... found that the committee of the Citizen Army were meeting and were engaged in reorganising the Army ... [Larkin] ... asked Capt. White what numbers of men he had in the Army and White replied about fifty. This was a tremendous shock to him. Larkin said: 'Oh, I think we have more than that.' Whereupon White said: 'No, rather less.' There was not much more said then.

The Army was reorganised and officers and officials appointed ... Capt. White continued to be in charge of the Army up until 14 May 1914, when he resigned because he disagreed with the attitude of the Army in criticising the [Irish National] Volunteers ... James Larkin was not in charge of the Army until May 1914.

James Larkin went to the United States on a lecture tour, leaving Dublin in October 1914. James Connolly came from Belfast, where he was secretary for the Union, to act as general secretary in Dublin, and took over at that time. He also took over the chairmanship of the Citizen Army.

Up to that time the Citizen Army was accustomed to parade and keep order at public meetings, but engaged in no serious work that would be expected from an army. Connolly changed all that and insisted upon having it reorganised as a revolutionary force. A number of uniforms were made in Arnott's in Dublin ... Sean O'Casey was secretary. O'Casey and some others who agreed with him took action against Madam Markievicz, who was a member both of the Citizen Army and of the Volunteers. As a result the Committee of the Army proposed to expel her from the Army unless she gave up membership of the Volunteers ... Seeing the strong feeling in favour of Madam Markievicz [Larkin]...tried to settle up the matter and pressed O'Casey to withdraw his opposition to her. O'Casey refused and thereupon left the meeting and never had any more to do with the Citizen Army ...

W O'Brien, *Forth the Banners Go*
(Dublin: Three Candles Press, 1969), pp 118-122

68 Augustine Birrell: Depths below nationalism

Birrell continued as the cabinet minister responsible for Ireland, running the country with an increasingly light rein until the 1916 Rising ended his career. His letters to (a) a relative and (b) the prime minister are shrewd assessments of the Dublin crisis, while giving little impression of a statesman in control of a difficult situation.

(a) A Birrell to Sir Charles Tennyson   20 Sept. 1913

... everything is as bad as bad can be in Dublin. It pours with rain, the people are starving, the Corporation are a pack of knaves and fools, the Executive is unpopular, and the Police have for the nonce established a reign of *terror* that may at any time disappear. However, there are still optimists who believe that this World will someday be fit for human inhabitation ...

Liverpool University Library: Birrell Collection, MS 8.2 (1)

(b) A Birrell to H H Asquith   26 September 1913

...The dispute is only about Larkin and his methods, which everybody in all ranks, outside the anarchical party, agree are impossible ... The whole atmosphere is still charged with gunpowder, and the hooligans in the city are ripe for mischief. From the Redmond point of view this state of things is very awkward. The *Irish Times*, very kindly, is always rubbing in the impotency of the four members [of Parliament] of the city, and of the Catholic Church, and quotes what Larkin is fond of saying, that 'home rule does not put a loaf of bread into anybody's pocket'. Larkin's position is a very peculiar one. All the powers that are supposed to be of importance are against him: the Party, the whole Catholic Church, and the great body of Dublin citizens, to say nothing of the Government, and yet somehow or other he has support and is a great character and figure. The fact is that the dispute has lifted the curtain upon depths below Nationalism and the Home Rule movement, and were there to be an election in Dublin tomorrow, it is quite likely that two of the four gentlemen I have just referred to [the Nationalist MPs for Dublin] would lose their seats.

Bodleian Library: Asquith Papers, MS 38

69 John Dillon: Larkin is a malignant enemy

The Nationalist MP John Dillon lived in central Dublin, and was better informed than most of his colleagues about changing public opinion in Ireland. This letter to a London-based colleague indicates clearly the party-political focus of the home rule movement's opposition to Larkin.

John Dillon MP to T P O'Connor MP   16 October 1913

As regards the situation in Dublin, nothing could be more mixed and mischievous. Larkin is a malignant enemy and an impossible man. He seems to be a wild international syndicalist and anarchist and for a long time he has been doing his best to burst up the Party and the National movement.

The employers have been led into a false position by Murphy. It is a devilish situation and I feel that any attempt on our part to interfere in any way will do *nothing but harm*. One overwhelming objection to your attending the [London] meeting called by the Gaelic League [to express support for the strikers] is that your action will immediately be commented on in Beresford Place by P.T.Daly, Larkin and co. and contrasted with the *brutal* attitude of Mr Redmond and Mr Dillon who, although on the spot, etc etc ...

The English Labour leaders have, it seems to me, acted in a most weak and contemptible manner. They all hate Larkin and condemn his methods, and he does not conceal his contempt for them, but openly denounces them as humbugs and traitors. Yet they are financing Larkinism in Dublin, and thereby prolonging this wretched strike and threatening Dublin with absolute ruin. And sowing a horrible crop of bitterness and hate which it will take years to get rid of.

TCD: John Dillon Papers, MS 6740

70 Patrick Pearse: The people who wept in Gethsemane

Aside from the issue of land tenure, radical or left-wing views on social questions were not a central feature of Irish nationalism in the early twentieth century. Leading Sinn Féiners like the Dublin journalist Arthur Griffith (1871-1922) were no more sympathetic to Larkin than were the parliamentarians. Outside the Labour movement, only the militant republicans of the Irish Republican Brotherhood supported the Dublin strikers or showed any general interest in organising the urban working class. Patrick Pearse (1879-1916), a private-school headmaster, writer, and IRB man who was to lead the 1916 uprising, voiced such sentiments in a typically vague and high-flown – and some have said blasphemous – way, in the last pamphlet he wrote, in March 1916.

The gentry have uniformly been corrupted by England and the merchants and middle-class capitalists have, when not corrupted been uniformly intimidated, whereas the common people have for the most part remained un-bought and un-terrified. It is, in fact, true that the repositories of the Irish tradition, as well the spiritual tradition of nationality as the kindred tradition of stubborn physical resistance to England, have been the great, splendid, faithful, common people – that dumb multitudinous throng which sorrowed during the penal night, which bled in '98, which starved in the Famine; and which is here still – what is left of it – un-bought and un-terrified. Let no man be mistaken as to who will be lord in Ireland when Ireland is free. The people will be lord and master. The people who wept in Gethsemane, who trod the sorrowful way, who died naked on a cross, who went down into hell, will rise again glorious and immortal, will sit on the right hand of God, and will come in the end to give judgement, a judge just and terrible.

'The Sovereign People', in P H Pearse,
Political Writings and Speeches (Dublin, 1924), p 345

71 John Redmond: Dollar dictator

The Liberal government of 1905-9 secured the co-operation of the Irish Party by 'governing according to Irish ideas', which meant extending full consultation to Redmond and Dillon in matters of public patronage but otherwise differed little in practice from the Tory policy of 'killing home rule with kindness'. Even the ill-fated attempt to set up an administrative council in 1907, vetoed by the Irish Party, had its origins in the devolution scheme evolved under Wyndham's administration. The Liberals, faced increasingly with resistance to their measures from the House of Lords, were reluctant to put an Irish issue in the forefront of their programme. The Lords' rejection of the 1909 budget seemed a much more attractive battleground. But by-election trends indicated clearly that the massive overall majority of 1906 was unlikely to recur, that the Liberal party would need, at the least, Irish support to win a number of crucial seats in British constituencies and, quite possibly, the support of Irish Party MPs to form a working majority in the House of Commons. Thus John Redmond could address Liberal cabinet ministers (and Irish-American financial backers) with an authority not possessed by an Irish leader since Parnell in 1886. A copy of the following letter found its way to the prime minister, Asquith, who declared a few days later that a future Liberal government would be entirely free to deal with the Irish question along the lines of full legislative home rule.

John Redmond to John Morley   27 November 1909

The political conditions in Ireland are such that unless an official declaration on the question of home rule be made, not only will it be impossible for us to support Liberal candidates in England, but we will most unquestionably have to ask our friends to vote against them ... as you know very well, the opposition of Irish voters in Lancashire, Yorkshire and other places, including Scotland, would mean the loss of many seats.

Declarations of individual candidates in favour of home rule are of no use to us. We cannot acquiesce in the present situation being continued. There is a large majority in the government and in the House of Commons in favour of home rule, and yet their hands are tied by reason of the fact that the home rule issue was deliberately withdrawn from the consideration of the electors at the last election. We must, therefore, press for an official declaration which will show clearly that the home rule issue is involved in the issue of the House of Lords by declaring that the government shall be free to deal with it, not on the lines of the Council Bill, but on the lines of national self-government, subject to imperial control, in the next parliament ...

Bodleian Library: Asquith Papers MS 36

72 The Constitutional Conference of 1910

Two general elections, in January and December 1910, could not dislodge the Irish Party from its new position of strength in relation to its Liberal allies. An attempt to reach a settlement by means of a bi-partisan agreement between the major British parties, occasioned by the death of Edward VII in May 1910, ultimately came to nothing, as the following document from the Conservative camp makes clear. Thus, when the year 1911 opened, a government programme was clear at last. The House of Lords, under threat of the mass creation of Liberal peers by George V, was to pass a Parliament Bill reducing its power of veto to a temporary stay of two years, leaving the way clear for Irish home rule to be brought forward in 1912.

Note by Sir Robert Finlay MP of A. J. Balfour's Report to Conservative leaders on the breakdown of the Constitutional Conference of 1910 18 December 1910

... On 16 October the Conference broke off on the difficulty of home rule. A. J. B[alfour] proposed that if a home rule bill was twice rejected [by the Lords] it should go to a plebiscite. Lloyd George, while admitting the reasonableness of this, said it was impossible for the Government to assent to this.

The Conference met again last Tuesday. Government proposed compromises.

One was that a general election should intervene on the next occasion on which a H[ome] R[ule] bill, having passed the H[ouse] of C[ommons], was rejected in the H[ouse] of L[ords], but only on this occasion, and that H.Rule bills if introduced afterwards should be treated like ordinary bills.

... A.J.B. made the statement ... and asked whether we should go on or break off. A.J.B. expressed no opinion but from an expression he let fall I inferred that he was averse to going on on such terms. Lansdowne, Cawdor and A[usten] C[hamberlain] were for breaking off. This was the decision arrived at. Alfred Lyttelton gave no opinion and Walter Long had doubts though he concurred with the majority.

I expressed myself strongly against the proposed settlement and in favour of breaking off the negotiations. My chief grounds were:

(a) The joint sitting with the whole of the H. of C. and a selection from the H. of L. giving Unionists only 45 or so of a majority was purely illusory.

(b) There was no principle in the proposal about home rule, that only one attempt should be safeguarded by a general election and it would leave it open to any government to get H.R. passed on subsequent occasions without consulting the people, for such subsequent bills would be treated as ordinary legislation, and there was no safeguard whatever as to constitutional changes other than H.R. unless they touched the Crown, the Protestant succession or the Act embodying the agreement arrived at by the Conference. I said that I did not believe that the Unionist Party in the H. of C. would give their support to carry into law any such arrangement ...

A Chamberlain, *Politics from Inside*
(London: Cassell, 1936), pp 295-97

73 Ulstermen prefer the Kaiser, 1911?

The Irish Unionists continued to oppose home rule altogether, although their only real strength lay in Ulster. The Liberals and the Irish Party went ahead with their plans on the assumption that any Ulster resistance would be party-political, both in character and in essence. It gradually became clear, however, that the attitude such as that taken in the press interview given by a prominent Ulster Unionist MP, Captain James Craig (1871-1940), was not the bluff which it was at first taken for.

Neither Mr Redmond nor the English people has any conception of the deep-rooted determination of the sturdy men and women of Ulster, or of the silent preparations that are being made to meet by armed resistance the encroachment on their civil and religious liberties that would naturally follow the establishment of a parliament in Dublin.

Further, there is a spirit spreading abroad which I can testify to from my personal knowledge – that Germany and the German Emperor would be preferred to the rule of John Redmond, Patrick Ford [editor of the American newspaper, *Irish World*] and the Molly Maguires. That sentiment has been doubtless strongly augmented by the number of kidnapping cases that have recently come to light consequent upon the Church of Rome decree *(Ne Temere)* put into full force with rigour in Ireland, but successfully resisted in Germany. There are a very large number of people in other parts of the

United Kingdom who are unwilling or unable to believe that Ulster will, if forced, adopt Lord Randolph Churchill's advice: 'Ulster will fight, and Ulster will be right.' Such steps will be taken when the proper moment arises as will convince those unbelievers and the whole of the British public that if the need arises armed resistance of the most determined character will be resorted to sooner than submit to the dominance of the Church of Rome which any parliament in Dublin would spell to the people of Ulster.

Morning Post, 9 January 1911

74 Bonar Law: No length of resistance

The third Home Rule Bill at last saw the light of day on 11 April 1912. Two days earlier an estimated 100,000 Ulster Protestants had marched past the platform in military formation at a protest demonstration in Belfast's Balmoral grounds. Sir Edward Carson (1854-1935), the Dublin-born lawyer who became leader of the Irish Unionist group in the Conservative party in 1910, made it clear both that he associated himself with the armed resistance spoken of by Craig and that, apparently, he intended to use that resistance to thwart nationalism altogether – 'if Ulster succeed, home rule is dead', he declared in the House of Commons in June 1912. A few months earlier, the sophisticated but seemingly lethargic Arthur Balfour had been replaced as Tory leader by Andrew Bonar Law (1858-1923), a Scots Canadian with Ulster family connections who gave full endorsement to the style and tone of the Ulster resistance. Law and Carson were the main platform speakers at the Balmoral demonstration. In July, Law went even further in his commitment to the Ulster cause, at a mass meeting held in the grounds of Blenheim Palace, family seat of the Duke of Marlborough.

In our opposition ... we shall not be guided by the considerations or bound by the restraints which would influence us in an ordinary constitutional struggle ... They may, perhaps they will, carry their home rule bill through the House of Commons, but what then? I said the other day in the House of Commons and I repeat here that there are things stronger than parliamentary majorities.

... Before I occupied the position I now fill in the party I said that, in my belief, if an attempt were made to deprive these men [Ulster Unionists] of their birth-right – as part of a corrupt parliamentary bargain – they would be justified in resisting such an attempt by all means in their power, including force. I said it then, and I repeat it now with a full sense of the responsibility which attaches to my position, that, in my opinion, if such an attempt is made, I can imagine no length of resistance to which Ulster can go in which I should not be prepared to support them, and in which, in my belief, they would not be supported by the overwhelming majority of the British people.

The Times, 29 July 1912

75 Ulstermen humbly rely on their God, 1912

To underline further the strength of Ulster Protestant feeling, and to achieve an even greater show of numbers, the local Unionist leaders declared 28 September 1912 to be 'Ulster Day', on which about 450,000 men and women signed a document or supporting declaration based in concept on the seventeenth-century Scottish Covenant. Carson signed with a silver pen. Some lesser political lights signed in their own blood. (See Volume 1, illustration 25).

Ulster's solemn league and covenant

Being convinced in our consciences that Home Rule would be disastrous to the material well-being of Ulster, as well as of the whole of Ireland, subversive of our civil and religious freedom, destructive of our citizenship, and perilous to the unity of the Empire, we, whose names are underwritten, men of Ulster, loyal subjects of His Gracious Majesty King George V, humbly relying on the God Whom our fathers in the days of stress and trial confidently trusted, do hereby pledge ourselves in solemn Covenant throughout this our time of threatened calamity to stand by one another in defending for ourselves and our children our cherished position of equal citizenship in the United Kingdom and in using all means which may be found necessary to defeat the present conspiracy to set up a home rule parliament in Ireland. And in the event of such a Parliament being forced upon us we further and mutually pledge ourselves to refuse to recognise its authority. In sure confidence that God will defend the right, we hereto subscribe our names. And further we individually declare that we have not already signed this Covenant. God Save the King.

The Times, 20 September 1912

76 Willoughby de Broke: Every white man

Their very adoption of the name 'Unionist' after 1886 acknowledged a measure of commitment on the part of English Conservatives. But the scale and intensity of their opposition to home rule between 1911 to 1914 was something new. Historians have seen this trend variously as part of the 'Ulster bluff', as determination to prevent dismemberment of the United Kingdom, and as a cynical exercise by a thrice-defeated political party. Evidence can be found to lend support to all these interpretations. But for many Conservatives, like the backbench English peer Lord Willoughby de Broke (1869-1923), the 'Ulster struggle' took on a symbolic significance. De Broke had taken an active part in the ineffective resistance to the Parliament Bill in 1911. It seemed to him that the traditional values of the British Empire were being swept away by radicals who held power only with the support of Irish nationalists. In this context Ulster, where Protestant and 'loyal' feelings had assumed such militancy and cut across class barriers, became an ideal issue and location for a defiant stand This extract is from a speech made by de Broke at Dromore, Co Down, in September 1912.

The Unionists of England were going to help Unionists over here, not only by making speeches. Peaceable methods would be tried first, but if the last resort was forced on them by the Radical government, the latter would find that they had not only Orangemen against them, but that every white man in the British Empire would be giving support, either moral or active, to one of the most loyal populations that ever fought under the Union Jack.

Belfast Newsletter, 27 September 1912

77 Winston Churchill: A combination of rancour and fanaticism

Even before the third Home Rule Bill was introduced, the Liberal cabinet had privately resolved to consider special treatment for Ulster if it became necessary and, Asquith reported to the king, intended making 'careful and confidential inquiry...as to the extent and character of the Ulster resistance'. Whether that special treatment would take the form merely of some local autonomy within an Irish framework, or whether it would mean exclusion of Ulster from the settlement, whether it would be permanent, indefinite, or strictly temporary, was not made clear. It appeared to the Government that there was probably no bargaining advantage to be gained from premature concessions, and certainly no prospect of securing Irish Party support for them in the absence of extreme duress. It was not until the unrevised Home Rule Bill had made its second journey through the Commons in 1913 that modification was seriously discussed between the parties. A letter from Winston Churchill (1874-1965), then First Lord of the Admiralty, in August 1913 typifies the cautious way in which the matter was being broached with the Nationalists. Churchill was the first member of the government to take up the question of Ulster, and was shortly to threaten resignation from the cabinet if Ulster was coerced. There is some evidence to suggest that he may even have been considering Ulster as an issue over which he might return to the Conservative party, which he had deserted nine years earlier on the question of free trade.

Winston Churchill to John Redmond   31 August 1913

... I do not believe there is any real feeling against home rule in the Tory party apart from the Ulster question, but they hate the government, are bitterly desirous of turning it out, and see in the resistance of Ulster an extra-parliamentary force which they will not hesitate to use to the full. I have been pondering a great deal over this matter, and my general view is just what I told you earlier in the year – namely, that something should be done to afford the characteristically Protestant and Orange counties the option of a moratorium of several years before acceding to the Irish parliament ... Much is to be apprehended from a combination of the rancour of a party in the ascendant and the fanaticism of these stubborn and determined Orangemen ...

NLI: Redmond Papers

78 *The Bishop of Raphoe: A queer autonomy*

The partition of Ireland was not a solution that had ever before been seriously countenanced. But a letter to *The Times* in favour of compromise from a veteran home ruler and Liberal elder statesman, Lord Loreburn (1846-1923), in September 1913 and a public speech by Churchill a few days later, brought discussion into the open. The bishop of Raphoe, Patrick O'Donnell (1856-1927), the Irish Party's most active supporter within the ranks of the Catholic hierarchy, was quick to call attention to the position of the Catholic minority in north-east Ulster. Even under a scheme for giving 'Ulster' separate treatment within the general jurisdiction of a home rule government, let alone any proposal for omitting Ulster from home rule altogether, he argued, the situation would be intolerable for nationalists. Interestingly enough, however, in the light of later developments, he placed the unity of the Irish Party above any attempt to create a distinct voice for nationalist Ulster – a voice which in the long run might have been less of a challenge to Ulster Unionism than to the official Nationalist leadership.

Bishop of Raphoe to John Redmond   9 October 1913

... There is no length to which any of us would refuse to go to satisfy the Orangemen at the starting of our new government, provided Ireland did not suffer seriously, and provided also the Nationalist minority did not suffer badly. But it is not hard for Mr Churchill to realise that under the bill as it stands, the set of Protestants who patently need no protection are the Ulster Unionists, and that, with the home rule of the bill, the Catholic and Nationalist minority in the N.E. corner remain under the domination in all local things which they have endured so long, until the spirit of freedom sets things right, as it would in a few years. But he may not see the point that nothing could justify cutting this minority off from their claims under the bill, and deliberately leaving them under a harrow that might be worse than what they have endured.

Autonomy in education etc. for the N.E. corner would be queer autonomy for them.

On matters of this kind there is a good deal of feeling that the Nationalists of Ulster should form a special committee, organise, and speak out, and insist on being represented as fully as the Orangemen at any conference. My own view has been that we in the interests of home rule should avoid forming a second camp in Ulster ...

NLI: Redmond Papers MS 15217 (4)

79 John Redmond: Ireland is a unit

In private correspondence amongst themselves, the leaders of the Irish Party acknowledged frankly that if the government offered, and persuaded the Unionists to submit to, home rule for Ireland with the option of exclusion for the four counties with Protestant majorities – Antrim, Armagh, Down and Londonderry – it would be difficult for them to object. But no such firm offer had been made, and in the meantime, Redmond, as he did in a speech at Limerick on 12 October 1913, could do no more than hint at the possibility of some local autonomy for Ulster within home rule.

Irish Nationalists can never be assenting parties to the mutilation of the Irish nation; Ireland is a unit. It is true that within the bosom of a nation there is room for diversities in the treatment of government and of administration, but a unit Ireland is and a unit Ireland must remain ... The two-nation theory is to us an abomination and a blasphemy ...

As cited in: D Gwynn, *The Life of John Redmond*
(London: Harrap, 1932), p 232

80 Joe Devlin: No trouble from the north-east corner

The Government's first serious attempt to apply pressure to the Nationalists to accept a compromise settlement to the Ulster difficulty was made in February and March 1914, as the Home Rule Bill came before the House of Commons yet again. This brought the leading Ulster member of the Nationalist party, Joe Devlin (1871-1934) to the forefront of events. Many on the Unionist side of affairs, including the Irish correspondent of *The Times*, appear to have thought that Devlin was on the brink of breaking with his Party leadership over the question of compromise. But senior Liberals had better grounds for believing that Devlin would put party unity, and loyalty to the leadership of Redmond and Dillon, above all other considerations. Great party organiser that he was, Devlin was ultimately content to use these skills to support a strategy devised by others. By March 1914 he has persuaded local and regional leaders of Nationalism in Ulster to agree to the temporary exclusion of the four counties of Antrim, Armagh, Down and Londonderry from the Home Rule Bill, in the interests of the wider movement.

(a) 'Mr Devlin's Memo'   20 February 1914

...We do not believe the reality of the threats of civil war indulged in by Sir Edward Carson and his followers. We have exceptional sources of information in regard to the Ulster Volunteer movement, and we are convinced that its danger is grossly exaggerated. The main ground for this conviction is the fact that in Belfast, the headquarters of the Carsonite movement, where the Catholic and Protestant home rulers would be amongst the first victims of any outbreak among the Orangemen, the home rulers regard the whole thing with absolute contempt, and are astonished that anybody outside Belfast should take it seriously ...

We believe the case could be met by permitting 'Ulster' to claim exclusion after, say, ten years if her representatives were not satisfied with their treatment in the Irish Parliament ... The record of Catholic and Nationalist Ireland, now and always, is proof of its toleration ... The inclusion of 'Ulster' with the right of going out after a trial period, affords the best means of practically testing its reliability ...

... We would be in favour of giving 'Ulster' extra representation in the Irish Parliament ... [and] ... such an arrangement of the Senate as would afford them an additional safeguard ...

NLI: John Redmond Papers, MS 15181 (3)

(b) Lloyd George Memo in reply to Devlin   23 February 1914

... I am therefore strongly of the opinion that the proposal must have two essential characteristics:

(1) It must be an offer the rejection of which would put the other side entirely in the wrong as far as the British public is concerned; and

(2) It must not involve any alteration in the scheme of the bill; so that if it is rejected the Unionists cannot say 'Why, you yourselves admitted that your bill needed amendment'.

I can only think of one suggestion which would meet these two fundamental conditions ... I would therefore suggest that any county in Ireland that wished to submit its case once more to the British electorate for decision should be allowed to contract out of the Act. The opinion of the counties would be taken by means of a plebiscite of the electors in each county ... The great advantage of this scheme lies in the fact that it is in no sense an admission that any part of the present bill is defective ... It would make the course of the Government very much clearer if the Unionists accept the responsibility for rejecting the proposal and countenance resistance.

As to the general considerations urged in Mr Devlin's memorandum, they are more or less common ground. Information in the possession of the Ministry indicates, however, that he underestimates the danger of civil disturbance in Ulster. I agree that the words 'civil war' are much too portentous a description to accord to the events which are likely to follow the setting up of an Irish parliament. All these elaborate preparations which have been made for some sort of resistance may, however, produce riots on a large and menacing scale, and the Government could hardly hope to quell them without some effusion of blood ... That contingency we are prepared to face, but before doing so we are anxious to make it clear to every reasonable mind in Great Britain that the rioters have refused all reasonable accommodation of their troubles ...

The Plunkett proposal [Ulster right of opt-out after a ten year trial] which is favoured by Mr Devlin's memorandum, would be an admirable way of out of the difficulty on one condition, and one condition only, i.e. that it should be accepted by the Unionists of Ireland. If the Ulster Unionists state that the moment they are forced in even temporarily they will take up arms and riots as a matter of fact ensue, a blood feud will have been set up between the Irish Parliament and the Ulster Protestants. Ten years count as nothing in a bloodstained quarrel of this kind, and at the end of that experimental period the defeated Protestants and their sympathisers would certainly under such circumstances vote the exclusion of Ulster ...

The Scheme which I placed before the Irish leaders is not open to the objections which I noted as applicable to the Plunkett plan. As the Protestants of the North-east could if they so desired remain temporarily under the Imperial Parliament, they have no excuse for rioting against conditions which have not yet been imposed upon them, and which we afford them an opportunity of appealing against to the electorate before they are forced to submit to them at the end of the term.

HLRO: Lloyd George
Papers C/20/2/7

(c) Devlin to John Redmond   Belfast, 6 March 1914

... I held a conference at the hotel today to which I invited all those people I thought it advisable to see ... The whole situation was discussed in the most reasonable and friendly spirit and everyone spoke out frankly and freely on the situation and there was almost unanimity. I made a statement, and each of them spoke, and all agreed that everything had been done that reasonably could be done; and they gave me the authority to say that, as far as they were concerned – and I believe a more representative meeting could not be called in this way – that the Party would have behind it, in the attitudes it decided to take up, not only their acquiescence but their fullest and most unqualified approval and support ... I am quite certain that, wherever else trouble may arise, none will come from the North-east corner.

NLI: Redmond Papers MS 15181 (3)

81 Sir Edward Carson: Ulster has a strong right arm

Carson too, notwithstanding dramatic gestures and close identification with paramilitary preparedness, at last began to hint publicly at a retreat from root-and-branch opposition to home rule of any kind, and at focusing resistance on the exclusion of Ulster.

... Ulster looms very largely in this controversy, simply because Ulster has a strong right arm, but there are Unionists in the south and west who loath the bill just as much as we Ulster people loath it, whose difficulties are far greater, and who would willingly fight, as Ulster would fight, if they had the numbers. Nobody knows the difficulties of these men better than I do. Why, it was only the other day some of them ventured to put forward as a business proposition that this bill would be financial ruin to their businesses, saying no more, and immediately they were boycotted, and resolutions were passed, and they were told that they ought to understand as Protestants that they ought to be thankful and grateful for being allowed to live in peace among the people who are there. Yes, we can never support the bill which hands these people over to the tender mercies of those who have always been their bitterest enemies. We must go on whatever happens, opposing the bill to the end. That we are entitled to do; that we are bound to do. But I want to speak explicitly about the exclusion of Ulster ... If the exclusion of Ulster is not shut out, and if at the same time the prime minister says he cannot admit anything contrary to the fundamental principles of the bill, I think it follows that the exclusion of Ulster is not contrary to the fundamental principles of the bill ... On the other hand I say this, that your suggestions – no matter what paper safeguards you put, or no matter what other methods you may attempt to surround these safeguards with for the purpose of raising what I call 'your reasonable atmosphere' – if your suggestions try to compel these people to come into a Dublin parliament, I tell you I shall regardless of personal consequences, go on with these people to the end with their policy of resistance.

H C Deb 5th series, vol 58, cols 175-6 (11 February 1914)

82 Eoin MacNeill: The North began

The organisation and drilling of 100,000 members of the UVF was becoming a source of concern not only to the Government, but to other interests as well. The two years of debate which had occupied the entire attention of the Irish Party leaders caught the imagination of active nationalists less than did the activities of the Ulstermen. In November 1913 a history professor at the new University College, Dublin, Eoin MacNeill (1867-1945), published an article in the Gaelic League newspaper under the heading 'The North began'. It purported to welcome the UVF as a rejection by a group of Irishmen of British leadership, but on a more practical level it proposed the establishment of an 'Irish National Volunteer Force' along similar lines. MacNeill was not known as an extreme nationalist, but was soon approached discreetly by others who were, as a result of which he summoned a huge meeting in Dublin on 25 November 1913 when the new body was founded. For the Irish Party leaders this apparent emulation of Carson's departure from constitutionalism seemed nothing other than embarrassing. But too many of their own supporters were involving themselves in it for a straight denunciation to be advisable. Accordingly they sailed anxiously with it until June 1914, when they felt in a position to deliver an ultimatum to the leadership of the movement and gain half the places on the provisional committee for 'Mr Redmond's nominees'.

... The Ulster Volunteer movement is essentially and obviously a home rule movement. It claims, no doubt, to hold Ireland 'for the Empire'; but really it is no matter whether Ireland is to be held for the Empire or for the Empyrean [ie Heaven], against the Pope, against John Redmond, against the man in the moon. What matters is *by whom Ireland is to be held* ...

The true meaning of this extraordinary development is dawning painfully on English Unionists. They are beginning to understand that Sir Edward Carson has knocked the bottom out of Unionism ... In any case, it appears that the British Army cannot now be used to prevent the enrolment, drilling and reviewing of Volunteers in Ireland. There is nothing to prevent the other twenty-eight counties from calling into existence citizen forces to hold Ireland 'for the Empire'. It was precisely with this object that the Volunteers of 1782 were enrolled, and they became the instrument of establishing self-government and Irish prosperity ...

The more responsible section of English Unionist opinion has taken alarm and is tentatively drawing away from the two-edged sword of 'Ulster' ... Sir Edward Carson proclaims that, in launching his new Ulster policy, he has not counted the cost. It looks like it.

... I do not say that Sir Edward Carson is insincere. Probably he, too, like the Orangemen and Presbyterians, is at heart a home ruler, and thinks that the sort of home rule that he wants is best guaranteed by the semblance of government from outside. His English allies, however, hoped that his master move would do effective electioneering work for them, and the fact that since he 'drew the sword' in Ulster he has devoted most of his energies to a political tour in Great Britain shows that he has lent himself to the game ...

It is evident that the only solution now possible is for the Empire either to make terms with Ireland or to let Ireland go her own way. In any case, it is manifest that all Irish people, Unionist as well as nationalist, are determined to have their own way in Ireland. It is not to follow, and it will ʃ ot follow, that any part of Ireland, majority or minority, is to interfere with the liberty of any other part. Sir Edward Carson may yet, at the head of his Volunteers, 'march to Cork'. If so, their progress will probably be accompanied by the greetings of ten times their number of National Volunteers, and Cork will give them a hospitable and memorable reception ...

> From *An Claidheamh Soluis*, 1 November 1913, cited in
> F X Martin & F J Byrne (eds) *The Scholar Revolutionary:*
> *Eoin MacNeill and the Making of the New Ireland*
> (Shannon: Irish University Press,1973), pp 381–84

83 The impact of a new university

The founding of the National University and its constituent University College, Dublin, in 1908 established a new academic and student body in the capital alongside that of the predominantly Unionist Trinity. Some of the influences in the new college, like that of the professor of national economics, T M Kettle – an ex-Irish Party MP who later met his death as an officer in the British army – were moderate ones. But the prevailing tone of the more politically conscious students was 'Irish-Ireland'. They remembered less the Irish Party's role in the creation of their university than the subsequent opposition of its leaders to the implementation of compulsory Irish for matriculation. They were at best independent of Irish Party thinking, and were to provide the basis of an officer corps for the Irish Volunteers in 1916.

Since the gigantic meetings, organised by students some years ago, on behalf of Irish as an essential subject in the matriculation of the National University, no event of a kindred significance has called forth the public response of students of University College as did the opening public meeting of the Irish Volunteers.

... Practically every male student of University College, whose movements were not restricted by a special discipline, attended at the inception of the 'Irish Volunteers'. To the meeting at the Rotunda about three hundred and fifty students went – a large proportion of them marching as a body. And this number may be taken as fairly close to the total aggregate of male students.

> *The National Student, IV*, ii (December 1913), cited in:
> F X Martin (ed), *The Irish Volunteers, 1913-15*
> (Dublin: Duffy & Co 1963), pp 120-1

84 Patrick Pearse: We may shoot the wrong people

A revived Irish Republican brotherhood was secretly very active within the new Volunteer movement, its membership increased by the addition of Irish language enthusiasts like Patrick Pearse, a former moderate raised by the possibilities of the new movement to a pitch of revolutionary excitement.

I have come to the conclusion that the Gaelic League, as the Gaelic League, is a spent force; and I am glad of it. I do not mean that no work remains for the Gaelic League, or that the Gaelic League is no longer equal to work; I mean that the vital work to be done in the new Ireland will be done not so much by the Gaelic League itself as by men and movements that have sprung from the Gaelic League or have received from the Gaelic League a new baptism and a new life of grace. The Gaelic League was ... a prophet and more than a prophet. But it was not the Messiah. I do not know if the Messiah has yet come, and I am not sure that there will be any visible and personal Messiah in this redemption: the people itself will perhaps be its own Messiah, the people labouring, scourged, crowned with thorns, agonising and dying, to rise again immortal and impassible ... If we had not believed in the divinity of our people, we should in all probability not have gone into the Gaelic League at all. We should have made our peace with the devil, and perhaps might have found him a very decent sort; for he liberally rewards with attorney generalships, bank balances, villa residences, and so forth, the great and the little who serve him well. Now, we did not turn our backs upon all these desirable things for the sake of *is* and *tá*. We did it for the sake of Ireland. In other words, we had one and all of us ... an ulterior motive in joining the Gaelic League ... Our Gaelic League time was to be our tutelage: we had first to learn to know Ireland, to read the lineaments of her face, to understand the accents of her voice; to repossess ourselves, disinherited as we were, of her spirit and mind, re-enter into our mystical birthright ... To every generation its deed. The deed of the generation that has now reached middle life was the Gaelic League: the beginning of the Irish Revolution. Let our generation not shirk its deed, which is to accomplish the revolution ... I am glad, then, that the North has 'begun'. I am glad that the Orangemen have armed, for it is a goodly thing to see arms in Irish hands. I should like to see the AOH armed. I should like to see the Transport Workers armed. I should like to see any and every body of Irish citizens armed. We must accustom ourselves to the thought of arms, to the sight of arms, to the use of arms. We may make mistakes in the beginning and shoot the wrong people; but bloodshed is a cleansing and a sanctifying thing, and the nation which regards it as the final horror has lost it manhood. There are many things more horrible than bloodshed; and slavery is one of them.

'The Coming Revolution', (November 1913),
in P H Pearse, *Political Writings and Speeches* (Dublin, 1924), pp 91-99

85 Mutiny at the Curragh, March 1914

While the Ulster Volunteer Force continued to perform its drill with dummy rifles under the leadership of out-of-office politicians and retired army officers, as was the case throughout 1912-13, it was easy for both the Government and the Nationalists to take it lightly. But on the night of 24-25 April 1914 a shipload of 20,000 German rifles from Hamburg was landed at the Ulster port of Larne by Major Fred Crawford (1861-1952) and distributed overnight to UVF units throughout the province. (See Volume 1, illustration 27.) Carson and the local Unionist leaders were fully aware of the plan in advance. The coolness and efficiency of this operation threw into sharp relief the clumsiness of the War Office's handling of events at the Curragh military camp a few weeks earlier, when seventy British army officers led by Brigadier-General Hubert Gough extracted an agreement from the Secretary of State for War, which Prime Minister Asquith later sought unconvincingly to refute, that the army would not be used to enforce home rule in Ulster.

(a) Major P. Howell to a friend   Curragh Camp, 22 March 1914

You have probably heard by now full details of the trouble here, but some notes direct may interest you. Who exactly is responsible I know not, but we are pretty well agreed that the crisis is due not to political passion but to an absurd want of tact! 48 hours ago the Grand Military and the like were the sole topic of conversation – all are sick to death of the subject of 'home rule' and for weeks I've never heard it mentioned in the mess or hunting field.

Then suddenly a bolt from the blue – officers all summoned and told that they must within two hours undertake to fight against Ulster to the end, or resign, and that resignation meant dismissal. 5th and 16th Lancers resigned in a body at once. Hogg and I realised that there must be some fatuous mistake and persuaded our officers to wait for further information. We suspected Goughie's hot-headedness at first, but it was soon evident that he was not to blame, for the other generals all confirmed his views. However, we persuaded Gough to hold up the resignations and then drafted a letter to which after hours of discussion the whole brigade eventually agreed, and quiet was more or less restored.

Then next morning (Saturday) down came 'A.P.' himself [Sir Arthur Paget, Commander-in-Chief, British Army in Ireland] and in about half an hour with, no doubt, the best intentions in the world, succeeded in wholly upsetting the applecart again. How much he said on his own and how much by instruction I do not know, but the general impression left upon those who kept calm was this, that there'll be no Army left in Ireland unless we can get at its head someone who will talk both sense and tact ...

I think that had this affair not arisen it is just possible that the troops might have drifted into active operations against the Ulstermen: but that is out of the question now. If we do anything at all it must clearly be for 'law and order' and nothing else. I suppose that I'm about as moderate and impartial as anyone here, for in principle I'm a home ruler and not swept away by Ulster heroics ...

On the whole the greatest danger seems to me leaving the conduct of a very delicate situation in the hands of a pompous old ass – whom no one respects [i.e. Sir Arthur Paget]. I don't know how they can get rid of him now, or whom they can put in his place, but go he certainly ought to ...

(b) 2nd Lieutenant E.G.Miles to his Father   Dublin, 21 March 1914

At 11 o'clock this morning the Colonel called a conference of all officers and put forward the following question: 'If the regiment is ordered to take action against Ulster in the interests of the preservation of peace, etc are you prepared to go or do you wish to resign your commission? ... If you resign your commission, you will be dismissed the service *without* a pension unless you are a resident of Ulster ... '

...We all loathed the idea of going to Ulster for the sake of a few dirty Nationalists who loathe the army and are most unloyal to anything to do with Britain, and yet we wondered what on earth we should do if we left ... [at first Miles chose to resign, but later the same day he and many regimental colleagues withdrew their names].

The disgrace about the whole affair is that the Govt want to find out how many officers they will have. So they made us decide instantaneously whether we would go or not, without stating any facts as to what we might have to do ...You cannot imagine a more trying ... day, when in a matter of an hour or so we had to decide between 'shooting down Loyalists and starting a fresh job on nothing ...'

I F W Beckett (ed) *The Army and the Curragh
Incident, 1914* (London: The Bodley Head for The Army
Records Society, 1986), pp 90-91, 102-104)

86   *The Buckingham Palace Conference, July 1914*

The Army's loyalty was never put to the test, and during the late spring and summer of 1914 political negotiations continued. From 21 to 24 July an eight-man conference of

Liberal, Irish Party, Conservative and Ulster Unionist leaders met at Buckingham Palace. They discussed details of which counties might be excluded from the settlement and possible mechanisms for excluding them, but they could find no way round the crucial issue of whether the exclusion was to be temporary or permanent.

The Prime Minister ... indicated that, in his opinion, the two serious outstanding points were (1) the area of exclusion, and (2) the time limit. As it was generally understood that there was no possibility, with any advantage, of discussing any settlement except on the liens of exclusion of some sort, the Prime Minister urged that the question of area should be first discussed.

Sir Edward Carson strongly argued that the question of time limit should be discussed in the first place ... Mr Redmond strongly dissented, and said that ... his views in reference to the time limit might be influenced in various ways by the decision come to on the question of area ... Finally it was decided to take the question of area first.

Sir Edward Carson then ... made a strong appeal to Mr Redmond and Mr Dillon to consent to the total exclusion of [nine-county] Ulster in the interest of the earliest possible unity of Ireland. He argued that if a smaller area were excluded, the reunion of the whole of Ireland would be delayed. Mr Redmond ... indicated in reply ... that it would be quite impossible from him, under any circumstances, to agree ...

Mr Redmond then read the following memorandum: The Irish National party have all along been, and still strongly are, strongly of opinion that no satisfactory settlement of the Irish question can be obtained by the exclusion of any portion of Ireland from the operation of the Home Rule Bill. They are, further, of opinion that there is no considerable section of any political party in Ireland in favour of such a settlement ... The Irish Party only consented to negotiate on the basis of exclusion because the leaders of the Ulster Unionists repeatedly and emphatically refused to consider any other proposal ...

Having examined carefully all possible methods of carrying out that principle [ie exclusion based on the wishes of local inhabitants], the National Party came to the conclusion that the only practical method ... was by giving each administrative county an option to exclude itself by ballot from the operation of the Act.

... let it be assumed ... that four of the nine counties of Ulster and the borough of Belfast would exclude themselves; and that five counties and also the borough of Derry would vote for inclusion ... If it be contended that it is an injustice to the Protestant minority in the five counties to be included ...

is it not an equal injustice to the Catholic minority in the four counties to be excluded? ... for while the number of the Protestant minority in the included counties would be ... 179,113, the number of Catholics in the excluded counties would be 293,483 ... Sir Edward Carson, Lord Lansdowne and Mr Bonar Law declared that upon the basis of county option no agreement was possible.

... Carson repeatedly stated that, so far as Tyrone was concerned, he was unable, even if his judgement led him in that direction, to agree to the inclusion of any part of that county in the jurisdiction of the home rule parliament. Mr Redmond made a similar declaration with reference to the exclusion of any part of Tyrone. The same situation, in substance, arose with regard to Co. Fermanagh and, eventually Sir Edward Carson substituted, for his demand for the exclusion of the whole of Ulster, the exclusion of a block consisting of the six counties ... all to vote as one unit. Mr Redmond intimated that he could not seriously consider this proposal, any more than the proposal for the total exclusion of Ulster.

It became apparent that a deadlock had arisen, and the question was raised as to whether it was of any value to continue the Conference ...

... Mr Redmond desired formally to ask whether any settlement not based on exclusion would be considered ... Sir Edward Carson said he would consider no settlement of any kind unless based on exclusion ...

... Mr Redmond [in a private audience with King George V after the failure of the Conference] said that he was convinced that no agreement could be come to until the Home Rule Bill was on the Statute Book. After that he believed both parties would be in a position to make larger concessions ...

NLI: Redmond Papers, cited in D Gwynn,
The History of Partition (Dublin: Brown & Nolan, 1950), pp 119-131

Chapter 7

The Easter Rising

87 *The one bright spot, August 1914*

The failure of the Buckingham Palace Conference left the Government and the Nationalists without a policy. What the next step might have been is not clear, although the emulation of the Larne gun-running on a smaller scale by the Irish National Volunteers at Howth, Co Dublin, on 26 July – leading to an incident in Dublin in which soldiers fired on a crowd, killing three and wounding thirty-eight – did not bode well for future peace. Many feared that the continued growth of the rival volunteer forces could only end in civil war. The sudden and, in the short view, unexpected involvement of Britain in a European conflict, announced by Sir Edward Grey to the House of Commons on 3 August 1914, brought new priorities to the situation. Redmond, without consulting his colleagues, declared Ireland's immediate support for the war and pledged the co-operation of the Irish National Volunteers in the defence of Ireland.

I hope the House will not consider it improper on my part, in the grave circumstances in which we are assembled, if I intervene for a very few moments. I was moved a great deal by that sentence in the speech of the Secretary of State for Foreign Affairs in which he said that the one bright spot in the situation was the changed feeling in Ireland. In past times, when this Empire has been engaged in these terrible enterprises, it is true – it would be the utmost affectation and folly on my part to deny it – the sympathy of the Nationalists of Ireland, for reasons to be found deep down in centuries of history, has been estranged from this country. Allow me to say, sir, that what has occurred in recent years has altered the situation completely ... and today I honestly believe that the democracy of Ireland will turn with the utmost anxiety and sympathy to this country in every trial and every danger that may over take it ...

I say to the Government that they may tomorrow withdraw every one of their troops from Ireland. I say that the coast of Ireland will be defended from foreign invasion by her armed sons, and for this purpose armed Nationalist Catholics in the South will be only too glad to join arms with the armed Protestant Ulstermen in the North. Is it too much to hope that out of this situation there may spring a result which will be good, not merely for the Empire, but good for the future welfare and integrity of the Irish nation?

H C Deb 5th series, vol 65, cols 1828-9 3 August 1914

88 The means and ends of volunteering

By the summer of 1914 the Irish National Volunteers had become, nominally, a very large body indeed – perhaps as many as 180,000 men – although the proportion of these who were effectively trained, equipped or armed was small by comparison with the UVF. The guiding spirit of the movement, *pace* Redmond's intervention in June, was revolutionary: frank hostility to England and a less frank affectation that the INV and the UVF were pulling essentially in the same direction. But at the grass-roots level, different factors operated: on one level, especially in the north, members of the INV felt that they might somehow or other 'fight for home rule'; on another level there were many, especially southern Protestants with military experience, who thought it realistic to come to terms with the inevitability of home rule, to provide 'responsible' leadership for a potentially formidable force, and who saw in Redmond's speech of 3 August a bridge to their Catholic neighbours and ex-tenants. The only lasting importance of this development was the negative Irish impact it had on the popularity of the INV, for it lent credence to the Sinn Féin charge that the Irish Party was out to 'conscript the people'. This correspondence from the files of the Inspector-General of the INV gives some indication of the difficulties brought to the nationalist movement by its new accretions.

Major S C Hickman to Col. Maurice Moore Newmarket-on-Fergus, Co. Clare

(a) 13 August 1914

I am not sure if it was you I used to know in the good old soldiering days, anyhow I will write you a few lines. Though I have hitherto done nothing in the Irish National Volunteer movement it is not because I have not approved of it, I always have ... I may tell you from the start that I am very much on the home rule side – but I want unity in Ireland ...

In this county the I.N. Volunteer scheme is badly done I think – in fact not done at all – if I could take up the job and organise it a bit here I am willing to do so. I have done twenty years in the R[oyal] H[orse] A[rtillery] my reserve service expired a little time ago, and though I would give my eyes to go with the army and have offered my services, of course there is no chance – can't put back the clock alas!

(b) 16 September 1914

After seeing the report of a meeting of the County Board of the I.N. Vols. in Ennis – and that they seemed to wish for an inspecting officer of their own choosing, I sent you a wire to appoint whoever they wanted in my place – it is better so ... I could not stand taking orders from some of the people who appear to be in authority on the County Board. I am very sure you would not care to be under their orders. I confess I am a bit afraid of the whole thing – if it is to be run by some people I hear about here, good fellows in their own way – but it wants a different class of man at the head, or it seems to me the movement may lead to great trouble in the future. I was undertaking the job to work under you and be a sort of restraining force as well as working it – but from what I gather that seems impossible. The idea among the country people is that the Nat.Vols. are to be trained, and armed with American rifles, and then be ready to fight Ulster any day! And the way people talk encourages all this too much I think ... I feel awfully ashamed of us all in the south not enlisting in the Irish Division, and this movement has a lot to do with it.

NLI: Maurice Moore Papers, MS 10547/5

89 John Redmond: Recruiting sergeant

Redmond's speech on 3 August 1914 appears to have been a unilateral gesture, independent of any pledge from the government. But during September Asquith pursued a course which met the immediate concerns of the Irish Party, and effectively postponed the home rule crisis for the time being. The Home Rule Act was placed 'on the statute book', but further legislation suspended its operation until the end of the war, and until an additional measure could be implemented to settle the Ulster difficulty. Two days after the passing of this agreement, on 20 September, Redmond made an apparently unplanned appearance at a Volunteer parade at Woodenbridge, near his home in Co Wicklow, and called for unqualified enlistment in the British army. Irish nationalists, he now argued, should be prepared to fight for the Allied cause in the front line of the conflict, and not just in Ireland itself.

The duty of the manhood of Ireland is twofold. Its duty is, at all costs, to defend the shores of Ireland against foreign invasion. It is a duty more than that, of taking care that Irish valour proves itself on the field of war as it has always proved itself in the past. The interests of Ireland – of the whole of Ireland – are at stake in this war. The war is undertaken in defence of the highest principles of religion and morality and right, and it would be a disgrace for ever to our country, and a reproach to her manhood, and a denial of the lessons of her history, if young Ireland confined their efforts to remaining at home to defend the shores of Ireland from an unlikely invasion, and shrunk from the duty of proving on the field of battle that gallantry and courage which has distinguished our race all through its history. I say to you, therefore, your duty is twofold. I am glad to see such magnificent material for soldiers around me, and I say to you, 'Go on drilling and make yourselves efficient for the work, and then account yourselves as men, not only in Ireland itself, but wherever the firing line extends, in defence of right, of freedom, and of religion in this war.

D Gwynn, *The Life of John Redmond*
(London, 1932), pp 391-2

90 The Volunteer split

The founders of the Irish Volunteers ('National' only crept into the movement's name under Redmondite influence) had only accepted Redmond's intervention through fear that his denunciation would destroy them. But it was clear, even before the war started, that the body was a heterogeneous grouping of attitudes, unlikely to be capable of effective action. Redmond's recruiting speech at Woodenbridge provided an ideal opportunity for the original Volunteer leadership to break with him by making an appeal to national sentiment which also held obvious attractions for Volunteers with no taste for enlistment in the army. The following manifesto was accordingly issued on 24 September 1914, immediately splitting the movement into Irish Volunteers (about 10,000 members, mostly strongly committed to militant nationalism) and National Volunteers (many times greater in number, but with a large proportion of merely nominal members).

To the Irish Volunteers

Ten months ago a Provisional Committee commenced the Irish Volunteer movement with the whole purpose of securing and defending the Rights and Liberties of the Irish people. The movement on these lines, though thwarted and opposed for a time, obtained the support of the Irish Nation. When the Volunteer Movement had to become the main factor in the Irish position, Mr Redmond decided to acknowledge it and to endeavour to bring it under his control.

Three months ago he put forward the claim to send twenty-five nominees to the Provisional Committee of the Irish Volunteers. He threatened, if the claim was not conceded, to proceed to the dismemberment of the Irish Volunteer Organisation.

… The Provisional Committee, while recognising that the responsibility in that case would be altogether Mr Redmond's, decided to risk the lesser evil and to admit his nominees to sit and act on the Committee …

Mr Redmond addressing a body of Irish Volunteers on last Sunday, has now announced for the Irish Volunteers a policy and programme fundamentally at variance with their own published and accepted aims and objects, but with which his nominees are, of course, identified. He has declared it to be the duty of the Irish Volunteers to take foreign service under a Government which is not Irish. He has made this announcement without consulting the Provisional Committee, the Volunteers themselves, or the people of Ireland, to whose service alone they are devoted.

… Those who, by virtue of Mr Redmond's nomination, have heretofore been admitted to act on the Provisional Committee accordingly cease henceforth to belong to that body …

At the next meeting of the Provisional Committee we shall propose ... To oppose any diminution of the measure of Irish self-government which now exists as a statute on paper, and which would not now have reached that stage but for the Irish Volunteers ... To repudiate any undertaking by whomsoever given, to consent to the legislative dismemberment of Ireland; and to protest against the attitude of the present Government, who, under the pretence that 'Ulster cannot be coerced', avow themselves prepared to coerce the Nationalists of Ulster ... To declare that Ireland cannot, with honour or safety, take part in foreign quarrels otherwise than through the free action of a National Government of her own; and to repudiate the claim of any man to offer up the blood and lives of the sons of Irishmen and Irishwomen to the service of the British Empire while no National Government which could speak and act for the people of Ireland is allowed to exist ...

F X Martin (ed) *The Irish Volunteers, 1913-15*
(Jas Duffy & Co Ltd, Dublin, 1963) pp 152-4

91 *Mortal men and pocket patriots*

The split in the Volunteers was for some while less clear-cut at local level than it was centrally. Local officers might find their decisions reversed by the men; companies where neither Irish Party nor Sinn Féin partisanship was strong, might be genuinely undecided; real confusion and misunderstanding also existed. Now that Redmond had come out for full army recruiting, it was difficult to see any immediate political purpose which the National Volunteers could serve. Their real function was to keep as many men as possible out of the ranks of the rival Irish Volunteers, and so a flurry of activity and organisation was necessary. Many Irish Party MPs, like Redmond's brother William who was later killed at the front, took an active part at this stage. The second extract is an interesting sidelight on the mechanics of grass-roots nationalism.

(a) Col. Maurice Moore to William Redmond M. P.   19 October 1914

There are many Volunteers who don't know much about the matters in dispute and if they parade for us at all will join in all right afterwards. They are not Sinn Féiners, but don't want to go off to fight in Belgium, and your speech will probably have the desired effect.

(b) Father M. Gilligan, C.C. to National Volunteer Headquarters, Dublin
21 April 1915

Volunteer companies in some places have broken up and in other places been seriously injured through the self-interest of publicans. They have managed in many places to get themselves appointed commanders and then have the drilling carried out at back or front of their premises. I know of one case where the publican – a very prominent man in the county – marched the men from the drilling ground through the village and gave them the 'dismiss' in front of his premises – needless to say there is no Volunteer company in that parish now, and it was not the split that broke it up either ... I had to fight the same difficulty in my own parish. Bung [D P Moran's name for the liquor trade] has captured and controlled the Gaelic Athletic Association for his own benefit. Will he be allowed to do the same thing with the Volunteers? He is very patriotic, but in many cases his patriotism is in his pocket.

NLI: Maurice Moore Papers, MS 10547/5

92 Ireland prefers the Kaiser, 1915?

In May 1915 the last Liberal government came to an end when criticism of its conduct of the war forced Asquith to form a coalition administration. Redmond was offered a cabinet place, but replied that 'the principles and history of the party I represent make the acceptance of your offer impossible'. Carson's status in his party was such that he could not be passed over, nor did he share Redmond's difficulties over acceptance. In these circumstances the Irish Party's objections to his inclusion have something of a dog-in-the-manger quality about them. And yet its dilemma was a hopeless one, for acceptance of office by any of its leaders would almost certainly have wrecked the party, while it seemed clear that one of the main tasks of the coalition government would be to implement military conscription in Britain and, it had to be assumed, in Ireland as well. The outburst of the Bishop of Killaloe (Michael Fogarty, 1859-1955) coming from a member of the Catholic hierarchy previously sympathetic to the Irish Party, is indicative of the changing climate of opinion in nationalist Ireland.

(a) John Dillon MP to Sir Matthew Nathan (Under Secretary, Dublin Castle)
28 May 1915

.. .A *great deal* of mischief has already been done – from the recruiting point of view – in this country by the formation of the coalition government, and the inclusion of Carson. If you are consulted as to the question of conscription – I think you should represent *strongly* that any attempt to enforce conscription in Ireland will have *most serious* and deplorable results.

Bodleian Library, Nathan Papers, MS 451, f 268

(b) Bishop of Killaloe to John Redmond MP   3 June 1915

The English have got all they wanted from Ireland, and don't care two pence about her feelings. Such is our reward for her profuse loyalism and recruiting. The people are full of indignation, but are powerless ...

As far as Ireland is concerned, there is little to choose between Carsonism and Kaiserism, of the two the latter is a lesser evil: and it almost makes me cry to think of the Irish Brigade fighting not for Ireland but for Carson and what he stands for – Orange ascendancy here.

Home rule is dead and buried and Ireland is without a national party or national press. The *Freeman* is but a government organ and the national party but an imperial instrument. What the future holds in store for us God knows – I suppose conscription with a bloody feud between people and soldiers. I never thought that Asquith would have consented to this humiliation and ruin of Irish feeling. There is a great revulsion of feeling in Ireland.

NLI: Redmond Papers, MS 15188/5

93 *Problems of recruiting 1915*

Rising prices, low wages, underemployment and relatively attractive War Office separation allowances (payable to wives) for family men, encouraged voluntary recruiting in Irish towns during the first year or so of the war. In rural areas, however, the situation was different. Although that large Irish class known as 'farmers' sons' was to a great extent agricultural labour surplus to requirements in a strictly economic sense, and therefore ideal recruiting material, in practice higher prices for farm produce provided more family income to keep such men at home, and more incentive to farm intensively. As the pace of voluntary recruiting inevitably slackened once the willing were creamed off, recruiting authorities began to look for ways round this difficulty.

Circular Letter from the Central Council for the Organisation of Recruiting in Ireland   11 August 1915

... Steps so far taken have failed to attract considerable numbers of recruits from the farming and commercial classes in Ireland. This failure is, we believe, reacting unfavourably upon recruiting among the labouring classes who naturally resent the abstention of others who should share the burden of the war.

We are satisfied that a much larger number of recruits could be obtained from the classes named were it not for their reluctance to enter upon their training with recruits from the labouring classes. This class prejudice is probably much more pronounced in Ireland than elsewhere in the United Kingdom.

The abstention of the classes named has undoubtedly produced a further and serious obstacle to general recruiting – in so far that anti-war propaganda has made special headway among farmers' sons and commercial [ie shop] assistants. The most certain way to counteract this tendency is to attract recruits from their ranks.

NLI: Maurice Moore Papers, MS 10561/1

94 Problems of the Irish Party, 1916

Many members of the Irish Party, most notably John Dillon, attributed a fair measure of blame for the war to Britain's foreign policy under Sir Edward Grey, and never consented to appear on recruiting platforms. Once home rule had been put 'on the statute book' and shelved, however, John Redmond and some others in the party committed themselves to whole-hearted support for the British and 'Imperial' war effort. Both Redmond's brother and his son became wartime army officers. In March 1916, after conscription had been introduced in Britain, Redmond invited all the Party's MPs to attend a conference with a view to stimulating Irish recruiting. Some of the replies he received give an interesting impression of the state of the various localities on the eve of the Easter Rising.

William Doris MP to John Redmond MP Westport, Co. Mayo

8 March 1916

... As to this western part of the county, I fear we have very little chance of getting recruits, and the calling of public meetings for the purpose would only show our weakness in this respect. On all questions (but this important question of the hour) the vast majority of the people are with the Party.

Most of our young fellows emigrate as they grow up and the small landowners will not listen to a suggestion that any of their few remaining sons should enlist. The Protestant farmers' sons in this district are even more hopeless slackers than our own people. Our shop assistants – mostly small farmers' sons – became such extreme nationalists all in a moment that they could not dream of 'fighting for England', and they are now regarded as Sinn Féiners ...

The landlord party here (Lord Sligo and co.) took control of the recruiting movement, and thus gave the 'extreme patriots' a further pretext for opposing it – 'Just imagine Doris, the old Land Leaguer, on Lord Sligo's platform', etc.

The leading disturbers and pro-Germans here are a few disappointed placehunters. If Dublin Castle gave them the appointments they looked for we would have very little pro-Germanism in the Westport district. I fear I would not be of any assistance at your conference, but if you think otherwise you have only to let me know.

NLI: Redmond Papers, MS 15262/3

95 Two views on the state of Ireland, 1914

Before the end of 1914, recruiting and the general question of support for the war had replaced home rule as the central issue in Irish politics. At first recruiting in Dublin, Belfast and the larger towns was maintained at a reasonable level. But the Irish Volunteers, and the general movement known 'Sinn Féin' – although that term embraced a trend of opinion considerably wider than the Sinn Féin party proper – found in 'England's war' a potentially more effective propaganda weapon than extreme nationalism had possessed for more than a generation. This correspondence between one of the Irish Party leaders and the Under-Secretary, chief public official in the Irish administration, reflects the concerns which now dominated the situation.

(a) John Dillon MP to Sir Matthew Nathan   28 November 1914

This war coming just before we finally secured home rule has created a position of terrible difficulty and embarrassment for us, and up to the beginning of this month the War Office and other government authorities have done nothing but add to our difficulties. Yet we have retained the confidence and the leadership of about twenty to one of the nationalists of Ireland and secured their goodwill to England in this war. And according to my information we have completely paralysed the attempts of the Germans to secure the co-operation of the Irish in America in influencing American opinion against England. I do not believe that the Sinn Féiners and pro-Germans are making any headway against us in Ireland.

But because certain Tory newspapers, and rabid anti-Irish Unionists in the House of Commons, clamour for coercion measures, the government are about, I fear, to embark on that dangerous course ... My strong feeling is – and I speak only for the myself in this matter – that so far from helping us, or promoting recruiting, the suppression of these wretched, scurrilous rags will only increase our difficulties and raise fresh obstacles in the path of recruiting from the ranks of Irish nationalists.

Had it not been for the perversity of the War Office in treating with contempt any suggestion we made, a very large number of nationalists would have entered the New Army before now.

There is a considerable movement in favour of recruiting since the Irish brigades were really put in working order, and I think that movement would be largely strengthened by other measures if the War Office could be got to adopt them.

But I greatly fear that the suppression of the papers, with the consequences which will probably follow, may have a very evil influence on the whole situation.

(b) Sir Matthew Nathan to John Dillon   30 November 1914

... From my very short experience in this country I believe Irishmen are affected by what they hear and read, probably more than more phlegmatic peoples. When you and Mr Redmond hold anti-hatred meetings in the country I am quite sure you pull out people from the Sinn Féin ranks. But the Sinn Féin leaders are very active; they seem always on the move and, so far as I can judge from the reports I receive, to be constantly getting new recruits. Their cleverly worded and insidiously scattered papers spread all over the country and in the distribution of leaflets they and their American allies have the field practically all to themselves. I sometimes wish there had been a stronger newspaper and leaflet 'reconciliation' campaign and wonder whether the strength of the hatred party has not been underestimated by the regular press in Ireland.

I lay no special stress on the recruiting aspect of the question because I am doubtful whether this is much affected by the Sinn Féin movement. A peasant proprietor or tenant population has a natural tendency 'to watch the harvest ripen, its herds increase' rather than to go out and fight like the labourer who does so without giving up anything. Besides, those who are wavering between 'reconciliation' and 'hatred' are probably not the sort of men to come as recruits should they decide on reconciliation. But the more of them that are known to decide on hatred, the greater the inducement for a foreign army to come over to Ireland.

Bodleian Library, Nathan Papers,
MS 451 f 218, MS 462 f 191

96 The Republic declared, 1916

Events in Dublin during Easter week 1916 were to knock the bottom out of Irish recruiting altogether. The week-long rising, in which somewhat over 400 (the majority civilian and crown forces) were killed and about 1,000 wounded, took the Irish Party and the government by surprise. The Irish administration continued, until the last minute, to accept the Irish Party view that to take strong action against 'the Sinn Féin element' would only 'create martyrs'. Thus the Irish Volunteers were able to train and drill quite openly from 1914 right up until the Rising, the majority of them, including their nominal chief-of-staff Professor Eoin MacNeill, in the belief that their purpose was defensive and that they would act only if it was necessary to resist suppression. This was an ideal arrangement for the secret IRB group within the movement, who were able to plan a rising, and indeed publicly announce mobilisation for 'manoeuvres', in circumstances where the government had decided on avoidance of provocation as its first priority. In the final event things ran less smoothly for the Volunteers – the German ship bringing arms for the country areas was captured, and due to misunderstanding (only a small part of which was wilful) the country outside Dublin almost entirely failed to rise. The Volunteers in Dublin acted *en masse* however, now under the direction of their real IRB leaders, augmented by the republican socialist Connolly, acting as a self-styled provisional government. Of the other signatories to the proclamation, Pearse, MacDonagh and Plunkett were teachers and poets, Ceannt was also a Gaelic League activist, MacDermott had worked for some years as an organiser for Sinn Féin, while Clarke was a much older man who had served fifteen years in Portland prison for dynamite offences.

Poblacht na h-Éireann
The Provisional Government of the Irish Republic
to the People of Ireland

Irishmen and Irishwomen: In the name of God and of the dead generations from which she receives her old tradition of nationhood, Ireland, through us, summons her children to her flag and strikes for her freedom.

Having organised and trained her manhood through her secret revolutionary organisation, the Irish Republican Brotherhood, and through her open military organisations, the Irish Volunteers, and the Irish Citizen Army, having patiently perfected her discipline, having resolutely waited for the right moment to reveal itself, she now seizes that moment, and, supported by her exiled children in America and by gallant allies in Europe, but relying in the first on her own strength, she strikes in full confidence of victory.

We declare the right of the people of Ireland to the ownership of Ireland, and to the unfettered control of Irish destinies, to be sovereign and indefeasible. The long usurpation of that right by a foreign people and government has not extinguished the right, nor can it ever be extinguished except by the destruction of the Irish people. In every generation the Irish people have asserted their right to national freedom and sovereignty; six times during the past three hundred years they have asserted it in arms. Standing on that fundamental right and again asserting it in arms in the face of the world, we hereby proclaim the Irish republic as a sovereign independent state, and we pledge our lives and the lives of our comrades-in-arms to the cause of its freedom, of its welfare, and of its exaltation among the nations.

The Irish republic is entitled to, and hereby claims, the allegiance of every Irishman and Irishwoman. The republic guarantees religious and civil liberty, equal rights and equal opportunities to all its citizens, and declares its resolve to pursue the happiness and prosperity of the whole nation and of all its parts, cherishing all the children of the nation equally, and oblivious of the differences carefully fostered by an alien government, which have divided a minority from the majority in the past.

Until our arms have brought the opportune moment for the establishment of a permanent national government, representative of the whole people of Ireland, and elected by the suffrages of all her men and women, the Provisional Government, hereby constituted, will administer the civil and military affairs of the republic in trust for the people. We place the cause of the Irish republic under the protection of the Most High God, whose blessing we invoke upon our arms, and we pray that no one who serves that cause will dishonour it by cowardice, inhumanity, or rapine. In this supreme hour the Irish nation must, by its valour and discipline, and by the readiness of its children to sacrifice themselves for the common good, prove itself worthy of the august destiny to which it is called.

Signed on behalf of the provisional government,
THOMAS J CLARKE, SEAN MACDIARMADA, THOMAS MACDONAGH, P H PEARSE, EAMONN CEANNT, JAMES CONNOLLY, JOSEPH PLUNKETT.

The Times, 1 May 1916

Chapter 8
The rise of Sinn Féin

97 The Republic smashed

The Rising, restricted in the event to the hopeless defence of a few bastions, lasted only as long as it took the authorities to flood the city with troops. After a week Pearse surrendered on behalf of the Irish Volunteers, and martial law was declared throughout the country. The seven signatories of the proclamation of the republic and eight other men were shot following summary courts martial between 3 and 12 May. Another 75 death sentences were commuted to terms of imprisonment, including that passed on Eamon de Valera (1882-1975), whilst of the remaining 81 who faced courts martial 10 were found not guilty and 71 received prison sentences ranging from six months' hard labour to penal servitude for life. In addition, 1867 unconvicted prisoners were interned at Frongoch, in north Wales, or at other camps and prisons in England. By June 1917 all had been released, convicted and unconvicted, including 11 who had received life sentences. The available evidence does not seriously weaken the traditional view that the Rising – or rather the executions and general aftermath, for the Rising itself was visibly unpopular with the mass of Dubliners – was primarily responsible for stimulating the great upsurge of militant nationalist feeling which swept Ireland in 1916-18. John Dillon's bitter speech to the House of Commons, disliked and despised as it was by English Unionists and even moderate Liberals, reflects accurately the change which overtook Irish national feeling, even down to the alarmism and exaggeration over the harsh events which were taking place

... I asked the Prime Minister, first of all, whether he would give a pledge that the executions should stop. That he declined to give. Secondly, I asked him whether he could tell whether any executions had taken place in Ireland since Monday morning; the last we had official notification of before I left there. The reply of the Prime Minister was 'No, Sir, so far as I know, not'. On Monday twelve executions had been made public. Since then, in spite of the statement of the Prime Minister, I have received word that a man named Kent had been executed in Fermoy, which is the first execution that has taken place outside Dublin. The fact is one which will create a very grave shock in Ireland, because it looks like a roving commission to carry these horrible executions all over the country ...

[On 26 April a well-known Dublin intellectual, Francis Sheehy-Skeffington, and two journalists were arrested in the street and, though not implicated in the Rising in any way, shot without trial on the orders of a demented captain of the Royal Irish Rifles] ... All Dublin was ringing with this affair for days. It came to our knowledge within two or three days after the shooting ... A more lurid light on military law in Ireland could not possibly be imagined than that a man is to be shot in Portobello Barracks – it must have been known to at least 300 or 400 military men, the whole city of Dublin knew it, his poor wife was denied all knowledge of it until her husband was lying buried in the barrack yard for three or four days – and the military authorities in Dublin turn round and say they knew nothing whatever about it until the 6th of May. How on the face of these facts, which I shall explain more fully in a few moments, can we blame the population of Dublin if they believe, as they do believe, that dozens of other men have been summarily shot in the barracks?

... It is the first rebellion that ever took place in Ireland where you had a majority on your side. It is the fruit of our life work. We have risked our lives a hundred times to bring about this result. We are held up to odium as traitors by those men who made this rebellion, and our lives have been in danger a hundred times during the last thirty years because we have endeavoured to reconcile the two things, and now you are washing out our whole life work in a sea of blood ...

Here are some of the facts that I know to be true, and I want to put it to the House of Commons, do you approve of this action? One of the practices going on in the barracks is that these unhappy persons, and they have taken numbers of them, are threatened with instant death in order to force them to become informers. They are given half-an-hour of life, and then put up against a wall, and several of them have given evidence against their comrades. Is that approved of by the House of Commons without any trial? Do they approve of that form of torture, because it really is torture?

... The great bulk of the population were not favourable to the insurrection, and the insurgents themselves, who had confidently calculated on a rising of the people in their support, were absolutely disappointed. They got no popular support whatever. What is happening is that thousands of people in Dublin, who ten days ago were bitterly opposed to the whole of the Sinn Féin movement and to the rebellion, are now becoming infuriated against the government on account of these executions, and, as I am informed by letters received this morning, that feeling is spreading throughout the country in a most dangerous degree ...

H C Deb 5th series, vol 82 cols 935-48 (11 May 1916)

98 Nationalists, bishops and partition, 1916

The Rising had made nonsense of the Redmondite and government preoccupation with recruiting problems in Ireland. In a desperate effort to salvage the situation, Lloyd George instituted talks during May and June 1916 with both Ulster Unionist and Irish Party leaders in the hope of implementing home rule at once. But reconciliation foundered once more on the question of whether the exclusion of Ulster should be permanent or temporary. In the long run the only significant feature of the episode was that Redmond and his Belfast colleague Joe Devlin persuaded a large gathering of Ulster Nationalists to agree voluntarily to the temporary exclusion of six counties from the settlement. The Irish Party could thus be branded with some degree of justification, if not with entire fairness, as 'partitionist' by its republican rivals, and Ulster Nationalists treated as 'acquiescent' by British governments.

(a) Devlin to Redmond   Belfast, 3 June 1916

I saw the Bishop of Down & Connor ... and he would not entertain the proposals. The Bishop of Derry rejected them contemptuously. The Bishop of Raphoe said the Party would not survive the offer of such proposals to the country. This, in brief, is the net result of my enquiry so far ... The Bishop of Down & Connor is not a politician in the sense of [the Bishop of] Derry or Raphoe, but his opposition would influence a section of his clergy. He thought the Party now had a better chance than ever of obtaining united support from the country. The laity in Belfast – Pat Dempsey, Dan McCann and others – would accept, but they now recognise that it would be impossible to get the Nationalists of Tyrone and Fermanagh and Derry City to agree.

The Bishop of Derry said the proposals were 'rot'; that the Party had no mandate to accept them, as they were a home rule party, and the proposals were neither home rule nor leading up to home rule. He said the feeling in his diocese – in Tyrone and in Fermanagh – was stronger against the Government than he ever remembered, and scouted the idea of the proposals being entertained for a moment. He would agree to exclusion by county vote, but that was the limit ... He did not think the Party had lost the support of the country, but that support had waned latterly. It could, however, be revived and retained by a definite and clear-cut policy ...

I saw Bishop O'Donnell today at Letterkenny. He considered the proposals carefully in detail and appeared anxious to accept them if he could. But his conclusion was that they were impossible; that you could not exclude Fermanagh, Tyrone and Derry City without a vote [ie referendum by county]; and that, if it became known that the Party backed such proposals, the country would divided against the Party. He appreciated the difficulties of the situation, but thought that pressure should be put on the Unionists to make them concede something ...

My own diagnosis of the situation is that the bishops will be very hostile; that the people in the districts outside Belfast will be equally hostile; and that the only support for these proposals will come from the people of this city. In face of this, do you think I should call any Conference? If so, I will do it; but the result would be merely that the proposals would be turned down ...

NLI: Redmond Papers MS 15181/3

(b) Devlin to T.P.O'Connor   Belfast, 19 June 1916

... I am having interviews every moment of the day with people calling upon me from every part of Ulster, and am now more hopeful. I am sanguine of this, at all events: whatever comes or goes, we will have a great support of our friends, who are rallying to us with marvellous Ulster loyalty. There's a rapidly-developing change in opinion. The [Irish] Independent, now that the issue is known and that we have faced it, is becoming absolutely discredited.

HLRO: Lloyd George Papers, D/14/3/26

(c) W.H.Owen's Reports to Lloyd George   Belfast, 20 & 23 June 1916

[20.6.16] You asked me last week to go to Belfast and ascertain as far as possible the extent to which the Nationalists of the North were prepared to give support to their leaders, and the prospects of a settlement on the lines of your proposals ... The conclusions which I think are to be derived from the situation are these.

(1) Influence of the priests – The majority of the Roman Catholic priests in the six counties proposed to be excluded are not friendly to the suggestion of settlement ... but their opposition is tempered by two important consideration, first that they have no alternative scheme to offer, and secondly, that Mr Devlin's personal influence in and around the Belfast Catholic diocese is sufficient to bring nearly all the priests therein to conformity with the proposals ...

(2) Newspaper influence. The Irish Independent, owned by Mr William [Martin] Murphy of Dublin, is pursuing an unscrupulous policy of opposition to a settlement, making an appeal to the worst faction elements, but is being met to some extent by the influence of the Irish News, which Mr Devlin controls ...

... The most successful arguments that are being used in favour of a settlement are (a) the statement that there is no alternative scheme save a continuance of military dictatorship; (b) that a home rule parliament once set up in Dublin can never be abolished, but is certain to expand, and, (c) that the creation thus early of a home rule parliament is the best possible memorial to the leaders of the late rebellion ...

... Mr Devlin still remains pessimistic as to the result of Friday's Convention, but this appears to be part of a good leader's desire that no stone should be left unturned to secure victory ... he regards the fight now as a straight one between himself and the priests of Ulster ... He reaffirms that Mr Redmond, Mr Dillon and himself have made a compact to resign if the proposals are defeated ...

[23.6.16] The day of the great Convention of Ulster Nationalists arrived ... Unfortunately I was not permitted to be present at the beginning of the proceedings ... On entering the hall I found the Very Rev. Canon Keown of Inniskilling [sic] speaking against the proposals ... The speaker followed the common lines of the factionists: (1) laying stress on the doubt as to the temporary nature of the scheme (2) suggesting that a separate executive was to be set up in Belfast, and (3) that an exhibition of courage and determination in opposing the present scheme, would result in other and more acceptable terms being offered by the Government.

... Mr Joseph Devlin rose to speak ... He firmly believed that if the proposals were adopted and an Irish Parliament set up in Dublin, the benefits attendant upon a scheme of that nature would soon become evident to the excluded counties and they would of their own accord very soon seek to be included under the jurisdiction of an Irish Parliament ... It is not too much to say that Mr Devlin's words turned the tide in favour of the proposals ...

The voting was in the majority of 210 in favour of the proposals [475 to 265]. The decision was taken by open vote, the name of every delegate being read out from the chair and the delegate rising in his place and declaring his vote 'yes' or 'no'. An analysis of the voting shewed that over 100 of the total of 265 votes recorded against the proposals were cast by the priests, the strength of the opposition lay vote being in the counties of Tyrone and Derry ...

HLRO: Lloyd George Papers D/14/3/21 & D/15/1/15

99 Volunteers and wire-pullers

The collapse of Lloyd George's scheme for immediate 26-county home rule quickly nullified the Irish Party's 'victory' at the Belfast Conference, although the full extent of the Party's decline did not become apparent for a little longer. At a by-election in West Cork in December 1916, an unofficial candidate who pledged himself to the Irish Party was successful against two independent nationalists, one of whom claimed to be a Sinn Féiner. But this was to be the Party's last shred of real electoral hope. The victory at North Roscommon, in February 1917, of papal Count George Plunkett (1851-1948), father of one of the men executed in 1916, over an official Party candidate, stimulated the development of a real political movement out of the ashes of 1916 and marks the beginning of the visible collapse of the Irish Party.

The message of North Roscommon was hammered home by another by-election defeat for the Irish Party in South Longford early in May – this time at the hands of an imprisoned Volunteer. The Irish Party no longer offered inspiration to the nationalist electorate, and as a result it began also to lose more calculating supporters. But there was as yet no organised alternative party to turn to, only an assortment of pre-war Sinn Féiners, Irish Volunteers (whose leaders were still mostly in prison) and others, held together by a general feeling of *ex post facto* support for the Rising and a vague policy of withdrawal from Westminster. Plunkett, father of a martyr and of two other Volunteers, though elderly and lacking any political experience, filled the vacuum for several months. In Cork city and county, where for years William O'Brien and his moderate All-for-Ireland League had managed to keep most of the parliamentary seats out of the hands of the Irish Party, the situation in 1917 was especially complicated. Mary MacSwiney (1872-1942) was a republican activist in Cork, and was later a leading opponent of the 1921 Treaty in the second Dáil.

Mary MacSwiney to Count Plunkett   Cork City, 30 May 1917

... I am very puzzled by the invitation [to you] ... which has ... not emanated from the usual Irish Volunteer sources, but from certain local politicians, who will only be prepared to act as politicians. You will, I am sure, forgive me for the sake of our common cause, for telling you that here in Cork it is necessary to be particularly careful of political wire-pulling. You are a 'trump-card' at present, you know. There are all over the country many earnest and convincing and, in their way, sincere politicians who would like to play that 'trump-card' and win; but I assure you the only friends it is safe to trust the organisation of an independent Ireland to must be sought – in Cork – in the ranks of the Volunteers and Cumann na mBan. You will not find them so pushing, or perhaps on the surface so capable, but you will find that both in the city and the county of Cork they are trusted because they are known to be honest. Unless your executive is composed mainly of them and controlled by them it cannot succeed. Any man who was ever prominent here either as an O'Brienite or a Redmondite will not command the confidence of the county. You would see that for yourself if you knew how high party feeling has risen here and what bitterness still exists. Both parties are watching, and if there is any attempt at an O'Brienite capture of the new movement it is damned at once ...

NLI: Count Plunkett Papers, MS 11383/6

100 The state of Ireland, 1916: Amnesty the key?

Attempts at settlement having failed in the summer of 1916, Irish Party leaders had to look elsewhere for ways of demonstrating their continued efficacy to the electorate. The Irish Party leader sent this letter to Asquith a few days before he was ousted as prime minister by Lloyd George.

John Redmond to H.H.Asquith   30 November 1916

The condition of Ireland, though still far from satisfactory, has vastly improved within the last two months, and that improvement has been due, amongst other causes, to the release of over a thousand of the interned prisoners, and the confident expectation, which has been spread by us, that the government contemplated a policy of conciliation, involving the removal of martial law and military rule, and the release of the remainder of the interned prisoners. Recent events and widely spread statements in the press have confirmed that impression, and if, in this matter of the interned prisoners, the popular expectations are disappointed the result will be a fresh outbreak of bitterness and exasperation, which may undo all the good effected during the last two months.

The effect of a refusal to release these men will be most dangerous to the position and influence of the National Party in Ireland, and will be pointed to by all those in Ireland who are hostile to constitutional and parliamentary action as a fresh proof that the British government attach no weight to the wishes of the Irish people expressed through their parliamentary representatives. An amnesty movement is already on foot, and, in the event of a refusal to release the prisoners, it will inevitably rapidly assume immense proportions. We shall feel it necessary to support this movement with all our influence. It will also be supported actively by the Catholic Church in Ireland. Great meetings and processions will be organised, and the difficulties of the government in Ireland will be immensely increased.

After months of furious and angry agitation the prisoners will, of course, be released, when infinite mischief has been done, and the release can have no healing effect on the Irish situation, but would be hailed by Sinn Féiners and extremists as one more proof that violent agitation is the only argument to which the British government will listen.

In the course of an amnesty movement a platform will be afforded to all the bitterest enemies of the Irish Party, and of any agreed Irish settlement, to make inflammatory and bitter speeches, passions will be excited, old race-hatred lashed to fury, and there will be the gravest danger of bloody collision between the people and the police and military.

I feel that it is unnecessary for me to enlarge on the effect of such a condition of things in Ireland, on foreign opinion, and on the conduct of the war. Exaggerated and highly coloured accounts of hostile and bitter speeches in Ireland will be scattered all over the world, and no censorship will be able to prevent the circulation of such reports ...

If now Ireland is to be thrown into a fresh tempest of anger and agitation by the refusal of the government to release 560 untried men at the request of the representatives of the overwhelming majority of the Irish people, the feeling in the dominions, and in the United States, which has recently shown signs of improvement, will be intensified against Great Britain ...

In conclusion, I feel it right to say that I am under no delusion as to the dangers of the Irish situation, or as to the attitude which will be adopted by these prisoners when released. But I and my colleagues feel strongly that they can do much more harm as prisoners in Frongoch than at liberty in Ireland.

NLI: Redmond Papers, MS 15262/9

101 The state of Ireland, 1917: Abstention the key?

By Christmas 1916 all the Rising internees had been released, but popular dissatisfaction with the Irish Party continued to grow. The 'abstention from Westminster' tactic advocated by Sinn Féin, Count Plunkett and others appeared to some to be equally threadbare, but its significance at this stage was less as a policy than as a touchstone of the new 'republican' nationalism, differentiating it clearly from the waning orthodoxy. Col Maurice Moore (1854-1939), Inspector-General of the now-defunct National Volunteers, took a pessimistic, but essentially accurate view of the situation.

Col. Maurice Moore to John Dillon   4 March 1917

I have been about the country, specially in Mayo, and have had an opportunity of discussing the political situation with very many people; with Priests, Party followers, Independents and Sinn Féiners, both there and in Dublin. I feel that it is right to inform you on this matter, even if the information is disagreeable. For many reasons I am in a better position to hear the real views of the people than members of the party or their agents. In the first place practically all the young men are Sinn Féiners in more or less degree. Your speeches and actions ought to have mitigated hostility, but they have not; the prisoners and Sinn Féiners believe that the late arrests were instigated by the Party and that the speeches in the House were merely bluff. They are hostile both to the policy, the members and leaders of the Party, and would change all if possible. The older and more responsible men, as an example of whom I might take the parish priests, are gravely dissatisfied with the party policy; they desire much more vigorous action both by *vote* and speech against any government that refuses Irish demands: they are not hostile to the leaders, whose past services they remember, but they would like to see them more active and determined – *not in talk only*. They have lost faith in the Home Rule Bill, and demand control over all taxation, and over trade, customs, and excise, and an abolition of concurrent legislation; these are the three main items.

Both the young men, and the older men to whom I have referred, have lost confidence in the rank and file of the party, and will certainly change it at the next election. Local men, who were formally popular are regarded with aversion; this is a sudden and unexpected revulsion of feeling, but quite understandable when one considers the strong national feelings that have taken hold of the people.

There are some farmers who stick by the Party remembering past favours, and some shopkeepers; but both these classes are wavering and becoming amenable to the pressure of opinion. You may remember the same change gradually working in 1879 and '80.

In one parliamentary division I discussed matters with ten out of fifteen parish priests, and without exception they took the views I have reported above. I am informed the other five are not exceptions. Many of the curates go further ...

This is a serious state of affairs and no speech-making in Parliament will change it, though *your* speeches might under other circumstances have been effective. If something decisive be not done the revolution may go to the extreme of changing the whole party, leaders and all.

As to what policy would be approved there is a difference of opinion, and the majority of the people are undecided. Any policy adopted will I think be attacked by some of the violent Sinn Féin papers, but the bulk of the people would, I think, agree to a really live hostility to the Government. What that is to be is worthy of consideration; no policy is suitable to every emergency; circumstances alter and policy with them. Independent opposition, party support, obstruction, rebellion, Carson's Ulster bluff, passive resistance, each is appropriate to a set of circumstances, and each has been effective in its time, and each is subject to grave difficulties at other times. I have never been an advocate for abstention from Parliament; it has not hitherto been a suitable weapon, but it may be now.

It is necessary to attract the eyes of Europe and America, and induce the Colonies to act for us. It would put England in a false position, and the Colonial Conference is approaching. If it is to be done at all it should be done with dramatic effect. The coming debate on Wednesday gives the opportunity; consider what would be the effect of 80 members walking out of the House together, after Lloyd George's speech postponing action.

The Sinn Féin proposal to bring the matter before the Peace Conference may be impracticable, but there is nothing impossible about the Imperial Conference. Some such suggestion was made by Lloyd George's settlement proposal, and moreover the Irish trade amendment can hardly be discussed without raising the question of self-government.

The danger is that it is very difficult to resume parliamentary action if objectionable legislation is threatened. It would certainly be necessary for the whole party to return to Dublin, and call together a conference of persons representative of all Ireland – not deputies from party organisations – but Chairmen of county councils, mayors and chairmen of town councils, representatives of trades, manufacturers, labour, professions, journalists and so on; some three hundred in all, and keep them in conference for a week at a time; recalling them as often as possible.

This policy will not be acceptable to cautious men; but the present dangers are imminent and an alternative is difficult to find.

NLI: Maurice Moore Papers, MS 10561/9

102 The power of the press

The *Freeman's Journal* was in practice the Irish Party's official daily newspaper. It reported the speeches of party leaders and the business of branches in mind-numbing detail, and its editorials increasingly followed the party line. But the paper's style and presentation took little heed of the journalistic innovations being made by Northcliffe's popular press. The *Irish Independent*, owned by a leading Dublin businessman, William Martin Murphy (1844-1921), was Ireland's largest-selling daily paper, and it tended to reflect the independent nationalist views of Murphy's friend T M Healy and his All-for-Ireland League associate, William O'Brien. Although it was bitterly hostile to the Rising – Murphy had been the main object of Larkin's and Connolly's strike activity in Dublin in 1913 – the *Independent's* criticism of the official party line gave important help to rival movements.

Frank Barrett to John Redmond MP   Cork, 12 October 1916

May I draw your attention to a most vital consideration. Circulation of the *Freeman's Journal* in this city is about 80 copies. Circulation of the *Irish Independent* well over 1500. I believe the same thing prevails right throughout Ireland. It is a great pity that something cannot be done to reduce the size of the *Freeman* and also its price to one halfpenny. The *Independent* has done, and is doing, a lot of damage to the great nationalist movement of which you are the great leader. Its 'taproom logic' has weakened and poisoned the minds of many of your supporters, who foolishly buy it daily, for its war news and general news in a brief form, such as they dish up. Halfpenny papers are the papers of today ...

NLI Redmond Papers, MS 15262/5

103   Sinn Féin: The doctrine of suppressed sovereignty

Sinn Féin ('Ourselves') had been founded as a political party by a Dublin journalist, Arthur Griffith (1871-1922), in 1905. Its goal of a dual monarchy for Britain and Ireland, on the Austro-Hungarian model, and its policy of achieving this through complete withdrawal from British institutions and the unilateral establishment of an alternative structure, attracted little serious attention. Only its name made any impact, for the anti-Redmondite Irish Volunteers of 1914-16, whose real policy was in fact the apparently very different one of securing an independent republic by military means, were erroneously dubbed 'Sinn Féin Volunteers' by police, press and people. Sinn Féin thus took no part in the 1916 rising, although Griffith and some of his associates were interned nonetheless. Differences in temperament and emphasis between Sinn Féin and the Volunteers were considerable. But the unco-ordinated election successes in 1917 brought the various leaders into closer co operation, and placed a premium on the early resolution of differences. At Sinn Féin's tenth annual convention in October 1917 its constitution was revised in such a way as to satisfy the Volunteers, and Griffith made way for de Valera as president. The aims of the movement were declared to be 'the international recognition of Ireland as an independent Irish republic', after which 'the Irish people may by referendum freely choose their own form of government'. How this was to be achieved is not entirely clear: talk of another rising was played down, and more publicity given to Griffith's plan for an appeal to the international peace conference which was expected to follow the war.

Ireland's claim to be at the Peace Conference was based on a doctrine of international law, the doctrine of suppressed sovereignty. They could not in Ireland secure belligerent rights unless they became, *de facto*, master of the country. As Bulgaria's claim was put forward on the doctrine of suppressed sovereignty, Ireland's claim was also good ... Their case was strong and their case must be heard. It could only be heard on two conditions. The first was that they destroy the representation that at present existed in the English Parliament. The very existence of that representation in the English Parliament denied Ireland's claim to sovereign independence ... In addition, they must have in Ireland before that Conference met, and the sooner they had it the better, a constitutional assembly chosen by the whole people of Ireland which could speak in the name of the people of Ireland ...

Cork Examiner, 26 October 1917

104 Irish-Ireland revived

The release of all convicted Volunteers, including Eamon de Valera, in June 1917 coincided exactly with his nomination for another by-election vacancy in East Clare, adjacent to his native county of Limerick. Still no formal organisation had been found to give full coherence to the new political spirit, but that such a spirit existed was amply confirmed - both by the welcome given to the returned convicts as they passed through Dublin, in contrast to the lukewarm reception experienced by the internees earlier – and more especially by the shattering victory of de Valera in East Clare, with over 71 per cent of the poll in a straight fight with an Irish Party candidate. The following brief comments from D P Moran's *Leader* convey some impression of the new spirit.

(a)...The new movement, miscalled Sinn Féin, is really the Irish–Ireland movement reinforced and stimulated by the Maxwell [military] regime, and by the new value given to small nations as a result of the world war ...

(b) ...What the Irish Party are up against today is not a policy but a protest. It serves their logic-chopping purposes to assume that they are up against a policy, and then they proceed to ask what is the policy ... The new movement at present has not reached the stage of political definiteness ... [It is] ... a national insurrection ...

(c) ...The Irish language and Irish industry were, we believe, planks in the United Irish League – it is all a question of the verb to do rather than, if we may put it so, the verb to plank...

The Leader, 22 & 29 September, 3 November 1917

105 Irish-America: A new desertion every day

The Easter Rising caught the imagination of Irish-America in a way that the Irish Party had been unable to do since the home rule policy had begun to crumble in 1914. With constituency associations in Ireland collapsing and the *Freeman's Journal* close to bankruptcy, Redmond and Dillon were in desperate need of new financial resources.

When America entered the war in April 1917 it was decided to ask another senior MP, T P O'Connor (1848-1929), to make an extended American tour in the hope that the allied war effort might have created new sympathies amongst Irish-Americans. Although O'Connor remained away for a year, and achieved a modicum of success in fund-raising, his initial impression reflected accurately enough the true facts — the bonds between constitutional nationalism and Irish-American opinion, which Parnell had forged forty years before, were now broken.

T P O'Connor to John Redmond   Washington DC, 9 July 1917

I have found my task more difficult than ever I anticipated. Feeling here about the executions and England was far more violent even than in Ireland. Indeed, it became clear to me before I was twenty-four hours in New York that the Irish here — at least of the masses — had just got back to the old position; and had learned nothing and forgotten nothing since 1846. We were scarcely in the hotel when a manageress, a big Irishwoman, announced to Hazelton [Nationalist MP] that he wasn't an Irishman at all; spoke of Tirpitz to me as the grandest man of the War because he had done the most injury to England. Then every post brought me abusive letters, some signed, some not; the language in some of them was coarse beyond imagination. The *Gaelic American* made an even more blackguardly attack, and the *Irish World*, though not so personal as the *Gaelic American*, was fierce enough, calling me the Benedict Arnold of the Irish movement.

M.J.Ryan [President of the United Irish League of America], to whom we sent a telegram on our arrival, merely replied that he had suggested to Jordan [UIL Secretary] that he should come and see us; since then not a word from Ryan. All these things brought home to me clearly that for the moment we were down and out so far as great masses of the people were concerned; and that if I had thought of attempting a public meeting it would have ended in disorder. Some women interrupted even the memorial service for poor Willie [Redmond] in New York.

I found it also a miscalculation that the entrance of America into the war would have put any stop to the Clan-na-Gael activities. It hasn't that effect in the least yet, though it may by and by. The campaign against me is active and widespread, apart from the newspapers ...

My main work at the present moment is propaganda through the Press ... I have reason to hope that this active propaganda will do good; our side of the question has never been put; and the only purely Irish papers that are read by our people are against us. I have no reason to doubt that the majority of clerical opinion is either hostile to the War or not very enthusiastic. None of them have come to see me yet. [Cardinal] Gibbons, I should say, is the only one whole-heartedly with the Allies.

P.S. I feel almost like James II – a new desertion every day.

NLI: Redmond Papers, MS. 15215/2

106 Nationalists, Bishops and the Irish Convention, 1917-18

The reorganisation and expansion of Sinn Féin was the most significant political development in Ireland between the rising and the end of the European war. Efforts by the Irish Party and the government to find a way of taking the steam out of the new republicanism met with no success. Lloyd George's attempt to buy time by transferring responsibility for a settlement back onto Irish shoulders, through the Irish Convention of 1917-18, in practice meant time for Sinn Féin to reorganise and expand its popular support. The Convention met in Trinity College, Dublin, under the chairmanship of Sir Horace Plunkett, from July 1917 until May 1918. Its participating membership of about ninety consisted of an assortment of Irish Party and Ulster Unionist MPs, local councillors, peers and landlords representing Southern Unionist opinion, and leading clergymen of the main denominations. Sinn Féin condemned the whole affair, and even John Dillon remained sceptically on the sidelines. In the key phase of the debate both sides split: Redmond and a small majority of his Irish Party colleagues reached provisional agreement with Lord Midleton's Southern Unionist group to recommend home rule without partition, though also without control of customs and associated duties or defence, but they were thwarted by the total opposition of the Ulster Unionists and the refusal of most of the leading Nationalists, other than Redmond, to cooperate unless the Ulster Unionists also concurred. By the time that the Convention ended in total failure, Redmond had been dead for several weeks.

(a) John Dillon to T.P.O'Connor   10 January 1918

... The situation is extremely critical and very bad. The Ulstermen are more stiff and irreconcilable than they were two years ago. The Southern Unionists led by Lord Midleton have come a long way and are agreed with the Nationalists on all points but 'customs' ... Redmond has, I fear, gone too far on the road of concession and is, I gather, anxious to agree with Lord Midleton ... And I am *convinced* that if the Nationalists were to agree with the Southern Unionists and surrender the customs, in the present state of Ireland, we and the Southern Unionists would be swept off the field in a few weeks. Sinn Féin, linked with [William Martin] Murphy and the *[Irish] Independent* and three-quarters of the priests, would carry the country hands down ... It would be the July [1916] negotiations over again in a much worse form...

TCD: Dillon Papers MS 6742/435

(b) John Redmond to Bishop Patrick O'Donnell   14 January 1918

... You will notice that this amendment of mine (to Lord Midleton's motion) does not commit anyone to giving up customs unless the Government accepts the scheme and gives it legislative effect *forthwith*. If they did this I am quite convinced that we would be guilty of a great dereliction of duty if we did not accept the compromise, quite regardless of what Sinn Féiners might say ...

NLI: Redmond Papers, MS 15217/4

(c) Bishop O'Donnell to Redmond   14 January 1918

The agenda containing your notice of amendment reached me yesterday morning in Letterkenny. It surprised me. At the meeting in the Mansion House, on your suggestion, it was accepted that nothing would be done as regards notices of amendment until we came to a decision; and I can only say that if I had had the chance I would most earnestly advise against notice of the amendment that stands in your name.

In my opinion, should the Government not carry through the proposed agreement, the Nationalist who votes for it cannot stand where he stood before ... The principle is given away. If Ulster had come in, or promised to come in, we could give something away. But with Ulster out, we never agreed to give anything away, and in my opinion it would be fatal to do so ... The proposition would be drowned in scorn and ridicule before it was a week before the public ...

No man has influenced my views [O'Donnell, Dillon and Devlin had dined together on 9 January]. My views are my own. But I entertain them so strongly that at any sacrifice I must express them ... In my opinion the very worst service that can be done to the chances of legislation on the Midleton lines would be by our concurrence in the absence of a promise from Ulster to come in.

May God direct us. It is needless to say with what pain I write in this way.

NLI: Redmond Papers, MS 15217/4

...Bishop O'Donnell came into the open as a wrecker ... When the division was taken, after nine months of deliberation, the result was foregone. Three months before there were only two known dissentients out of ninety-six, the vote of the twenty-one Ulstermen being, according to the definite statement of their leader, uncertain but not averse. Now the figures cast were: for the settlement forty-seven; against forty-one ... the Ulster twenty-one, combining with the men they most distrusted in Ireland, assisted in a body at the wreckage ... The Catholic Church had once more proved itself the strongest element in Ireland and Rome shortly afterwards rewarded Bishop O'Donnell, the chief actor, with the Archbishopric of Armagh and a Cardinal's hat.

The Earl of Midleton, *Ireland: Dupe or Heroine*
(London: William Heinemann, 1932) p 120

107 'Repeal that Act!': the conscription crisis, April 1918

Far more important than the failure of the Convention, from the point of view of Irish public opinion, was the Government's passage in April 1918 of a new Military Service Bill. This gave the Government discretionary power to introduce conscription in Ireland by order-in-council whenever it wished, without further debate. Opposition to conscription brought about a temporary unity of purpose among Nationalists, Republicans and Catholic Church leaders but, once the Government had swept aside the Irish Party's opposition to the Bill at Westminster, that unity could only be based on Sinn Féin tactics. As he and Dillon fought against the Bill at Westminster, Devlin asked the Dublin journalist Robert Donovan to report on the current situation in Ireland.

(a) Robert Donovan to Joseph Devlin   Dublin 15 April 1918

... Undoubtedly the popular expectation is that the passive resistance movement should have your backing, and that united action is essential. If Sinn Féin appears to occupy or arrogates itself the position of expressing the united will, the political consequences must be bad. I cannot imagine conscription succeeding. The feeling abroad is unlike anything that I can remember since Parnell's arrest. I do not think it can evaporate. The idea that the alternative to resistance is death or mutilation under incompetent generalship in Flanders, for no result, is universal in the simplest minds and will stiffen the resistance of the slackest. The defeat of this thing is, therefore, all but certain, and if Sinn Féin should be able to claim it as the result of its solitary action the effect must be deplorable ...

TCD: Dillon Papers 6730/193

(b) REPEAL THAT ACT!

Denying the right of the British Government to enforce compulsory service in this country, we pledge ourselves solemnly to one another to resist Conscription by the most effective means at our disposal.

...We are convinced that this anti-Conscription Pledge was read in all the 1,115 [Catholic] parishes ... Probably 500,000 Irishmen of all ages between 18 and 80 signed the Pledge yesterday ...

Mr John Dillon presided over a very full meeting of the Irish National Party in Dublin on Saturday, and the leader and his colleagues resolved 'that in the present crisis we are of opinion that the highest and most immediate duty of the members of this Party is to remain in Ireland, and actively co-operate with their constituents in opposing the enforcement of the Compulsory Military Service Bill in Ireland'.

Irish News editorial, 22 April 1918

(c) Report on the Present State of Ireland, Especially with Regard to Conscription, prepared for Lloyd George and the War Office by the Duke of Atholl, 29 April 1918

Ireland appears at the present moment to be solidly united against conscription from north to south – I fancy that there is equal antipathy to it in Ulster, although a certain number of people engaged in shipbuilding may possibly speak in favour of it, knowing that they are safe [from being conscripted]. With the exception of one or two wounded men returned from the front, I have not heard one word in favour of it, but on the contrary, bitter hatred is shown by all classes of people other than the class which may be known as 'Society'.

From a military point of view, the game appears to be hardly worth the candle – it can only be justified by results. I am convinced that there would be the very greatest difficulty getting the conscripts, and when you have got them, I believe they will do more harm than good to the Army, and be of more trouble than they are worth. The general attitude appears to be one of passive resistance on the part of every single individual, and every obstacle will be put in the way that the ingenuity of Irish men and women can devise ...

The people in their present temper have almost forgotten their desire for home rule, and conscription holds the board to the exclusion of every other topic. The Nationalist leaders aver that the Government has let them down – that they were doing their very best to fight Sinn Féin, had won three by-elections, but all of a sudden, without consulting them, the Government brought in conscription ... At the present moment their power is almost negligible, but they still look upon themselves as likely to be the dominant party in the long run. They dare not, however, for the sake of their own skins, suggest conscription or voluntary enlistment. I am convinced that the Church in Ireland is not really hostile to conscription, or voluntary enlistment in itself, but they have joined forces against it for exactly the same reason as the Nationalists, otherwise their power would be entirely gone ...

The only chance seems to me to lie in home rule – otherwise the danger of civil war is run, and very possibly the loss of the European campaign. It is the appalling thought of the latter which convinces me that whatever our feelings may be with regard to home rule, it must be conceded now with as little delay as possible ...

HLRO: Lloyd George Papers F/94/3/45

108 The one bright spot, June 1918

'Conscription' for Ireland remained on the statute book, but was never implemented. A few weeks later almost all the Sinn Féin and Volunteer leaders were re-interned on the basis of their alleged involvement in a highly improbable 'German plot' for another rising. The impact of these events was described by Hugh Law (1872–1943), a Protestant landowner from Donegal, who was one of the more moderate Irish Party MPs.

Moreover, alas over every proposal, even the best, hangs the shadow of conscription. By a tragic accident (for such I must suppose it) the Report of the Convention appeared in the Irish press on the same day as the announcement of the Cabinet's resolve to extend the Military Service Acts to Ireland: and the Prime Minister has indicated his intention of associating with the 'tender' of a new home rule bill an Order-in-Council bringing these Acts into operation. Conceive the plight of the Irish ministry whose first task it will be to cooperate in enforcing conscription!

No-one who has not been in Ireland during the past six weeks can possibly realise how passionate is the resentment which has been aroused. Those who blame the Roman Catholic bishops and the Parliamentary Party for the share they have taken in the anti-conscription movement have little sense of realities. If these had not intervened to regularise and moderate popular action, there might well have been bloodshed; and this, not in certain specially disturbed areas, but all up and down the country. My own constituency [West Donegal] has for at least a quarter of a century been completely free from agrarian or other troubles. During the sixteen years I have represented it in the House of Commons, I cannot recall a single instance of boycotting, intimidation, or similar outrage. Yet there, as elsewhere, I know that men were, and are, ready to take to the hills or die fighting in their homes rather than be compelled to join the Army. The tension is extraordinary, and the wildest stories find belief. Thus the visit of a single RAMC officer to a disused workhouse which it was thought might serve for a convalescent home at once produced a rumour that 500 soldiers had arrived in the district to commence a drive for conscripts; and quick on its heels came the statement that these were Gurkhas, specially trained to hunt men through the mountains and kill them with knives. To Englishmen it may well seem incredible that fellow-subjects of theirs should credit their rulers with intentions such as are here implied. Nevertheless, it is not only peasants who believe that the aim of an influential section here and in Ireland is not so much to gain recruits for the Army as to find a pretext for a pogrom in which the troublesome aspirations of Ireland after self-government may be once and for all quenched in blood, and the work half-done by Cromwell completed. To this pass has a country come which in August 1914, was the 'one bright spot on the horizon' ...

Contemporary Review, vol cxiii, p 606 (June 1918)

109 Volunteers and land-grabbing

Although the political programme of Sinn Féin had been revised by de Valera, Arthur Griffith and others during the autumn of 1917, social policy was always likely to be more divisive, and for that reason were mainly avoided by the new party. But during the winter of 1917-18 a number of schemes of varying degrees of ingenuity were devised to translate 'Sinn Féin' ('Ourselves') into terms which had more practical appeal to the common man. Talk of a famine caused by the mass export of Irish farm produce to England was met by imaginative publicity stunts such as the impounding of consignments of pigs at the dockside by Volunteers. On a wider scale, graziers (who tended to employ very little labour) were encouraged to obey the Department of Agriculture's order to till at least ten per cent of their land, by decisions of local Sinn Féin clubs to march out and plough up their grass. The memoirs of a policeman who later became sympathetic to Sinn Féin describe one such episode in early 1918. Shortly afterwards the Sinn Féin standing committee acted firmly to stifle such class-conscious and socially divisive operations, but not before they had provided an effective boost to party recruitment in western grazing districts.

When ... the Volunteers began to divide ranches the British government had to sit up and take notice. It was well for the Volunteers and Sinn Féin that it did so, as otherwise there would have been chaos in the country.

My first experience of land division was at a farm in a place called Toberanania, about a mile from Ballintogher village. The local Sinn Féin club decided to divide a farm among 'deserving small farmers' in the district. Since all the farmers around were 'deserving' and 'small' they all turned up on the appointed day at the farm due for division. The local secretary, who was himself a 'small' farmer, got up on a cart and announced that he was about to divide the farm. 'Hands up', he said, 'all who want an addition to their farms'. Every hand went up. I was half tempted to put up my own hand so as not to feel odd in that great forest of hands. As there were only about eighty acres to be divided it would have required a miracle almost equal to that of the loaves and fishes to satisfy that crowd of land-hungry men and women. It was at that moment that the secretary showed real leadership. 'Ladies and gentlemen', he said, 'we did not anticipate so many applications and, as you are all aware, our one ambition is to see that everybody is satisfied. We have decided to take all the names and each case will get our personal and sympathetic attention. In the meantime we shall confine ourselves to marking out the plots with the ploughs and taking over the farm in the name of the Irish Republic'. The cheering in response to this announcement could be heard miles away and after the secretary had made a few concluding remarks all present, except the police, shouted in chorus 'Up the Republic', and 'Down with British tyranny'. A few ploughmen then went into action and ploughed single furrows in a very large field to mark off divisions of land. As most of the land in question was of poor quality and too swampy for the horses, the division of the rest of it was deferred to that day week when another 'monster' meeting was to be held at the same time and place. Fortunately for the leader, he was safely behind the bars of Sligo jail that day week. When he came out some months later he was met by the bands and acclaimed a local hero. In the meantime the division of Toberanania farm was postponed indefinitely.

J A Gaughan, *Memoirs of Constable Jeremiah Mee, RIC*
(Dublin: Anvil Books, 1975), pp 512

110 'Workers would willingly sacrifice': Labour and the 1918 election

An Irish Labour Party had been brought into existence by the Irish Trade Union Congress at its 1912 conference. During the War it had begun to contest elections in Dublin, but neither it nor the remaining branches of the British-affiliated Independent Labour Party in Belfast had won any parliamentary seats. During 1917 and 1918 however, rising food prices coupled with relative scarcity of labour gave a great boost to trade unionism in Ireland as workers sought to improve wage levels. The Irish Labour Party leadership was anxious to capitalise on this politically, but although the majority of activists in Dublin were closer to Sinn Féin than to the Irish Party, the national question continued to pose serious problems. William O'Brien of Dublin (1881-1968) and Thomas Johnson (1872-1963), the Belfast-based Englishman, were the movement's leading figures in the years after 1916.

(a)   In 1918 it was thought that the general election might come soon and accordingly we [the leaders of the Irish Labour Party] had several talks with representatives of Sinn Féin. We had difficulties about the matter which they did not seem to understand. Sinn Féin had, of course, a fully political organisation and the adherents of it were under the control or inspiration of their elected officials. Labour was not in that position at all. Labour was made up of the trade unions, and the members of the trade unions were not pledged supporters of Sinn Féin; many of them, in fact, were opponents.

The actual general election changed this very much, but in the meantime we had difficulties. The question of attendance at Westminster was one of them ... There was also the question of the Republican oath, which many of the older people in the trade union movement might be opposed to ... The representatives of the Sinn Féin movement wanted to get us to agree with them about the general election. Labour, however, had made up its mind to a round number of candidates, particularly in Dublin City.

In this respect the spokesman for Labour was the executive of the Irish Trade Union Congress ... When it came close to the election ... it seemed to me that unless there was an agreement about certain things there might be trouble and it might result in Labour candidates and Sinn Féin candidates in conflict and on a split vote the old Irish Party might get in, in a number of places ... I decided to urge the Congress executive not to put forward any candidates ... We got it through and it created a very friendly feeling between us and Sinn Féin.

W O'Brien, *Forth the Banners Go: Reminiscences*
(Dublin: Three Candles, 1969), pp 160-161

(b) A call comes from all parts of Ireland for a demonstration of unity on this question such as was witnessed on the conscription issue. Your Executive believes that the workers of Ireland join earnestly in this desire, that they would willingly sacrifice for a brief period their aspirations towards political power if thereby the fortunes of the nation can be enhanced ...

The main purpose of the Irish Labour Party is not the election of one or two or two dozen members of parliament, but the building up of an organised political labour consciousness in this country, definitely democratic, not on a single issue, but on every democratic policy ...

If the North had made up its mind to run candidates on the programme of the Irish Labour Party ... the Executive's decision would have been a very different one. If the South has responded heartily to the [earlier] decision of the Irish Labour Party Executive five or six weeks ago the decision might have been very different.

> Speech to ITUC Executive by Thomas Johnson,
> *Irish Times* 2 November 1918, *Voice of Labour*
> 9 November 1918. Cited in A Mitchell,
> *Labour in Irish Politics, 1890-1930*
> (Dublin: Irish University Press, 1974), pp 99-100

111 'Any and every means available': Sinn Féin and the 1918 election

The war came to an end without the implementation of conscription in Ireland. But from April until October 1918 the threat had been close enough to serve Sinn Féin as a formidable propaganda weapon until the very last days of the war. The general election of December, following only six weeks after the termination of hostilities, returned Lloyd George and his coalition convincingly to power in Britain as 'the men who won the war'. But in Ireland the same pace of events was to the advantage of Sinn Féin: their resistance to conscription was remembered, while their policy of an 'appeal to the peace conference' could not yet be put to the test. The Irish Party was annihilated at the polls, winning only six seats, five of which were in Ulster (and four of those as the result of a pact with Sinn Féin to avoid losing the seats to Unionists). Sinn Féin, whose election manifesto appears below, won seventy-three seats and immediately set about establishing Dáil Éireann as a republican constituent assembly.

Manifesto to the Irish people

The coming general election is fraught with vital possibilities for the future of our nation. Ireland is faced with the question whether this generation wills it that she is to march out into the full sunlight of freedom, or is to remain in the shadow of a base imperialism that has brought and ever will bring in its train naught but evil for our race. Sinn Féin gives Ireland the opportunity of vindicating her honour and pursuing with renewed confidence the path of national salvation by rallying to the flag of the Irish Republic. Sinn Féin aims at securing the establishment of that Republic.

1. By withdrawing the Irish representation from the British parliament and by denying the right and opposing the will of the British government or any other foreign government to legislate for Ireland.

2. By making use of any and every means available to render impotent the power of England to hold Ireland in subjection by a military force or otherwise.

3. By the establishment of a constituent assembly comprising persons chosen by Irish constituencies as the supreme national authority to speak and act in the name of the Irish people, and to develop Ireland's social, political and industrial life, for the welfare of the whole people of Ireland.

4. By appealing to the Peace Conference for the establishment of Ireland as an independent nation. At that conference the future of the nations of the world will be settled on the principle of government by consent of the governed. Ireland's claim to the application of that principle in her favour is not based on any accidental situation arising from the war. It is older than many if not all of the present belligerents. It is based on our unbroken tradition of nationhood, on a unity in a national name which has never been challenged, on our possession of a distinctive national culture and social order, on the moral courage and dignity of our people in the face of alien aggression, on the fact that in nearly every generation, and five times within the past 120 years our people have challenged in arms the right of England to rule this country. On these incontrovertible facts is based the claim that our people have beyond question established the right to be accorded all the power of a free nation.

Sinn Féin stands, less for a political party than for the nation; it represents the old tradition of nationhood handed on from dead generations; it stands by the Proclamation of the Provisional Government of Easter, 1916, re-asserting the inalienable right of the Irish people to achieve it, and guaranteeing within the independent nation equal rights and equal opportunities to all its citizens.

Believing that the time has arrived when Ireland's voice for the principle of un-trammelled national self-determination should be heard above every interest of party or class, Sinn Féin will oppose at the polls every individual candidate who does not accept this principle.

The policy of our opponents stands condemned on any test, whether of principle or expediency. The right of a nation to sovereign independence rests upon immutable natural law and cannot be made the subject of a compromise. Any attempt to barter away the sacred and inviolate rights of nationhood begins in dishonour and is bound to end in disaster. The enforced exodus of millions of our people, the decay of our industrial life, the ever-increasing financial plunder of our country, the whittling down of the demand for the 'Repeal of the Union', voiced by the first Irish Leader to plead in the Hall of the Conqueror to that of Home Rule on the Statute Book, and finally the contemplated mutilation of our country by partition, are some of the ghastly results of a policy that leads to national ruin ...

The present Irish members of the English parliament constitute an obstacle to be removed from the path that leads to the Peace Conference. By declaring their will to accept the status of a province instead of boldly taking their stand upon the right of the nation, they supply England with the only subterfuge at her disposal for obscuring the issue in the eyes of the world. By their persistent endeavours to induce the young manhood of Ireland to don the uniform of our seven-century old oppressor, and place their lives at the disposal of the military machine that holds our nation in bondage, they endeavour to barter away and even to use against itself the one great asset still left to our nation after the havoc of centuries ...

D Macardle, *The Irish Republic*
(London: Gollancz 1937; 4th edn
Irish Press, 1951), pp 919-20

Chapter 9

The War of Independence

112 Stirring up a hornet's nest

The 'first shots' in the military campaign were fired by a small group of Volunteers in Co Tipperary in January 1919. Apparently with the deliberate intention of bringing about a regular guerrilla campaign they ambushed a routine delivery of dynamite to Soloheadbeg quarry, near Tipperary town, shooting dead the two unsuspecting constables who guarded it. It was the first of a number of such incidents in 1919, resulting in the deaths of 14 policemen and soldiers during the year. A rather smaller number of civilians died at the hands of crown forces during the same period. Irish clerical and nationalist opinion at this stage drew a clear line between the earnest endeavours of Sinn Féin and Dáil Éireann to secure national independence, and the murders being perpetrated by small groups of Volunteers 'acting on their own initiative'. As time went on it became apparent that no such easy distinction could be made. Dáil ministers like Michael Collins (1890-1922) combined their key roles in the collection and distribution of the very large Republican Loan funds that were being raised in Ireland and America with the direction of what was becoming a systematic and cohesive guerrilla war. In 1920, 232 police and soldiers were killed, and later still 24 Volunteers were shot or hanged for murder, almost all of them between February and May 1921. From early 1920 onwards the mass importation of British soldiers, a new, ruthless Auxiliary Force and large numbers of 'black and tans' (Englishmen recruited into the Royal Irish Constabulary to replace the mass of Irishmen who were resigning) to deal with the worsening security situation led to repression and reprisals amongst the civilian population which effectively solidified nationalist opinion behind the IRA. In August 1919 relations between the Dáil and the IRA were put on a more formal basis, and although many churchmen continued to denounce Volunteer operations, and non-military members of the Dáil remained uneasy about developments, it was clear that the military campaign was what counted. Thus events which, in 1919, had seemed to many to be rather squalid or brutal episodes, assumed a more heroic stature as prospects of success loomed nearer, a stature which the nationalist framework of politics did not allow to diminish even many years afterwards.

SOLOHEADBEG MEMORIAL
Commemorating the Ambush at Soloheadbeg,
21 January 1919.
Unveiled by the President of Ireland
SEAN T. O CEALLAIGH
On Sunday 22 January 1950.

There is a saying: 'Where Tipperary leads all Ireland follows.' This saying is well borne out by what followed the lead given the country at Soloheadbeg on Tuesday, 21 January, 1919, the day on which the first Dáil Éireann unanimously adopted the Declaration of Irish Independence. On that date an engagement took place between members of the Irish Volunteers and an armed enemy party, resulting in two RIC constables being shot dead and their equipment and arms, and the explosives they were escorting, captured. It is our proud claim for Soloheadbeg, that it was the first deliberate planned action by a select party of the Irish Volunteers (shortly to be recognised as the Irish Republican Army) renewing the armed struggle, temporarily suspended, after Easter Week 1916 ... The men who took part in the Solohead ambush broke so far with tradition that they refused to fly the country after their coup. This course was urged upon them, but they determined to remain and carry on the fight against the enemy wherever and whenever they could, and with ever-increasing intensity. Their lead was an incentive to the rest of the country, and before long the British were finding that they had stirred up a hornet's nest. The rescue of Sean Hogan at the Station of Knocklong in the following May further increased the morale of the IRA by showing what a few ill-armed men could achieve when they were imbued with the determination to do or die. In collaboration with the Dublin Brigade the war was brought into the streets of Dublin, including the abortive attack on the then Lord Lieutenant at Ashtown in December 1919, which had, nevertheless, the effect of further stepping up the national morale. Barrack attacks, ambushes and raids on enemy communications followed, in all of which the Tipperary Volunteers took a leading part, leading up to the formation of regular Flying Columns in each area.

> Official Souvenir 1950, cited in D Breen, *My Fight for Irish Freedom* (Dublin: Anvil Books, 1964), pp 182-3

113 All legitimate methods of warfare

When the revolutionary Dáil - in fact little more than one-third of it, since the majority were either in prison or on business elsewhere – met on 21 January 1919 it declared Ireland to be an independent republic, and appointed de Valera, Griffith and Count Plunkett to present Ireland's claim at the Versailles peace conference. But despite the efforts of John Devoy and his associates in America, and of a leading Sinn Féiner in Paris itself, neither President Wilson nor the other allied leaders could be persuaded to admit the Irish delegation to the conference table. Many, possibly the majority, of the Sinn Féin electorate had no clear idea of what alternative strategy the party might adopt, other than passive resistance to the British administration. An editorial which appeared in the revived Volunteer journal indicated more clearly than did the publications of the Dáil what the immediate future was to hold.

The principle means at the command of the Irish people is the Army of

Ireland, and that Army will be true to its trust ... If they are called on to shed their blood in defence of the new-born Republic, they will not shrink from the sacrifice. For the authority of the nation is behind them, embodied in a lawfully constituted authority whose moral sanction every theologian must recognise, an authority claiming the same right to inflict death on the enemies of the Irish State, as every free national government claims in such a case. Dáil Éireann, in its message to the Free Nations of the World, declares a 'state of war' to exist between Ireland and England, a fact which has been recognised and acted on by the Volunteers almost from their inception; it further declares that the state of war can never be ended until the English military invader evacuates our country.

We have thus a clear issue laid down, not by any body that could be termed 'militarists' or 'extremists', but by the accredited representatives of the Irish people met in solemn session, in a document drawn up with the utmost care and a full sense of responsibility, and unanimously adopted.

The 'state of war', which is thus declared to exist, renders the National Army the most important national service of the moment. It justifies Irish Volunteers in treating the armed forces of the enemy – whether soldiers or policemen – exactly as a National Army would treat the members of an invading army. It is necessary that this point should be clearly grasped by Volunteers.

Every Volunteer is entitled, morally and legally, when in the execution of his military duties, to use all legitimate methods of warfare against the soldiers and policemen of the English usurper, and to slay them if it is necessary to do so in order to overcome their resistance. He is not only entitled but bound to resist all attempts to disarm him ...

An t-Oglach, 31 January 1919

114 David Neligan: Spying for Ireland

Prior to independence most of the administration and policing of Ireland, outside the North-East, was carried out by Irish Catholics. Many of these people remained loyal to the existing regime throughout the troubles. But many others switched their allegiance to the Sinn Féin side: some simply by turning a blind eye to republican activities, others by passing on occasional snippets of information. A few, like Eamonn Broy and David Neligan, established detectives of the Dublin Metropolitan Police's G Division now working at the heart of the British administration in Dublin Castle, became systematic, full-time spies, reporting to the intelligence network masterminded by IRA leader Michael Collins. They and others like them provided the kind of detailed information on the Government's plans which enabled the IRA to carry out a number of dramatic and morale-boosting operations.

... I resigned from the police [on 11 May 1920] ... Before I resigned I had seen Paddy Sheehan, who was on the Dáil staff and was sometime private secretary to De Valera, and had offered my services. Sheehan promised to enquire, returned and advised me to resign. [Tim] Kennedy ... told me that this was done without Collins's knowledge: that he would never have allowed me to resign ... I ... suggested to Kennedy that he should arrange for a few threatening letters to be sent to me at home in Limerick, ordering me to clear out, and I could show them to the [Dublin] Castle people ...

Kennedy had arranged a meeting for me with Austin Stack, a Kerryman then Minister for Home Affairs in the proscribed Dáil ... He told me that Collins wanted to see me and that arrangements would be made ... I went to the Wicklow Hotel where we met Liam Tobin. Tall, gaunt, cynical, with tragic eyes, he looked a man who had seen the inside of hell. He walked without moving his arms and seemed emptied of energy. Yet this man was, after Collins, the Castle's most dangerous enemy. Like all of us, a poor man, an ex-shop assistant, he had a great flair for intelligence, and was Collins's chief assistant. He ran a secret intelligence office within a stone's throw of the Castle. It was never discovered by the British. Untrained or self-trained as he was, he was an efficient counter-espionage agent and I believe would have been worth his place in any intelligence bureau. It is a measure of the G-men's impotence that they had not tagged Tobin ... His motive in meeting me was to safeguard Collins and the revolutionary movement against a possible enemy, as many 'friends' had been turning up sailing under false colours. By adroit questioning he sought to probe my mind ... The result ... must have been satisfactory as he arranged a meeting for me with Collins ...

... O'Reilly brought me to an old three-storey Dublin [public] house at the junction of Upper Abbey Street and Liffey Street, then an unfrequented place ... A tall, handsome man of about thirty who was alone rose from his chair and greeted us. This was my first glimpse of Michael Collins ... He was a friendly man with the fortunate manners of putting one at ease ... He said 'I know you and your brothers are all right (i.e. friendly to the revolution) ... You shouldn't have been let resign – there was a misunderstanding. I want you to go back to the Castle to work for us'. 'Mr Collins', I said, 'there's nothing I should hate more than to go back there; I'll do anything else for you: join a flying column or anything.' 'Listen, Dave', he said, 'we have plenty of men for columns, but on the other hand no one can fill your place in the Castle, for they trust you and we trust you'. Only the two of us were present at this conversation. After some further talk I agreed to go back.

... Having an escort was a two-edged weapon ... It had the disadvantage of pointing the finger at the person being escorted. This was proved in the case of Alan Bell ... Collins ... knew nothing of Mr Bell nor his activities. He was an ex-stipendiary, ie a paid magistrate, whose title in Ireland was Resident Magistrate. Curiously enough he was also an ex-district inspector of the RIC. Apparently a versatile fellow, he was now engaged in secret and lethal employment, to wit, investigating Sinn Féin funds ... Several millions had been scraped up at home and abroad ... In March 1920 [Bell] was given power ... to send for and interrogate bank managers and others in order to lay hands on that money. He lived beyond the Dalkey tramline and was escorted by RIC men to that tram every morning and met at the Dublin end by G-men. One of the latter told me who he was and what he was doing ... I ... suggested that he should be investigated. Soon afterwards, in May, Bell was shot at Merrion. No one filled his place. The fact that he had an escort, and one which stupidly gave him no protection on his journey, directed attention to him ...

The Dublin police, apart from the G-men, were very careful not to stick their necks out and escaped practically unscathed. The RIC, though, were in the thick of it and were boycotted. A lot of them resigned, some under duress, but those who remained had a very tough time, plenty of them being ambushed and killed. Ishmaels, they had every man's hand against them. Sinn Féin blundered where the RIC was concerned. Many of those poor devils were married with families, generally large ones, and had no resources apart from their pay. A vigorous propaganda was directed at them with the object of making them resign, but no effort was made by anybody to provide alternative employment or help them to return to civilian life. The result was that they could see nothing ahead but starvation. So literally they stuck to their guns and fought their own countrymen – to the last ... However, that is not to say that they were all hostile to Sinn Féin. Many RIC men helped actively and others turned a blind eye to the rebels. To my own knowledge, one county inspector, two or three district inspectors and countless sergeants and privates [sic] rendered the movement useful service ...

> D Neligan, *The Spy in the Castle* (London: MacGibbon & Kee, 1968, an imprint of HarperCollins Publishers), pp 68-81

115 *Shirkers and malcontents*

In the early stages of the war of independence, during the first half of 1919, it was not always clear that the various components of the Republican movement were working together as cohesively as hindsight had tended to suggest.

(a) The conscription danger brought a large accession of strength to our ranks. Many of the newcomers were undoubtedly men whose eyes had been opened to the necessity of the Irish Volunteers by this moment of national peril and who joined to take their part in the defence of the Irish people. Some, it is to be feared, were influenced by more selfish consideration, and were affected more by the sense of personal peril than the danger to the nation ... we have no time for shirkers or slackers ...

An t-Oglach, February, 1919

(b) Michael Collins to Austin Stack   17 May 1919

You will be interested to hear that all precedents have been abolished by the new standing committee [of Sinn Féin] ... The policy now seems to be to squeeze out anyone who is tainted with strong fighting ideas or I should say I suppose ideas of the utility of fighting. Of course any [sic] of the Dáil ministers are not eligible for the standing committee and only a third of the entire number may be members of the Dáil. The result is that there is a standing committee of malcontents, and their first act is to appoint a pacifist secretary and announce the absence of H[arry] B[oland]. Our own people give away in a moment what the Detective Division has been unable to find out in five weeks.

NLI: MS 5848

116 *The democratic programme: the duties of the nation*

When Dáil Éireann met for the first time on 21 January 1919, alongside a Declaration of Independence it also approved a document known as the Democratic Programme, intended as a blueprint for the social policy of the future state. A document which was clearly socialist in tone, it was later revealed that it had been drafted by Thomas Johnson, leader of the Irish Labour Party. A possible explanation for Sinn Féin's decision to make such a gesture is that it might have helped Irish Labour to win recognition of their claim to national representation at the first post-war assembly of European Socialists, notwithstanding the fact that the Dáil included no Labour Party representation. Michael Collins and the IRB had sought to suppress the document at the last minute, on the grounds that the Dáil's job was 'to get the English out of Ireland', and that decisions on social issues could be postponed. Instead, however, the document was modified, and appeared in the following revised form. All the declarations at the first meeting of the Dáil were passed without discussion, but cynics point out that as the opening session was conducted entirely in Irish, many delegates would not in any event have been able to contribute to the debate. The Democratic Programme was largely ignored, and had little impact on the future development of independent Ireland.

We declare in the words of the Irish Republican Proclamation [see Document 96] the right of the people of Ireland to the ownership of Ireland and to the unfettered control of Irish destinies to be indefeasible, and in the language of our first President, Pádraic Pearse, we declare that the nation's sovereignty extends not only to all men and women of the nation, but to all its material possessions; the nation's soil and all its resources, all the wealth and all the wealth-producing processes within the nation and with him we re-affirm that all rights to private property must be subordinated to the public right and welfare.

We declare that we desire our country to be ruled in accordance with the principles of Liberty, Equality and Justice for all, which alone can secure permanence of government in the willing adhesion of the people.

We affirm the duty of every man and woman to give allegiance and service to the commonwealth, and declare it is the duty of the nation to assure that every citizen shall have opportunity to spend his or her strength and faculties in the service of the people. In return for willing service, we, in the name of the Republic, declare the right of every citizen to an adequate share of the produce of the nation's labour.

It shall be the first duty of the Government of the Republic to make provision for the physical, mental and spiritual well-being of the children, to secure that no child shall suffer hunger or cold from lack of food or clothing or shelter, but that all shall be provided with the means and facilities requisite for their proper education and training as citizens of a free and Gaelic Ireland.

The Irish Republic fully realises the necessity of abolishing the present odious, degrading and foreign poor law system, substituting therefor a sympathetic native scheme for the care of the nation's aged and infirm, who shall no longer be regarded as a burden, but rather entitled to the nation's gratitude and consideration. Likewise it shall be the duty of the Republic to take measures that will safeguard the health of the people and ensure the physical as well as the moral well-being of the nation.

It shall be our duty to promote the development of the nation's resources ... It shall be the duty of the Republic to adopt all measures necessary for the recreation and invigoration of our industries, and to ensure their being developed on the most beneficial and progressive cooperative industrial lines ...

It shall devolve upon the national government to seek the cooperation of the governments of other countries in determining a standard of social and industrial legislation with a view to general and lasting improvements in the conditions under which the working classes live and labour.

D Macardle, *The Irish Republic* (London: Gollancz, 1937;
4th edn, Dublin, Irish Press, 1951), pp 274-6

117 The burning of Cork: Sanction of a higher authority?

After 1916 it became increasingly difficult for the Government to recruit Irish Catholics into the security forces, and from 1919 existing members began to resign in large numbers. During 1920 the Royal Irish Constabulary was greatly expanded by the enlistment of large numbers of new recruits from Britain, many of them ex-soldiers. Because of their makeshift uniforms they became known as 'the Black and Tans'. An entirely new elite force, the Auxiliary Police, was also established in 1920: small, and designed specifically for counter-insurgency work, it was recruited exclusively from former British Army officers.

During 1920 the IRA campaign became increasingly formidable, especially in the South-West and in Dublin. In parts of Munster police were forced to evacuate small barracks and villages and concentrate in the main towns; roads were cut, and even large motorised patrols were bombed and ambushed. The police and army forces were unused to the methods of guerrilla warfare, and not infrequently sought to retaliate against a hostile civilian population. But during the later months of 1920 suspicion began to grow, in both Ireland and Britain, that some of the reprisal actions, at least, were being undertaken with the connivance or even encouragement of the authorities at some level. One of the major acts of reprisal was the burning of Cork City, described here by the city IRA leader, Florence O'Donoghue.

The burning of Cork City by the British Army of Occupation on the night of 11 December 1920 was the most extensive single act of vandalism committed in the whole period of the national struggle from 1916 to 1921. But it would be a mistake to regard it as an isolated incident, or to accept in explanation of it the conventional excuse that the armed forces of England, drink-sodden and nerve-racked from a contest in which they were being worsted had run amok and destroyed the city in a fit of frenzy ...

The burning and looting of Cork was ... rather the large scale application of a policy initiated and approved, implicitly or explicitly, by the Government from which all authority of the British Forces in Ireland was alleged to derive ... In one month these 'forces of law and order' had burned and partially destroyed twenty-four towns; in one week they had shot up and sacked Balbriggan, Ennistymon, Mallow, Miltown-Malbay, Lahinch and Trim.

... The Auxiliaries were not uncontrolled soldiers of fortune, acting without authority, which they were sometimes conveniently represented to be; nor were their crimes the unpremeditated reaction of men exposed to the hazards of guerrilla warfare. Their actions had the sanction of a higher authority, although it was the policy at first to give an indignant denial to any charge made against these forces ...

... The British Labour Commission, which was in Ireland at the time investigating the outrages by the British forces, intimated their conviction, after investigation on the spot, that the fires were caused by Crown Forces ... When it became clear that no impartial enquiry into the burnings would be permitted by the British Government, the Sinn Féin organisation took the matter in hands and proceeded to collect evidence in connection with the events of the night of 11 December. Sworn statements were taken from nearly one hundred witnesses, including American citizens and Englishmen, as well as many local persons who were not in sympathy with the national movement. This evidence was detailed and specific, and was so overwhelmingly conclusive that no doubt could remain in the mind of any reasonable person but that the City of Cork had been deliberately burned by the British Army of occupation on that night.

With the IRA in the Fight for Freedom, 1919 to the Truce (Tralee: The Kerryman Ltd, nd), pp 129-137

118 Lord Mayor of Cork: A dangerous occupation?

Throughout 1920 Cork City had been in the thick of the troubles, with reprisals beginning at the level of tit-for-tat murders. The murder of the City's IRA Commandant, Tomás MacCurtain (1884-1920) shortly after his election as Lord Mayor of Cork, was only one example. The murderers were never brought to justice: early rumours in the British press of a republican feud were never substantiated, and a coroner's jury returned a verdict of wilful murder against the British Government and against three named police inspectors – one of whom, Swanzy, was quickly transferred to Lisburn, Co Antrim, where he too was murdered a few months later, provoking more reprisals (Document 149).

MacCurtain was succeeded, both as Cork City IRA Commandant and as Lord Mayor, by Terence MacSwiney (1879-1920). A few months later MacSwiney and colleagues were arrested in possession of IRA documents in the city hall, and ten men went on hunger strike in Cork jail in protest against the harassment of elected representatives. MacSwiney was quickly transferred to Brixton Prison, in London, where he died after a fast of 74 days. Two of the Cork hunger-strikers also died before Vice-President Arthur Griffith persuaded the others to end the protest.

MacSwiney's funeral was a massive propaganda success for Sinn Féin. After the procession through London described below in *The Times* – not a paper sympathetic to Irish republicanism – the coffin was seized by the authorities at Holyhead and taken by sea to Cork, to avoid the danger of a big political demonstration in Dublin. The mourning party nonetheless proceeded to Dublin and held the ceremony, presided over by the Archbishop, with an empty coffin, before continuing to Cork for the funeral itself.

(a) ... during the early hours of Saturday ... Alderman Thomas MacCurtin, the recently elected Lord Mayor of Cork, was murdered in his own house in mysterious circumstances. His residence is situated in ... an old and congested part of the city, where he conducted a flour and meal store. He and his family were in bed when they were awakened by a loud knocking at the door. Mr MacCurtin, believing that the police were about to arrest her husband, who was a prominent Sinn Féiner, opened the door. She was immediately brushed aside by two men with blackened faces who carried revolvers. These were followed by two others, similarly disguised, who carried rifles. Four other men rushed into the shop. The first four men rushed upstairs and called upon Alderman MacCurtin to come out of his room ... When he made his appearance two revolver shots were fired at him ... His assailants made off, leaving nothing apparently likely to lead to their identification ... before help could reach him the Lord Mayor died of his wounds.

Times, 22 March 1920

(b) The body of the late Lord Mayor of Cork [Terence MacSwiney] was yesterday born in procession through the streets of London to Euston, thence to be taken to Cork for burial. The coffin was wrapped in the yellow, white and green of Sinn Féin; the flag of Sinn Féin waved over the procession; men of the Irish Republican Volunteers acted as escort. Many thousands of Londoners looked on in silence. There was no disturbance ... The body had lain in state in St George's Roman Catholic Cathedral ... Irish people came from all parts of the Kingdom to be present, but the cathedral not being big enough to hold all, some whom had travelled far were disappointed ... The predominance of youth in this crowd was very noticeable ... When, in the early afternoon, the procession formed for the long march across southern and central London, the footpaths were occupied by a great gathering. It was a very long procession – a mile was a low estimate – and, though it walked briskly, took quite half an hour to pass ... As rank after rank of Irishmen and women went by – and, one was tempted to think, more women than men – the silence grew, if possible, more silent, and certainly more pervaded by sentiment ... Some of the men looked comfortable and prosperous; the women were more often poorly clad and hardened. Remembering what the procession meant – that it was in some sort a demonstration under the banners of Sinn Féin – the London crowd, so huge in its entirety ... said nothing, and did nothing but pay its tribute to the dead ...

The Times, 29 October 1920

119 Tom Barry: 'The highest expression of our nationhood'

As the struggle continued through 1920 and the early months of 1921 the IRA, in the South-West at least, became a sophisticated military force. 'Flying Columns' were formed, made up of men on the run and others who had become full-time fighters, which trekked through the hill country seeking surprise engagements with British units. Tom Barry

(1897-1980) in west Cork was one of the most active flying column commanders, leading 36 Volunteers in an ambush at Kilmichael on 28 November 1920 (17 Auxiliaries and 3 Volunteers killed). In an even larger engagement at Crossbarry on 19 March 1921 Barry led 103 Volunteers, spurred on by a piper, who counter-attacked encircling British forces, killing 35 and losing three of their own.

For me it began in far-off Mesopotamia, now called Iraq ... It was there in that land of the Arabs, then a battle-ground for the two contending imperialistic armies of Britain and Turkey, that I awoke to the echoes of guns being fired in the capital of my own country. It was a rude awakening, guns being fired at the people of my own race by soldiers of the same army with which I was serving. The echo of these guns in Dublin was to drown into insignificance the clamour of all other guns during the remaining two and a half years of war ...

In June 1915, in my seventeenth year, I had decided to see what this great war was like. I cannot plead that I went on the advice of John Redmond or any other politician, that if we fought for the British we would secure home rule for Ireland, nor can I say that I understood what home rule meant. I was not influenced by the lurid appeal to fight to save Belgium or small nations. I knew nothing about nations, large or small. I went to the war for no other reason than that I wanted to see what war was like, to get a gun, to see new countries and to feel a grown man. Above all I went because I knew no Irish history and had no national consciousness.

[After the war] ... I reached Cork in February 1919. In West Cork I read avidly the stories of past Irish history ... About the middle of 1919 whispers came of the volunteers again secretly drilling and reorganising. Names leaked through of local leaders and eventually I approached Sean Buckley of Bandon, telling him who I was and that I wanted to join the IRA. Buckley told me to return again, and at a later meeting asked me not to parade as yet with the local Company, but to act as Intelligence Officer against the British military and their supporters in the Bandon area. So began my connection with the IRA ...

In the summer of 1920 enemy pressure increased. Two thousand extra British troops were landed at Bantry and distributed throughout west Cork. IRA attacks had slowed down and nothing was hampering the British movements ... Desultory training of [IRA] companies proceeded irregularly. This was not satisfactory ... At the time this training policy was being discussed, GHQ in Dublin had sent a communication to all brigades that a flying column should be started in each brigade. The idea was enthusiastically accepted in west Cork ...

... Strange as it may seem, it was accepted in west Cork that the paramount objective of any flying column in the circumstances then prevailing should be, not to fight, but to continue to exist. The very existence of such a column of armed men, even if it never struck a blow, was a continuous challenge to the enemy and forced him to maintain large garrisons. Such a column moving around must seriously affect the morale of garrisons, for one day it would surely strike. It also remained the highest expression of our nationhood, The Flying Column of the Army of the People.

But the flying column would attack whenever there were good grounds for believing that it would inflict more casualties on an enemy force than those it would itself suffer. It would chose its own battleground, and when possible, would refuse battle if the circumstances were unfavourable. It would seek out the enemy and fight, but would not always accept an enemy challenge. It must avoid disaster at all costs ...

> T Barry, *Guerrilla Days in Ireland* (Tralee: Anvil Books,
> 1962; 1st edn Dublin: Irish Press, 1949), pp 7-27

120   Lloyd George: the ordinary rules of civilised warfare

At 9 am on Sunday 21 November 1920 members of the Dublin IRA, directed by Michael Collins, mounted synchronised attacks on the private homes of agents of the British Secret Service, plain-clothes men recently brought into Ireland - supposedly in secret – as part of an intended counter-insurgency operation. Fourteen agents and civilians were shot dead and only one of the killers (who later escaped) was captured.

That afternoon, lorry-loads of police and military interrupted a Gaelic football final at Croke Park, Dublin, apparently intending to search the crowd for evidence concerning the earlier attack. In the event Black and Tans opened fire on the crowd, killing more than a dozen and wounding many more. That night two leading figures of the Dublin IRA, and a visiting friend, were arrested by the Auxiliaries and killed shortly afterwards while 'attempting to escape' from Dublin Castle. A week later came the Kilmichael ambush in west Cork (Document 119).

The conflict in Dublin and the South-West seemed to be worsening daily. Prime Minister Lloyd George made two statements on Ireland to the House of Commons during these weeks, in the second of which martial law was proclaimed for the four south-western counties. Between his two statements various abortive efforts were made – by Father Michael O'Flanagan of Sinn Féin, by moderate Sinn Féiners on Galway Co Council, and by the Catholic Archbishop Clune of Perth, Western Australia – to find a basis for truce and negotiation between the two sides. But the IRA still refused to compromise on 'The Republic', while Lloyd George still believed that by persisting with a military policy he could drive a wedge between 'elected representatives' and 'the murder gang'.

(a) Sir WILLIAM DAVISON asked the Prime Minister whether he is aware that the House of Commons would be prepared at a single sitting to give him whatever powers may be necessary to stamp out the atrocious murder campaign in Ireland under which fourteen British officers and civilians were yesterday foully done to death in Dublin, and will he take immediate steps to introduce any necessary legislation to enable persons found in possession of arms or ammunition without a permit in any disturbed area in Ireland to be shot?

THE PRIME MINISTER: I appreciate the view and desire of my Hon. Friend, and share with him the horror we all feel about the cold-blooded murder of unarmed British officers by assassins in Dublin yesterday. The Government are resolved to suppress the murder conspiracy in Ireland. We always realised that to stamp out such a carefully organised and highly-subsidised plot would take time, but we are convinced, in spite of recent outbreaks, that the Irish authorities are gradually succeeding in their gallant efforts to break up the gang of assassins who have been terrorising Ireland. Should, however, experience show that the powers with which the Irish Government are equipped prove insufficient for the purpose, they will have no hesitation in asking Parliament for such further authority as may be necessary to achieve that end.

MR DEVLIN: May I ask the Prime Minister why it is, when a question is put to him and the Chief Secretary to recite all the horrible occurrences that have taken place last Sunday in Dublin, we have heard nothing about the appearance of the military forces at a football match at which ten people were killed [HON. MEMBERS: 'Sit down!']. I will not sit down, I want to know why the House of Commons has not been made acquainted, in the recital of these other things that have occurred, with the onrush of the military into a football field, with fifteen thousand people, indiscriminate shooting, and ten people killed ...

Grave disorder having arisen, MR SPEAKER suspended the Sitting ...

(b) The PRIME MINISTER: ... During the last few weeks the Government have been in touch with intermediaries who have been anxious to bring about a better understanding. The majority of the people of Ireland are anxious for peace and a fair and lasting settlement ... On the other hand the Government are also very regretfully convinced that the party, or rather the section, which controls the organisation of murder and outrage is not yet ready for a real peace, that is to say, for a peace that will accept the only basis on which peace can be concluded – a basis which would be consistent with the unbroken unity of the United Kingdom ...

In these circumstances the Government determined on the double policy which I propose now to declare. On the one hand they feel they have no option but to continue and indeed intensify their campaign against that small but highly organised and desperate minority who are using murder and outrage ... but on the other hand they are anxious to open every channel ... for an honourable settlement ...

We have decided to proclaim in that quarter of Ireland [the south west] martial law, and to mete out exactly the same treatment to these people as would be done if they were open rebels ... We are only meting out the ordinary rules of civilised warfare ... There will be a proclamation of martial law ... The effect will be that after a certain date unauthorised persons found in possession of arms in the specified areas to which martial law is applied will be treated as rebels, and will be liable on conviction by a military court to the penalty of death. The same penalty will be applied to the unauthorised wearing of the uniforms of any of His Majesty's forces and to the aiding and abetting and harbouring of rebels ...

> H C Deb 5th series, vol 135, cols. 39-40, 2602
> 2611 (22 November, 10 December 1920)

121 'Government attended by such consequences cannot be right'

During the early months of 1921 revulsion at the reprisals policy – which the Government appeared to be defending, if not initiating - spread widely in Britain. It began among political opponents such as Asquithian Liberals and Trade Unionists, was articulated through groups such as the Peace with Ireland Council (the Secretary of which body was, improbably, the young Sir Oswald Mosley, later founder of the British Union of Fascists), and was afterwards taken up by the main Protestant churches. The following declaration was issued by seven Church of England bishops and thirteen leaders of other Protestant churches in England and Scotland.

In opening the latest discussion on the Irish situation in the House of Lords, the Archbishop of Canterbury took occasion once more to protest strongly against the deplorable practice of indiscriminate and unauthorised reprisals by the irregular forces of the crown. He did so on the highest of all grounds – namely, the absolute unlawfulness of the attempt to overcome wrong, however flagrant and provocative, by means of further and equally indefensible wrong. With that protest we, the undersigned, desire earnestly to associate ourselves.

And we go further. While not entitled to commit our respective Churches, we feel constrained to say that we cannot regard the cruel and detestable outrages which have given rise to the whole reprisals policy, authorised and unauthorised alike, as a mere outbreak of criminality in the ordinary sense. Notoriously there lies behind them a long-cherished and deep-seated sense of political grievance which has been aggravated and inflamed by many untoward events, and which the concessions of the new [1920] Irish Government Act have altogether failed to appease ...

In these circumstances we join our voices with those who are appealing from many sides for the adoption of a different line of policy. We plead with the Government to arrange, if possible, a genuine truce, with a view to a deliberate effort after an agreed solution to the Irish difficulty. It may be that attempt will fail; but until it has been seriously and patiently tried we cannot acquiesce in any alternative course of action. The present policy is causing grave unrest throughout the Empire, and exposing us to misunderstanding and the hostile criticism even of the most friendly of other nations of the world ... It affords no prospect of the speedy restoration of law and order. Nor can we believe that it leads to the end all must desire – a peaceful and contented Ireland. On the contrary, its heaviest condemnation perhaps lies in the deepening alienation it is steadily affecting between this country and all classes of the Irish people. A method of government attended by such consequences cannot be politically or ethically right, and ought, we submit, to give place without delay to a policy of conciliation. What form this should take we do not presume to say. Various possibilities seem to be open. What the situation in our judgement requires is that the Government should take the initiative, and with resolute magnanimity pursue such a course, by the blessing of Heaven, to the end.

The Times, 6 April 1921

122 George V: 'May this historic gathering be the prelude...'

As these clergymen suggested, a more conciliatory security policy on the part of the British Government could only hope to be effective if combined with some sort of political initiative. The official opening of the Northern Ireland Parliament, on 22 June 1921, provided such an opportunity. Now that political security for the Unionist community in the North was at least provisionally established, the British Coalition Government could more readily countenance negotiations with Sinn Féin and the IRA without risking overthrow at the hands of the die-hards and the politically-discontented on their own back benches. The South African premier and influential Commonwealth leader, General J C Smuts, drafted a speech for King George V to deliver at the opening of the Northern Parliament, which set in train events in the South leading to truce and Treaty.

... This is a great and critical occasion in the history of the Six Counties, but not for the Six Counties alone, for everything which interests them touches Ireland, and everything which touches Ireland finds an echo in the remotest parts of the Empire ...

I am confident that the important matters entrusted to the control and guidance of the Northern Parliament will be managed with wisdom and with moderation, with fairness and due regard to every faith and interest, and with no abatement of that patriotic devotion to the Empire which you proved so gallantly in the Great War ...

My hope is broader still. The eyes of the whole Empire are on Ireland today – that Empire in which so many nations and races have come together in spite of ancient feuds, and in which new nations have come to birth within the lifetime of the youngest in this Hall. I am emboldened by that thought to look beyond the sorrows and the anxiety which have clouded of late My vision of Irish affairs. I speak from a full heart when I pray that My coming to Ireland today may prove to be the first step towards an end of strife amongst her people, whatever their race or creed.

In that hope I appeal to all Irishmen to pause, to stretch out the hand of forbearance and conciliation, to forgive and forget, and to join in making for the land which they love a new era of peace, contentment and good will. It is My earnest desire that in Southern Ireland too there may ere long take place a parallel to what is now passing in this Hall; that there a similar occasion may present itself and a similar ceremony be performed.

For this the Parliament of the United Kingdom has in the fullest measure provided the powers; for this the Parliament of Ulster is pointing the way. The future lies in the hands of My Irish people themselves. May this historic gathering be the prelude of a day in which the Irish people, North and South, under one parliament or two, as those Parliaments may themselves decide, shall work together in common love for Ireland upon the sure foundation of mutual justice and respect.

The Times, 23 June 1921

123 Truce at last, 11 July 1921

Three days after the King's speech Lloyd George, working through the Dublin Castle civil servant A W Cope, invited de Valera to a conference in London, 'in the spirit of conciliation for which His Majesty appealed'. De Valera insisted on a military truce as a precondition to political negotiations and, after further interventions by Smuts and by the southern Unionist Lord Midleton, a truce was agreed between British Armed Forces and the IRA. Signed on 9 July 1921, it came into force on 11 July.

On behalf of the British Army it is agreed as follows:

1. No incoming troops, RIC, and Auxiliary Police and munitions, and no movements for military purposes of troops and munitions, except maintenance drafts.

2. No provocative displays of force, armed or unarmed.

3. It is understood that all provisions of this truce apply to the martial law area equally with the rest of Ireland.

4. No pursuit of Irish officers or men [ie IRA] or war material or military stores.

5. No secret agents noting description or movements, and no interference with the movements of Irish persons, military or civil, and no attempts to discover the haunts or habits of Irish officers and men.

   Note: This supposes the abandonment of curfew restrictions.

6. No pursuit or observance of lines of communication or connection.

   Note: There are other details connected with courts martial, motor permits, and ROIR [emergency legislation] to be agreed later.

On behalf of the Irish Army it is agreed that:

(a) Attacks on Crown forces and civilians are to cease.

(b) No provocative displays of forces, armed or unarmed.

(c) No interference with Government or private property.

(d) To discountenance and prevent any action likely to cause disturbance of the pact which might necessitate military interference.

D Macardle, *The Irish Republic*
(London: Gollancz, 1937; 4th edn, Dublin,
Irish Press, 1951), pp 475-76

Chapter 10

The Anglo-Irish Treaty

124 *'Neither side accepts the position of the other '*

Following the Truce, de Valera had several meetings with Lloyd George in England. These were followed by an exchange of thirteen letters and telegrams over a period of ten weeks, in which the framework for a peace conference was established. With hindsight we may be tempted to dismiss all this as verbal shadow-boxing. But many peace conferences are delayed by pre-negotiations of this type, 'talks about talks' – for instance the 'shape of the table' discussions in Vietnam in 1975. It is always important for each side not to give ground inadvertently before its representatives enter the conference chamber. For much of this period Lloyd George was at Gairloch, in the northern highlands of Scotland and, bizarrely, the original intention had been for the peace conference to take place in Inverness Town Hall. By the time preliminary agreement was reached, however, the summer was over and the conference venue became London. Lloyd George was therefore unable to bring the Sinn Féin leaders to a Catholic and Gaelic-speaking region of Britain – although throughout the period of the conference he would take opportunities of conferring privately in Welsh with his political secretary Tom Jones.

(a) Lloyd George to De Valera   Gairloch, 18 September 1921

> I have received your telegram of last night, and observe that it does not modify the claim that your delegates should meet us as the representatives of a sovereign and independent state. You made no such condition in advance when you came to see me in July. I invited you then to meet me, in the words of my letter, as 'the chosen leader of the great majority in Southern Ireland', and your accepted that invitation. From the very outset of our conversations I told you that we looked to Ireland to own allegiance to the throne, and to make her future as a member of the British Commonwealth. That was the basis of our proposals, and we cannot alter it. The status which you claim in advance for your delegates is in effect a repudiation of that basis ... I must therefore repeat that unless the second paragraph in your letter of 12 September is withdrawn, conference between us is impossible.

(b) De Valera to Lloyd George   Dublin, 19 September 1921

> We have had no thought at any time of asking you to accept any

conditions precedent to a conference. We would have thought it as unreasonable to expect you as a preliminary to recognise the Irish Republic formally or informally as that you should expect us formally or informally to surrender our national position. It is precisely because neither side accepts the position of the other that there is a dispute at all, and that a conference is necessary to search for and discuss such adjustments as might compose it ...

(c) Lloyd George to De Valera   Gairloch, 29 September 1921

His Majesty's Government have given close and earnest consideration to the correspondence which has passed between us since their invitation to you to send delegates to a conference at Inverness. In spite of their sincere desire for peace and in spite of the more conciliatory tone of your last communication, they cannot enter a conference on the basis of this correspondence. Notwithstanding your personal assurance to the contrary, which they much appreciate, it might be argued in future that the acceptance of a conference on this basis had involved them in a recognition which no British Government can accord. On this point they must guard themselves against any possible doubt. There is no purpose to be served by any further interchange of explanatory and argumentative communications upon this subject. The position taken up by His Majesty's Government is fundamental to the existence of the British Empire, and they cannot alter it. My colleagues and I remain, however, keenly anxious to make, in cooperation with your delegates, another determined effort to explore every possibility of settlement by personal discussion. The proposals which we have already made have been taken by the whole world as proof that our endeavours for reconciliation and settlement are no empty form; and we feel that conference, not correspondence, is the most practical and hopeful way to an understanding such as we ardently desire to achieve. *We therefore send herewith a fresh invitation to a conference in London on 11 October, where we can meet your delegates and spokesmen of the people whom you represent, with a view to ascertaining how the association of Ireland with the community of nations known as the British Empire may best be reconciled with Irish national aspirations* [editor's italics].

(d) De Valera to Lloyd George   Dublin 30 September 1921

We have received your letter of invitation to a conference in London on 11 October, 'with a view to ascertaining how the association of Ireland with the community of nations known as the British Empire may best be reconciled with Irish national aspirations'.

Our respective positions have been stated and are understood, and we agree that conference, not correspondence, is the most practical and hopeful way to an understanding. We accept the invitation and our delegates will meet you in London on the date mentioned 'to explore every possibility of settlement by personal discussion'.

BPP: *Correspondence Relating to the Proposals of His Majesty's Government for an Irish Settlement 1921* [Cmd 1502], pp 10-11

125   Not shirking duty, but keeping the symbol untouched

One of several surprising features of the period surrounding the peace conference and treaty is the fact that De Valera chose not to take part in the talks. Although the British team of seven was led by the Prime Minister, Lloyd George, the man who was in the Sinn Féin view 'President of the Irish Republic' and head of state did not participate. The Irish team of five negotiators, appointed by the Dáil cabinet, was led by Vice-President Arthur Griffith, supported by IRA leader Michael Collins, the legal experts George Gavan Duffy and Eamonn Duggan, and the Anglo-Irish landowner, former British Army officer and now Sinn Féin politician, Robert Barton. De Valera's decision not to attend was confirmed in the private session of the Dáil on 14 September. He later gave his private view of these events to the leading American sponsor of Irish revolution, the Tyrone-born Philadelphia businessman Joe McGarrity (1874-1940).

(a) MR W.T.COSGRAVE: ... He [de Valera] had an extraordinary experience in negotiations. He also had the advantage of being in touch already. The head of the state in England was Mr Lloyd George and he expected he [De Valera] would be one of the plenipotentiaries ... They were sending over a team and they were keeping their ablest player in reserve ... The reserve would have to be used sometime and it struck him now was the time they were required ...

PRESIDENT DE VALERA: ... He [de Valera] really believed it was vital at this stage that the symbol of the Republic should be kept untouched and that it should not be compromised in any sense by any arrangements which it might be necessary for our plenipotentiaries to make. He was sure the Dáil realised the task they were giving to them – to win for them what a mighty army and navy might not be able to win for them. It was not a shirking of duty, but he realised the position and how necessary it was to keep the Head of State and the symbol untouched and that was why he asked to be left out.

Dáil Éireann, Private Session, 14 September 1921

(b) De Valera to Joseph McGarrity   21 December 1921

Through my conversations there with Lloyd George, I gathered that an offer of some form of Dominion Home Rule would be made, and I became convinced that if Ireland were willing to go within the Empire she could, by holding out, easily secure, on paper at least, the same nominal status and degree of liberty that Canada and Australia enjoy, except as regards Ulster and naval defence. On both these grounds Lloyd George would be afraid to give way on account of the political opposition his doing so would arouse in England. With such an offer, and no alternative before them except that of continuing the war for the maintenance of the Republic, I felt certain that the majority of the people would be weaned from us.

... On my return from London, when it became necessary to send a written reply to the British proposals, I proposed another way out – external association of Ireland with the group of free nations in the British Empire ... In entering such an association Ireland would be doing nothing incompatible with her declared independence ... This proposal in its main outline was accepted by the [Dáil] Cabinet and the whole Ministry (about 15 members were present when I made it) and I set out with the fixed determination of making peace on that basis. Lest I might in any way compromise the position of the Republic, and in order that I might be in a position to meet any tricks of Lloyd George, I remained at home myself, but the plenipotentiaries had agreed with my view, had had their instructions and even a preliminary draft treaty to guide them.

S Cronin, *The McGarrity Papers*
(Tralee: Anvil Books, 1972), pp 105–106

126 *De Valera and the Pope: Ambiguities in the name of the King*

The peace conference finally got under way on 11 October 1921. Within days the fragile negotiations were rocked by what seemed a fairly gratuitous exchange of telegrams. Pope Benedict XV and King George V exchanged general telegrams of encouragement, which de Valera regarded as a provocation. He objected, he later told Griffith, to the fact that 'the Vatican' had addressed King George V as if he were 'the common father of both disputant nations'. The Irish delegates privately regarded this as an unhelpful intervention; the London *Times* newspaper on 21 October described it as 'an act of impertinence' towards the Pope, and 'unmannerly to the point of churlishness' towards the King.

(a) Pope Benedict XV to King George V

We rejoice at the resumption of the Anglo-Irish negotiations and pray to the Lord with all our heart that He may bless them and grant to Your Majesty the great joy and imperishable glory of bringing to an end the agelong dissension.

(b) George V to Pope Benedict

I have received the message of your Holiness with much pleasure and with all my heart I join in your prayer that the Conference ... may achieve a permanent settlement of the troubles in Ireland, and may initiate a new era of peace and happiness for my people.

(c) President de Valera to Pope Benedict

The people of Ireland have read the message sent by your Holiness to the King of Great Britain, and appreciate the kindly interest in their welfare and the paternal regard which suggested it. I tender ... gratitude. They are confident that the ambiguities in the reply sent in the name of King George will not mislead you into believing that the troubles are in Ireland, or that the people of Ireland owe allegiance to the British King. The independence of Ireland has been formally proclaimed ... The trouble is between England and Ireland and its source that the rulers of Britain have endeavoured to impose their will on Ireland. We long to be at peace and in friendship with the people of Britain, as with other peoples; but the same constancy through persecution and martyrdom that has proved the reality of our people's attachment to the Faith of their Fathers proves the reality of their attachment to their national freedom and no consideration will ever induce them to abandon it.

F Pakenham, *Peace by Ordeal*
(London: Sidgwick & Jackson, 1972) pp 136-7

127 Lloyd George: Not the first time Britain has treated with rebels

Since the general election result of December 1918, Lloyd George's Coalition Government had become much more heavily dependent on Conservative support in Parliament. Between 1919 and 1922, ambitious backbench Conservatives became increasingly restive as they sought a political issue which they could exploit so as to weaken Lloyd George sufficiently to bring down the Coalition which their votes were maintaining in power This was why Lloyd George could not agree to the Sinn Féin demand for an Irish Republic outside the Empire. But subject to this constraint, Lloyd George was able both to retain the support of the Ulster Unionists and to prevent his backbench opponents from using either 'the Empire' or 'Ulster' as issues over which to topple him. On 31 October 1921 his Government defeated by 439 votes to 43 a censure motion brought by Tory die-hards opposed to negotiations with Sinn Féin.

(a) CAPTAIN CHARLES CRAIG [leader-designate of the Ulster Unionist Parliamentary Party]: It is almost a year since the Government of Ireland Act was passed and, as I said, all the preliminary steps have been taken towards setting up a government [of Northern Ireland] but without the powers I have referred to the House will realise that the Government [of Northern Ireland] is absolutely impotent ...

Therefore I make a very earnest appeal to the Prime Minister that he should hand over these powers to the Ulster Parliament at the earliest possible moment. The present position is utterly intolerable. I have no doubt that these powers, as I have said, would have been put into our hands long ago had it not been for the Conference [ie the Treaty negotiations]. I do not know what the Government's defence is for the delay which has taken place in these transfers. I think they will tell us that to give us these powers will require action under the Government of Ireland Act which would have the effect of irritating the Sinn Féiners and might in some way or other either jeopardise or prejudice the chances of agreement at the Conference ...

We do not propose to discuss further than I have done the merits or demerits of the Conference. The Ulster Government has from the very beginning taken up the position that this was a matter which did not vitally concern them. We have got our parliament ... Let me say to the many Hon. Friends who are about to support and vote for this Resolution that we have decided to take no part in the division, provided always, as we have every hope may be the case, we get a satisfactory answer from the Government with reference to the transfer of these powers ...

H C Deb 5th series, vol 147, cols 1389-93 (31 October 1921)

(b) THE PRIME MINISTER (Mr Lloyd George): My Hon. Friend has asked me a specific question, and he is entitled to an answer. I propose to dispose of that before I come to the Motion ... My Hon. Friend knows perfectly well that those powers were to be conferred upon the two parliaments simultaneously. If the Southern parliament did not come into existence, there was something in the nature of Crown Colony government to be set up ... Peace negotiations were interposed. We did not deem it advisable to set up Crown Colony government until we knew how these negotiations would eventuate. But I can quite see that that is paralysing the domestic activities of the Ulster Government, and therefore I will give my friend this pledge ...

Now I come to the Motion, which divides itself into two parts. The first is ... an expression of grave apprehension that the Government should have entered into negotiations ... with men who at the same time were engaged in a conspiracy against the authority of the crown ... The second point is that those negotiations ought to have been preceded by the sanction of Parliament to the actual proposals made inside the Conference ...

No pact entered into in the course of these negotiations can come into effect without the authority of Parliament. Every detail will have to be submitted to Parliament ... If you enter into negotiations, you must have some latitude ... Otherwise there is no use in having a conference ... There was the Act of Parliament of 1920. That was not a conference ... it was Parliament making a proposal. That did not accomplish its purpose. I was always in favour of a conference, if I could get it ...

I have repeatedly at this box stated ... that the Government were prepared to meet in discussion any representatives of the Irish people who could – I used the phrase – 'deliver the goods', that is, who were in a position to make good a bargain when it was made ... . The House of Commons must either trust its negotiators or replace them ...

It is not the first time that Britain has treated with rebels and it is not the first time that Britain has treated with rebels with good effects for the Empire. The point for the House of Commons to decided is not whether you are going to treat with rebels ... but whether you are going to enter into a conference at all ... or whether you are going to say that, first of all, you will crush the rebellion, and then deal with Ireland ...

Unless it be absolutely necessary for the honour and security of this country, this is not the time to come to the House of Commons and ask it to impose great additional burdens upon the taxpayers or ... to invite young men once more to risk their lives ... But I cannot conceal from the House the possibility that I may have to make the grim announcement that it is impossible to settle without danger or dishonour ...

H C Deb 5th series, vol 147, cols 1314–20
(31 October 1921)

128 The Treaty negotiations: One possible way out?

The conference continued in London from mid-October to early December 1921. The Irish delegates were supported by a large administrative team, and made several trips back to Dublin for discussions with the Dáil cabinet. But detailed discussions between individuals and sub-groups, and within the two teams, as well as full plenary sessions of the conference, took place in London through the two-month period. Tom Jones (1870-1955) deputy secretary to the British cabinet, was at the centre of events throughout the conference, and his extensive *Diaries* are our main source for what went on behind the scenes during these vital weeks.

(a) *Private Meeting of British Team, 25 October 1921.* Austen Chamberlain ... [reported that the Irish delegates said] they would give her [Ulster] all existing powers and possibly more on condition she accepted position of a provincial legislature and came into the central Dublin parliament ... They said they would not allow homogeneous Catholic districts which did not wish it to remain under an Ulster parliament. Chamberlain asked if it would be easier for them to accept the six counties, if that area came under a Dublin parliament? They said no.

They asked as they left, 'Why would we not allow county option?' Chamberlain said they could not put a more difficult question. Griffith said they could not recommend allegiance to the King unless they got the unity of Ireland ...

Winston Churchill [said that] 'We can't give way on six counties; we are not free agents; we can do our best to include six in a larger parliament plus autonomy. We could press Ulster to hold autonomy for six from them instead of from us.

[Lord] Birkenhead: 'I rather agree with Winston; our position re six counties is an impossible one if these men [Sinn Féin delegation] want to settle, as they do'.

Winston: 'I don't see how Ulster is damnified: she gets her own protection, and an effective share in the southern parliament and protection for the southern Unionists'.

(b) *7 November 1921.* ... From 5.0 to about 6.20 [Sir James] Craig was with the Prime Minister. About 6.30 the PM sent for me and I had about half an hour with him alone during which time he paced up and down the Cabinet room, more depressed than I had seen him at all since the negotiations began. He said – 'Craig will not budge one inch ... This means ... a break on Thursday'.

... He then said – 'There is just one other possible way out. I want to find out from Griffith and Collins if they will support me on it; namely that the 26 counties should take their own dominion parliament and have a boundary commission, that Ulster should have her present powers plus representation in the imperial parliament plus the burdens of taxation which we bear. I might be able to put that through if Sinn Féin will take it. Find out'.

(c) *8 November 1921.*   ... Griffith urged that the PM should stand up to Craig & co, that their rejection was a giant piece of bluff ... I assured them that the PM would put up the strongest possible battle but that we were bound to contemplate his failure ... I pointed out that if the PM resigned it was impossible to foretell the course of events ... There might be no general election immediately; if, for example, Bonar Law formed a new government he would be supported by the big Unionist majority in the House. It was in my opinion all important to try to keep the PM at the helm ...

(d) *9 November 1921.* I told him [Griffith] that the PM was prepared to play the boundary commission as an absolutely last card if he could feel sure that Sinn Féin would take it, if Ulster accepted. Griffith replied ... 'We would prefer a plebiscite, but in essential a boundary commission is very much the same. It would have to be not for Tyrone and Fermanagh only but for the six counties.' ...

About 5.45 I saw the PM alone. He was perfectly satisfied with what I reported but pointed out that the boundary commission would be for the nine counties ...

Tom Jones, *Whitehall Diary, vol. 3: Ireland, 1918-25* (London: Oxford University Press, 1971), pp 146, 154-7

(e) *Note drafted by Tom Jones, approved by Griffith on 13 November 1921.* If Ulster did not see her way to accept immediately the principle of a parliament for all Ireland, coupled with the retention by the Parliament of Northern Ireland of the powers conferred upon it by the Act of 1920 and such other safeguards as have already been suggested ... we should then propose to create such parliament for all Ireland, but to allow Ulster the right within a specified time ... to elect to remain subject to the Imperial Parliament for all reserved services. In this case she would continue to exercise through her own Parliament all her present rights; she would continue to be represented in the British Parliament, and she would continue subject to

British taxation ... In this case however, it would be necessary to revise the boundary of Northern Ireland. This might be done by a boundary commission which would be directed to adjust the line both by inclusion and exclusion so as to make the boundary conform as closely as possible to the wishes of the population.

F Pakenham, *Peace by Ordeal* (London: Jonathan Cape. 1935; Sidgwick & Jackson, 1972), pp 177-178

(f) *Jones to Lloyd George, 5 December 1921.* I saw Arthur Griffith at midnight for an hour alone. He was labouring under a deep sense of the crisis and spoke throughout with the greatest earnestness and unusual emotion. One was bound to feel that to break with him would be infinitely tragic. Briefly his case was −

1. That he and Collins had been completely won over to belief in your desire for peace and recognised that you had gone far in your efforts to secure it.

2. This belief was not shared by their Dublin colleagues and they had failed to bring them all the way, but were convinced they could be brought further. In Dublin there is still much distrust and fear that if the 'Treaty' is signed they will be 'sold'.

3. They are told that they have surrendered too much ('the King' and 'association') and got nothing to offer the Dáil in return. Cannot you − and this was the burden of his appeal − get from Craig a conditional recognition, however shadowy, of Irish national unity in return for the acceptance of the Empire by Sinn Féin ? Will he [Craig] not write you a personal letter, as AG did, saying Ulster will recognise Unity if the south accepts the Commonwealth? Then the south will give all the safeguards you want for the north and will not ask for the boundary commission − a most difficult thing to give up ...

4. Without something to offer the Dáil on these lines AG and MC could not carry more than about one-half of them ...

(g) *Sir James Craig to Austen Chamberlain 15 December 1921.* ... I think it only proper ... to give the most solemn warning regarding the situation created by the signing of the Treaty between the British and Sinn Féin representatives. I could, I believe, have carried the people of Ulster with me towards a peaceful settlement, had it not been for the inclusion in the terms of a proposal to set up a boundary commission ... I understood that when Ulster's interests were touched upon my colleagues and I would be invited to take part in a conference once an all-Ireland parliament was turned down and got out of the way ...

... So intense is local feeling at the moment that my colleagues and I may be swept off our feet, and contemporaneously with the functioning of the Treaty, Loyalists may declare independence on their own behalf, seize the Customs and other government departments and set up an authority of their own. Many already believe that violence is the only language understood by Mr Lloyd George and his ministers ...

T Jones, *Whitehall Diary vol 3: Ireland 1918-25* (London: Oxford University Press, 1971), pp 160, 189-90

129 The Anglo-Irish Treaty, 6 December 1921

At last, during the small hours of 5-6 December, the two delegations signed 'Articles of Agreement for a Treaty between Great Britain and Ireland'. Southern Ireland, the 26-county area, was to have full dominion status, rather than the limited devolution of the 1920 Act. If the Parliament of Northern Ireland opted to keep the six counties out of the new scheme, as it undoubtedly would, then Article 12 provided for a boundary commission with powers to modify the partition line – although to what extent was left undefined. A clinching factor in bringing about the settlement had been Lloyd George's last-minute reminder to Griffith of his earlier agreement (Document 128e) to settle the Ulster issue by means of a boundary commission. Griffith therefore committed himself to signing the Treaty, and his colleagues one by one followed suit.

1. Ireland shall have the same constitutional status in the community of nations known as the British Empire as the Dominion of Canada, the Commonwealth of Australia, the Dominion of New Zealand, and the Union of South Africa, with a parliament having powers to make laws for the peace and good government of Ireland and an executive responsible to that parliament, and shall be styled and known as the Irish Free State.

2. Subject to the provisions hereinafter set out the position of the Irish Free State in relation to the imperial parliament and government and otherwise shall be that of the Dominion of Canada ...

4. The oath to be taken by members of the parliament of the Irish Free State shall be in the following form: I ... do solemnly swear true faith and allegiance to the constitution of the Irish Free State as by law established and that I will be faithful to HM King George V, his heirs and successors by law in virtue of the common citizenship of Ireland with Great Britain and her adherence to and membership of the group of nations forming the British Commonwealth of nations.

5. The Irish Free State shall assume liability for the service of the public debt of the United Kingdom as existing at the date hereof and towards the payment of war pensions as existing at that date in such proportion as may be fair and equitable, having regard to any just claims on the part of Ireland by way of set off or counter-claim ...

7. The government of the Irish Free State shall afford to His Majesty's imperial forces:

(a) in time of peace such harbour and other facilities as are indicated in the annex hereto, or such other facilities as may from time to time be agreed between the British Government and the government of the Irish Free State; and

(b) in time of war or of strained relations with a foreign power such harbour and other facilities as the British Government may require for the purposes of such defence as aforesaid ...

11. Until the expiration of one month from the passing of the act of parliament for the ratification of this instrument, the powers of the parliament and the government of the Irish Free State shall not be exercisable as respects Northern Ireland, and the provisions of the Government of Ireland Act, 1920, shall, so far as they relate to Northern Ireland, remain of full force and effect, and no election shall be held for the return of members to serve in the parliament of the Irish Free State for constituencies in Northern Ireland, unless a resolution is passed by both houses of the Parliament of Northern Ireland in favour of the holding of such elections before the end of the said month.

12. If before the expiration of the said month, an address is presented to His Majesty by both houses of Parliament of Northern Ireland to that effect, the powers of the Parliament and Government of the Irish Free State shall no longer extend to Northern Ireland, and the provisions of the Government of Ireland Act, 1920 (including those relating to the Council of Ireland), shall so far as they relation to Northern Ireland, continue to be of full force and effect, and this instrument shall have effect subject to the necessary modifications.

Provided that if such an address is so presented a commission consisting of three persons, one to be appointed by the Government of the Irish Free State, one to be appointed by the Government of Northern Ireland, and one who shall be chairman to be appointed by the British Government shall determine in accordance with the wishes of the inhabitants, so far as may be compatible with economic and geographic conditions, the boundaries between Northern Ireland and the rest of Ireland, and for the purposes of the Government of Ireland Act, 1920, and of this instrument, the boundary of Northern Ireland shall be such as may be determined by such commission ...

17. By way of provisional arrangement for the administration of Southern Ireland during the interval which must elapse between the date hereof and the constitution of a parliament and government in accordance therewith, steps shall be taken forthwith for summoning a meeting of members of parliament elected for constituencies in Southern Ireland since the passing of the Government of Ireland Act, 1920, and for constituting a provisional government, and the British Government shall take the steps necessary to transfer to such provisional government the powers and machinery requisite for the discharge of its duties, provided that every member of such provisional government shall have signified in writing his or her acceptance of this instrument. But this arrangement shall not continue in force beyond the expiration of twelve months from the date hereof.

18. This instrument shall be submitted forthwith by His Majesty's Government for the approval of Parliament and by the Irish signatories to a meeting summoned for the purpose of the members elected to sit in the House of Commons of Southern Ireland ...

Articles of Agreement for a Treaty between
Great Britain and Ireland [Cmd 1560], 1921

130 The Conservatives and the Treaty: Convincing the medievalists

As we have seen (Document 127), the Coalition leaders trounced a die-hard revolt in the House of Commons soon after the commencement of the Treaty negotiations in October 1921. Even more important was the work of Tory Coalitionists Austen Chamberlain and Lord Birkenhead in persuading the Conservative Party Conference at Liverpool on 17 November to give a resounding endorsement to the negotiations. Lloyd George was of course delighted at this outcome, although he interpreted it as a sign of weakness on the part of Tory leader Bonar Law, who had left the Government some months before. In fact Law's health was deteriorating, and he was dead within two years. Law resisted all temptations to break with his former Coalition colleagues on the question of Ireland, though he was briefly Conservative prime minister in 1922-23 after helping to bring down the Coalition on a separate issue.

Sir Edward Carson, on the other hand, who was in private always a man of more flexible views on Ireland that his public persona suggested, was less cooperative, and denounced the settlement fiercely in his maiden speech in the House of Lords, an occasion which, custom dictated, called for a non-controversial speech. Birkenhead's cabinet colleague Lord Curzon wrote to him that Carson's speech was 'an outrage on every convention of the house and on decency, the speech of a prosecuting counsel at the Old Bailey'. The Government nonetheless won overwhelming parliamentary ratification for the Treaty, by 401 votes to 58 in the Commons and 119 to 47 in the Lords.

(a) Tom Jones' *Diary,*   17 November 1921

I dined at Hampstead and at 9.0 p.m. met the P[rime] M[inister] at Waterloo and told him the Liverpool figures [ie the overwhelming majority at the Conservative Party Conference in favour of continuing the Treaty negotiations with Sinn Féin]. I walked down the long platform with him and his first words were about Bonar Law and the unfriendly part he had played. He felt that Bonar had meant to make a bid for the leadership of the Conservatives and a break up of the Coalition. He reverted to the topic in No. 10 and said Bonar had not the necessary courage for supreme leadership. He missed his chance in 1916 for lack of courage and he had missed it again and it had passed to F.E.[Smith, Lord Birkenhead]. 'If you are going to lead a revolt you must go all out for it', said the PM, pacing up and down ...

T Jones, *Whitehall Diary vol 3: Ireland 1918-25*
(London: Oxford University Press,
1971), pp 167-8

(b) MR A. BONAR LAW: ... Many of them [the 'die-hards'] are intimate friends, and among them is one who, throughout the whole of my political life, has been most intimately associated with myself – Lord Carson. I do not think I have had more personal friendship with anyone with whom I have worked in political life. We differ now ... [but] I think it would be almost cowardly not to express my opinion.

... I am in favour of this Agreement ... I have noticed ... that there seems to be a bitter feeling growing up in Ulster on the ground that she has been betrayed. For what my opinion is worth, that would seem to me to be one of the most disastrous things that could happen ... I honestly think that that feeling is not justified by anything in this Agreement.

I will deal with one very serious objection to this Treaty. It has been urged by every speaker ... They say it is a surrender to a campaign of murder. I don't think it is, but if my right hon. friend the Prime Minister and his colleagues will allow me to say so, they are partly to blame for giving that impression ... The overwhelming mass of the people is in favour of this Agreement.

When I say I am in favour of this Agreement, I don't pretend to like it. I am sure the Government do not like it in many particulars. I don't pretend to like it, but I ask myself this: what is the alternative? Are we to go back to the condition of things which prevailed for the past year or two? Nobody would like that. We could do it ... but how much better off would we be? Throughout my whole life this Irish question has been a trouble to this country and to Ireland ... There is bound to be something like chaos in the South of Ireland for some time, but if they get a government which really tries to govern, then they perhaps have a better chance of restoring order than we would have.

H C Deb 5th series, vol 149 cols 196–209
(14 December 1921)

(c) LORD CARSON: ... If you tell your Empire in India, in Egypt and all over the world that you have not got the men, the money, the pluck, the inclination and the backing to restore order in a country within twenty miles of your own shore, you may as well begin to abandon the attempt to make British rule prevail through the Empire at all ...

... I did not know, as I know now, that I was a mere puppet player in a political game. I was in earnest, I was not playing politics. I believed all this. I thought of the last thirty years, during which I was fighting with others whose friendship and comradeship I hope I will lose from tonight, because I do not value any friendship that is not founded upon confidence and trust. I was in earnest. What a fool I was! I was only a puppet, and so was Ulster, and so was Ireland, in the political game that was to get the Conservative Party into power.

H L Deb, vol. 48 (14 December 1921)

(d) THE LORD CHANCELLOR (Lord Birkenhead): ... I say here perfectly plainly that I recede not by one iota from the position which I assumed throughout the whole of those old bitter controversies ... Lord Carson has publicly repelled and proscribed me from a friendship which had many memories for me, and which I deeply value ... I stood side by side with Lord Carson at grave and critical moments and neither he nor I knew what advice would be given to His Majesty's Government by those who were then [in 1912–14] the Law Officers of the Crown ...

It is perfectly true that we have changed our minds more than once in the last three years, and we may change them again. Our difficulties lie in attempting to convince the medievalists among us that the world has really undergone some very considerable modification in the last few years ... As for the speech of Lord Carson, his constructive effort at statecraft would be immature on the lips of a hysterical schoolgirl ... With the single exception of the Boundary Commission, those for whom the Noble Lord [Carson] stands will retain everything the [1920] Bill gave ...

Of one thing I am certain: that we have given a population which is overwhelmingly homogeneous the opportunity of taking their place side by side with the other communities in the British Empire. That is an immense moment in history. We believe there is a chance that this settlement will satisfy that sentiment of nationhood and if it does, year by year, the animosities that have poisoned our public life will disappear ...

Is your alternative any other than this, that we shall now resume the war, that we shall take and break this people, as we can with our military might take and break them? And when we have done that, how shall we be any better off? Shall we be nearer a settlement ... ?

H L Deb vol 48 (16 December 1921)

131 A Republican alternative: 'Document No 2'

The five Irish negotiators had signed the Treaty under threat of 'immediate and terrible war' by Lloyd George if they refused. They were not given an opportunity to return to Dublin for last-minute consultations, and they did not take advantage of the telephone for communication. The Treaty which they put before the Dáil for approval thus proclaimed neither a sovereign republic nor, with any degree of certainty, a united Ireland. De Valera found that the checks which he had built into the negotiating arrangements had been by-passed. He refused to be committed to so large a concession, and opposed the Treaty in the Dáil. But he had been aware since the summer truce that some degree of compromise would be necessary, and in the course of debate brought forward his alternative plan, known as 'Document No 2'. In its attempt to reconcile republicanism with the British Commonwealth, through the device of external association, it foreshadowed the arrangements which India and other new states were able to make in later years. Interestingly, it also accepted the basic Treaty position on Ulster. But de Valera already knew that such a formula would not be acceptable to the British Government, and in the circumstances the main function of Document No 2 was to provide the most conciliatory rallying-ground on which all the republican opponents of the Treaty could gather during the months of dispute that followed.

That inasmuch as the 'Articles of Agreement for a treaty between Great Britain and Ireland', signed in London on December 6th, 1921, do not reconcile Irish National aspirations and the Association of Ireland with the Community of Nations known as the British Commonwealth and cannot be the basis of an enduring peace between the Irish and the British peoples, Dáil Éireann, in the name of the Sovereign Irish Nation, makes to the Government of Great Britain, to the Governments of the other States of the British

Commonwealth, and to the peoples of Great Britain and of these several States, the following proposal for a Treaty of Amity and Association which, Dáil Éireann is convinced, could be entered into by the Irish people with the sincerity of goodwill ...

1. That the legislative, executive, and judicial authority of Ireland shall be derived solely from the people of Ireland.

2. That, for purposes of common concern, Ireland shall be associated with the States of the British Commonwealth, viz. The Kingdom of Great Britain, the Dominion of Canada, the Commonwealth of Australia, the Dominion of New Zealand, and the Union of South Africa.

3. That when acting as an associate the rights, status, and privileges of Ireland shall be in no respect less than those enjoyed by any of the component States of the British Commonwealth ...

6. That, for purposes of the Association, Ireland shall recognise His Britannic Majesty as head of the Association.

7. That, so far as her resources permit, Ireland shall provide for her own defence by sea, land and air, and shall repel by force any attempt by a foreign power to violate the integrity of her soil and territorial waters, or to use them for any purpose hostile to Great Britain and other associated States.

8. That for five years, pending the establishment of Irish coastal defence forces, or for such other period as the governments of the two countries may later agree upon, facilities for the coastal defence of Ireland shall be given to the British Government as follows:

(a) In time of peace such harbour and other facilities as are indicated in the Annex hereto, or such other facilities as may from time to time be agreed upon between the British Government and the Government of Ireland;

(b) In time of war such harbour and other naval facilities as the British Government may reasonably require for the purposes of such defence as aforesaid ...

13. That Ireland shall assume liability for such share of the present public debt of Great Britain and Ireland, and of payment of war pensions as existing at this date as may be fair and equitable, having regard to any just claims on the part of Ireland by way of set-off or counter-claim, the amount of such sums being determined in default of agreement, by the arbitration of one

or more independent persons, being citizens of Ireland or the British Commonwealth ...

16. That by way of transitional arrangement for the administration of Ireland during the interval which must elapse between the date hereof and the setting up of a Parliament and Government of Ireland in accordance herewith, the members elected for constituencies in Ireland, since the passing of the British Government of Ireland Act in 1920 shall, at a meeting summoned for the purpose, elect a transitional Government to which the British Government and Dáil Éireann shall transfer the authority, powers, and machinery requisite for the discharge of its duties, provided that every member of such transition government shall have signified in writing his or her acceptance of this instrument. But this arrangement shall not continue in force beyond the expiration of twelve months from the date hereof.

17. That this instrument shall be submitted for ratification forthwith by His Britannic Majesty's Government to the Parliament at Westminster, and by the Cabinet of Dáil Éireann to a meeting of the members elected for the constituencies in Ireland set forth in the British Government of Ireland Act, 1920, and when ratifications have been exchanged shall take immediate effect ...

ADDENDUM
NORTH-EAST ULSTER

Resolved:

That, whilst refusing to admit the right of any part of Ireland to be excluded from the supreme authority of the Parliament of Ireland, or that the relations between the Parliament of Ireland and any subordinate legislature in Ireland can be a matter for treaty with a government outside Ireland, nevertheless, in sincere regard for internal peace, and in order to make manifest our desire not to bring force or coercion to bear upon any substantial part of the province of Ulster, whose inhabitants may be unwilling to accept the national authority, we are prepared to grant to that portion of Ulster which is defined as Northern Ireland in the British Government of Ireland Act of 1920, privileges and safeguards not less substantial than those provided for in the Articles of Agreement for a Treaty between Great Britain and Ireland signed in London on December 6th, 1921.

The Times, 5 January 1922

132 Cathal Brugha: A draught of poison

Cathal Brugha, *angl.* Charles Burgess (1874-1922), was, like Patrick Pearse, of partly

English origin. As Minister of Defence in the revolutionary Dáil, he came into frequent contact with Michael Collins, the effective leader of the IRA, and was said to be very jealous of him. Brugha was an irreconcilable republican, who was to die a few months later in a gun-battle with Free State forces. His contribution to the debate on the Treaty illustrates both the attitude of the extreme republican group towards distinctions which others saw primarily as questions of terminology, and the way in which Document No 2 held the opponents of the Treaty together.

Now Mr Griffith has referred to the difference between this Treaty of his and the alternative that we have as being only a quibble; and yet the English government is going to make war, as they say they will, for a quibble. The difference is, to me, the difference that there is between a draught of water and a draught of poison. If I were to accept this Treaty and if I did not do my best to have it defeated I would, in my view, be committing national suicide; I would be breaking the national tradition that has been handed down to us through the centuries. We would be doing for the first time a thing that no generation thought of doing before – wilfully, voluntarily admitting ourselves to be British subjects, and taking the oath of allegiance voluntarily to an English king.

We are prepared to enter into an agreement, an association with the British Commonwealth of Nations as it is usually called, on the same or similar lines as that on which one business firm enters into association with another, or several others ...   Now, by entry into a combination, no firm sacrifices its independence as a firm. We are prepared, on the same terms, to enter into an association with the British Commonwealth of Nations, and for the purpose of that combination we are prepared to recognise the English government as the head of the combination ...   Now by entering into such arrangements we are not going into the British Empire; neither do we take any oath whatsoever; and there will be no representative of the British crown in the shape of a governor-general in Ireland. We are entering into that arrangement, into this association, as external associates ...

Dáil Éireann, Treaty Debates, pp 325-34 (7 January 1922)

133   Michael Collins: Find a better way

Collins's defence of the Boundary Commission idea demonstrated the essential ambiguity which lay behind the seeming flexibility of the approach: on the one hand the Protestant north would not be coerced; on the other hand the apparent plight of northern Catholics should give no cause for long-term concern because the Boundary Commission would shortly secure the unity of the country.

We have stated we would not coerce the Northeast. We have stated it officially in our correspondence. I stated it publicly in Armagh and nobody has found fault with it. What did we mean? Did we mean we were going to coerce them or we were not going to coerce them? What was the use of talking big phrases about not agreeing to the partition of our country. Surely we recognise that the Northeast corner does exist, and surely our intention was that we should take such steps as would sooner or later lead to mutual understanding. The Treaty has made an effort to deal with it, and has made an effort, in my opinion, to deal with it on lines that will lead very rapidly to goodwill and the entry of the Northeast under the Irish parliament (applause). I don't say it is an ideal arrangement, but if our policy is, as has been stated, a policy of non-coercion, then let somebody else get a better way out of it ...

Dáil Éireann, Treaty Debates, p 35 (19 December 1921)

134 Nationalist reaction to the Treaty: An unparalleled opportunity

There were strong grounds for believing that the majority of grass-roots Irish nationalist opinion in the south of Ireland was ready for peace, and was far less unhappy with the Treaty provisions than many members of the Dáil. Press editorials, declarations of public bodies, and a statement by the Catholic hierarchy all pointed in this direction. Even the Northern Catholic community's sole daily newspaper, controlled by Devlin and the moderate home rulers, came out strongly for a settlement that offered Northern nationalists no more than the promise of a boundary commission.

The accredited exponent of the views held by the Cabinet of 'Northern' Ireland said to a group of pressmen on Tuesday that much would depend on 'the spirit' in which it is intended to work the ... Treaty ... Really there is not a sane man or woman in Ireland who doubts for a moment that a vast majority of the Irish people are not merely willing but intensely anxious to 'work' this Agreement rationally and thoroughly, in the completest possible association and harmony with Great Britain and their own countrymen ... Of course, there are many people in Ireland whose judgements on certain issues have become so warped, twisted and deformed that they may fairly be regarded as politically and sectarianly insane ...

Ireland as a whole has welcomed the Agreement with the spirit of hope and goodwill. The country does not – nor can it afford to – forget past bitter disappointments and shameful betrayals; it realises keenly that a signed agreement is not a ratified treaty ready for use as an instrument of national progress and international amity; that many traps and snares must be avoided, many obstacles surmounted or removed, and many dangers faced and averted or overcome by peoples and statesmen before the final goal is reached. Therefore Ireland's enthusiasm is tempered by caution, even though it is inspired and strengthened by resolute determination.

... Let us hope that none of these perils will originate in Ireland or amongst Irishmen. An unparalleled opportunity for bringing an unexampled struggle to a satisfactory end is presented to all concerned ... As proof of the Government's earnestness as well as for the sake of justice, of peace in Ireland, and of the wronged men themselves, we welcome the announcement that the political prisoners 'interned' without charge or trial will be promptly released ...

Irish News, 8 December 1921

135 Sean MacEntee: Partition perpetuated

Most of the opposition to the Treaty in Dáil Éireann, like that of de Valera and Brugha, focused on the question of sovereignty. The only critic to place his emphasis elsewhere, on the Ulster question, was Sean MacEntee (1889-1984) himself a Belfast man, although his later life and ministerial career were to be in southern politics.

I am opposed to this Treaty because it gives away our allegiance and perpetuates partition. By that very fact that it perpetuates our slavery; by the fact that it perpetuates partition it must fail utterly to do what it is ostensibly intended to do – reconcile the aspirations of the Irish people to association with the British Empire. When did the achievement of our nation's unification cease to be one of our national aspirations?

MR MILROY: I desire to ask this Deputy if he is prepared to coerce all these northern counties to come in?

MR MacENTEE: I am not responsible for policy in this Dáil. If I were I might be prepared to lay a programme before you, but until I am sitting with a Government of the Republic it is not open to any man to ask me what I would do in such a case ... Mr Milroy stated that the economic advantages of the case in connection with the six counties were such that, sooner or later, they would be compelled to resume association with the rest of Ireland. Does Mr Milroy ... tell me that material or economic facts are the determining factors in nationality? Would he have said that when we were asking the people of Ireland to risk their economical welfare on the question of nationality three years ago? Ah! He would not, and if I had said that to him he would have regarded it as insulting. I say there is more in nationality and history than mere materialism; and I say because there are more than these things in history and nationality, this Treaty is the most dangerous and diabolical onslaught that has ever been made upon the unity of our nation, because, Sir, by the very effort in it we are going to be destructive of our own nationality ...

... the provisions of this Treaty mean this: that in the North of Ireland certain people differing from us somewhat in tradition, and differing in religion, which are very vital elements in nationality, are going to be driven, in order to maintain their separate identity, to demarcate themselves from us, while we, in order to preserve ourselves against the encroachment of English culture, are going to be driven to demarcate ourselves so far as ever we can from them. I heard something about the control of education. Will any of the Deputies who stand for it tell me what control they are going to exercise over the education of the republican minority in the North of Ireland? They will be driven to make English, as it is, the sole vehicle of common speech and communication in their territory, while we will be striving to make Gaelic the sole vehicle of common speech in our territory. And yet you tell me that, considering these factors, this is not a partition provision. Ah! Sir, it was a very subtle and ironic master-stroke of English policy to so fashion these instruments that, by trying to save ourselves under them, we should encompass our own destruction ...

The Minister for Finance [Michael Collins] referring again to the problem of secessionist Ulster, more or less washed his hands of the whole matter when he said: 'Well, after all, what are we to do with these people?' Well I am not responsible for policy, but of all the things I may have done, this one thing I would not do: I would not let them go. I would not traffic in my nation's independence without, at least, securing my nation's unity. I would not hand over my country as a protectorate to another country without, at least, securing the right to protect my countrymen.

Dáil Éireann, Treaty Debates, pp 152-8 (22 December 1921)

Chapter 11
The Irish Civil War

136 The Craig-Collins pact, 30 March 1922

Following the elections of May 1921 for the House of Commons of Northern Ireland, the Unionist Party began the development of a state machinery. By the end of the year it had assumed responsibility for law enforcement in the province and a new regular force, the Royal Ulster Constabulary, was in the process of formation. But the Treaty ended a patchy IRA truce in the North, while the inter-communal hostility between Catholics and Protestants – which had resulted in savage outbreaks of rioting and intimidation of Catholics from employment in 1920 – was an additional dimension to the northern problem. A large, armed Special Constabulary force, consisting of full-time 'A' men and part-time 'B' men, was formed by the Northern Government. This caused disquiet in some political circles in Britain, for its paramilitary nature appeared to conflict with the Northern Government's right to raise police but not military forces. Inevitably, since the purpose of the force was to defend the existence of the new state, its membership was exclusively Protestant and so, equally inevitably, it appeared to be a re-emergence of the old UVF of the previous decade, now with official sanction. Arguments that such arrangements made for peace by keeping the Protestant militants under disciplined control were countered by widespread Catholic allegations of misconduct by the Specials themselves.

For Collins and the new Provisional Government in the Free State, the situation was complicated. They had no wish to see the Northern state succeed and, struggling vainly to reconcile their anti-treaty IRA colleagues in the south, could scarcely be expected to give priority to squashing the northern IRA – and indeed evidence now suggests that Collins was covertly supporting it. On the other hand Protestant violence against Catholics in the north, often indiscriminate, exceeded the level of IRA activity, especially in Belfast during the early months of 1922. However much he might have expected the Boundary Commission to settle the long-term problems of northern Catholics, Collins could not disclaim all short-term responsibility for their safety. Equally it was imperative for Craig to show that his government could stabilise the north. He and Collins therefore came together in London on 30 March 1922, under the aegis of the British government, to sign a pact. It was intended only as a short-term measure, and was never effectively implemented, but it remains the only explicit attempt to implement 'minority protection' in Ulster prior to the 1970s.

Heads of agreement between the Provisional Government and Government of Northern Ireland:

1. Peace is today declared.

2. From today the two Governments undertake to cooperate in every way in their power with a view to the restoration of peaceful conditions in the unsettled areas.

3. The police in Belfast to be organised in general in accordance with the following conditions:

    (i) Special police in mixed districts to be composed half of Catholics and half of Protestants, special arrangements to be made where Catholics or Protestants are living in other districts. All Specials not required for this force to be withdrawn to their homes and their arms handed in.

    (ii) An Advisory Committee, composed of Catholics, to be set up to assist in the selection of Catholic recruits for the Special police.

    (iii) All police on duty, except the usual secret service, to be in uniform and officially numbered.

    (iv) All arms and ammunition issued to police to be deposited in barracks in charge of a military or other competent officer when the policeman is not on duty, and an official record to be kept of all arms issued, and of all ammunition issued and used.

    (v) Any search for arms to be carried out by police forces composed half of Catholics and half of Protestants, the military rendering any necessary assistance.

4. A Court to be constituted for the trial without jury of persons charged with serious crime, the Court to consist of the Lord Chief Justice and one of the Lords Justices of Appeal of Northern Ireland ...

5. A Committee to be set up in Belfast of equal numbers Catholic and Protestant with an independent Chairman, preferably Catholic and Protestant alternately in successive weeks, to hear and investigate complaints as to intimidation, outrages, etc, such Committee to have direct access to the heads of the Government. The local Press to be approached with a view to inserting only such reports of disturbances, etc. as shall have been considered and communicated by this Committee.

6. IRA activity to cease in the Six Counties, and thereupon the method of organising the special police in the Six Counties outside Belfast shall proceed as speedily as possible upon lines similar to those agreed to for Belfast.

7. During the month immediately following the passing into law of the Bill confirming the constitution of the Free State ... there shall be a further meeting between the signatories to this agreement with a view to ascertaining:

   a) Whether means can be devised to secure the unity of Ireland.

   b) Failing this, whether agreement can be arrived at on the boundary question otherwise than by recourse to the Boundary Commission outlined in Article 12 of the Treaty ...

9. In view of the special conditions consequent on the political situation in Belfast and neighbourhood, the British Government will submit to Parliament a vote not exceeding £500,000 for the Ministry of Labour of Northern Ireland to be expended exclusively on relief work, one-third for the benefit of Roman Catholics and two-thirds for the benefit of Protestants. The Northern signatories agree to use every effort to secure the restoration of the expelled workers.

The Times, 31 March 1922

137 *Winston Churchill: Staking everything on elections*

On 7 January 1922 the Dáil voted to approve the Treaty by the modest margin of 64 votes to 57. De Valera had resigned the Presidency of the Republic on the previous day, and was replaced by Arthur Griffith. Collins meanwhile took a parallel role as 'Chairman of the Provisional Government of the Irish Free State' under the Treaty. In practice the two men worked together, but the myth of an independent republic going into voluntary liquidation as the result of a Treaty freely concluded with Great Britain, was maintained. Equally the anti-Treaty party denied the right of any group to 'abolish the republic'. The split in the Dáil was soon paralleled by a split in the IRA, just as it was beginning to expand its numbers and take over occupation of barracks from the retiring British forces. But the Provisional Government resisted British suggestions that they should hold elections immediately so as to undermine the lack of democratic support for the anti-Treaty position. They still hoped, by procrastination, to avoid military confrontation with their former colleagues, though building up the Free State Army the while. The anti-Treaty wing of the IRA, however, seized the initiative and formed a 16-man Executive Council to direct their movement, independent of any political organisation. De Valera was acknowledged simply as a sympathetic political leader of cognate views. On 14 April 1922 the Council ordered the Dublin Brigade to occupy the Four Courts buildings, Dublin's main legal complex, and to fortify them. Other buildings in Dublin and elsewhere were also occupied by anti-Treaty (or 'Irregular') forces.

Some elements in the anti-Treaty IRA denied the right of politicians, on whatever authority, to bargain away the Republic, and wanted to establish an undisguised military dictatorship until it was achieved. Other anti-Treaty IRA leaders, like Sean O'Hegarty, made last-minute attempts to avert civil war by addressing the Dáil. At Westminster however, where Winston Churchill had become the minister responsible for relationships with Ireland, concern focused less on averting war in the South than on ensuring that the Provisional Government adhered to its Treaty commitments.

(a) Memorandum by Lord Stamfordham for King George V   4 May 1922

I saw Mr Churchill this morning and told him of the King's anxiety about the very grave condition of things in Ireland. Mr Churchill takes a very hopeful view of the situation, and the very fact that the Provisional Government's troops will fight, and have defeated the Irregular troops and turned them out of Kilkenny Castle and captured a large store of whiskey, which had been seized by the latter, is all to the good. In fact he would rather that the fighting continued than that the two sides should be negotiating truces or holding conferences. He is certain that De Valera is losing ground every day and a large proportion of the population is longing for peace. He also thinks that Michael Collins is right not to take violent and drastic measures in instances such as the seizure of the Law [Four] Courts and of the Kildare Street Club and that it is better policy to let the public generally realise that they are suffering inconvenience, discomfort, pecuniary loss and general derangement of business, than that they should have a grievance against the [Provisional] Government for the exercise of dragooning and Prussianised methods ...

Mr Churchill, however, stakes everything upon the elections, which he believes will take place within the next six weeks and that the result will be an overwhelming majority to the [Provisional] Government ...

M Gilbert, *Winston S Churchill, vol iv Companion pt 3* (London: Heinemann, 1977), pp 1882-3

(b) Address to Dáil by Sean O'Hegarty   3 May 1922

What did I find? I found an atmosphere of absolute hostility, personalities indulged in across the room and ... utter irresponsibility as to what the country was like and the conditions in it ...

The Army two days ago was drifting, but it is now drifting to destruction ...

...When a crisis occurs in a country it is not the name [ie mode] of the Government that counts. It is the men. And if you can get the best men in Ireland into the Government, it does not matter under what auspices you put them when the crisis comes, because when the opportunity comes to set up a Republic, it can be set up ...

If this [Dáil Peace] Committee is going to do anything, there must be a truce between the two armies. I have a report now that there is heavy fighting going on in Kilkenny and that eighteen have been killed [in fact there were, surprisingly, no deaths in this serious incident]. That is a good start, is it not? And people are sitting down here discussing whether they will compromise themselves by stopping it ...

Dáil Éireann, Debates, 3 May 1922, pp 357-367

138 The Collins-de Valera pact: 'The national position requires ...'

Whereas the British Government hoped that a clear verdict in favour of the Treaty by the Irish people would resolve the Provisional Government's difficulties, Collins and many others on the Pro-Treaty side saw that such a democratic outcome, highly likely as it was, would in fact push the anti-Treatyites into the arms of their military extremists. To the surprise of the Dáil, and the annoyance of Westminster, it was announced on 20 May 1922 that Collins and de Valera had made a pact, as Pro- and anti-Treaty leaders of Sinn Féin, for the two sides to contest the forthcoming general election as a coalition, each side putting up candidates in the 64:57 ratio of the existing Dáil's vote in favour of the Treaty.

1. That a National Coalition Panel for this Third Dáil, representing both parties in the Dáil and in the Sinn Féin Organisation, be sent forward, on the ground that the national position requires the entrusting of the Government of the country into the joint hands of those who have been the strength of the national situation during the last few years, without prejudice to their present respective positions.

2. That this Coalition Panel be sent forward as from the Sinn Féin Organisation, the number for each party being their present strength in the Dáil.

3. That the candidates be nominated through each of the existing party Executives.

4. That every and any interest is free to go up and contest the election equally with the National Sinn Féin Panel.

5. That constituencies where an election is not held shall continue to be represented by their present Deputies.

6. That after the election the Executive shall consist of the President, elected as formerly; the Minister for Defence, representing the Army; and nine other Ministers – five from the majority party and four from the minority, each party to choose its own nominees. The allocation will be in the hands of the President.

7. That in the event of the Coalition Government finding it necessary to dissolve, a general election will be held as soon as possible on adult suffrage.

D Macardle, *The Irish Republic* (London: Gollancz,
1937; 4th edn, Dublin, Irish Press, 1951), pp 712

139 *To fight in the swamps of Lough Erne?*

The situation in the south of Ireland had reached crisis point, and many British observers feared that the 1921 Treaty agreement was in process of collapsing. This concern inter-reacted with the party-political situation at Westminster, where Conservative back bench 'supporters' of the Coalition Government were increasingly restive, while ministers regarded one another with growing suspicion and viewed every crisis as their potential nemesis. Uncompromising Southern Unionist zealots like Field Marshal Sir Henry Wilson, recently embarked upon a new career as Ulster Unionist MP, pressed for renewed British confrontation with Sinn Féin. anti-Treaty IRA elements meanwhile seized a few square miles of land in the south-west corner of Northern Ireland, 'the Belleek triangle', which was entirely cut off from the rest of the province by the waters of Lough Erne. Churchill believed that he could not have appeared before Parliament 'with Belleek in hostile hands', and was willing to order British troops across the new border into Donegal in order to flush out the Irregulars. In the event the incident petered out with an Irregular withdrawal, but not before Lloyd George had given Churchill a stiff lecture.

(a) Sir Henry Wilson's Diary   31 May 1922

Winston [Churchill] made his statement [in Parliament] about Ireland and the Valera-Collins Pact. He admitted that the pact broke the Treaty but pleaded for patience and conciliation. In other words he agreed to this flagrant breach of the Treaty. The House was decidedly sceptical. Several spoke against him including myself and I extracted from him that the troops were being kept in Dublin in case a Republic was declared. Collins and Griffith were in the Distinguished Strangers Gallery ...

M Gilbert, *Winston S Churchill*, vol iv Companion,
pt 3 (London: Heinemann, 1977), pp 1907

(b) Tom Jones's Diary,   7 June 1922

... I went to bed but I could not sleep for hours as I feared that the troops were moving towards Belleek and that we might have some bloody business on the following day before the PM could intervene.

8 June: Breakfast 9.30. The PM at once said on appearing, 'I am going to *write* to Winston'. He wanted to have on record his views in case of a breakdown ...

[later that afternoon] ... I gathered from Curtis who had been with Winston when it [the letter] arrived that he was 'deeply moved' with anger ... The PM slept in the open after luncheon. We had tea about 4.00 and there was a good deal of talk about Churchill's disloyalty as a colleague. 'No Churchill was ever loyal', remarked the PM. 'Churchill is fancying himself as a leader of a Tory revolt ...' ... the PM compared Winston to a chauffeur who apparently is perfectly sane and drives with great skill for months, then suddenly he takes you over a precipice. He thought that there was a strain of lunacy ...

Tom Jones, *Whitehall Diary, vol 3: Ireland, 1918-25*
(London: Oxford University Press, 1971), pp 210-212

(c) Lloyd George to Winston Churchill   8 June 1922

I am profoundly disquieted by the developments on the Ulster border. We are not merely being rushed into a conflict, but we are gradually being manoeuvred into giving battle on the very worst grounds which could possibly be chosen for the struggle. I cannot say whether Henry Wilson and De Valera are behind this but if they are their strategy is very skillful. They both want a break and they both want to fight the battle on this ground. I am not convinced that a break is inevitable. On the contrary, with patience, with the adroitness of which you have such command, I believe we can get through in the end ... Ulster divides British opinion at home and throughout the Empire ... But if the Free Staters insisted on a Constitution which repudiated Crown and Empire and practically set up a Republic we could carry the whole world with us in any action we took. That is why the anti-Treatyites are forcing the issue on Ulster.

Moreover, our Ulster case is not a good one ... In two years 400 Catholics have been killed and 1200 have been wounded without a single person being brought to justice. It is true that several Protestants have also been murdered, but the murder of Catholics went on at the rate of three or four to one for some time before Catholic reprisals attained their present dimensions ...

Quite frankly, if we force an issue with these facts we shall be hopelessly beaten ... We shall have no opinion behind us that will enable us to carry through a costly strangling campaign. Let us keep on the high ground of the Treaty – the Crown, the Empire. There we are unassailable. But if you come down from the height and fight in the swamps of Lough Erne you will be overwhelmed ...

M Gilbert, *Winston S Churchill, vol iv Companion, pt 3* (London: Heinemann, 1977), pp 1914-15

140 Winston Churchill: The time has come ...

On 22 June Sir Henry Wilson was shot dead outside his house in London by two local IRA men one of whom, incredibly, had a wooden leg following wartime service in the British Army. The men were unable to make a getaway, and were subsequently convicted of murder and hanged. It is not clear which wing of the IRA authorised the murder, or what the motives were: de Valera, Griffith and the anti-Treaty IRA Executive all repudiated the crime, and some historians have attributed it to Collins, though the evidence is highly circumstantial The outcome was of course to raise the political temperature in Britain, encouraging the Government to increase pressure on the Free State Government to implement the Treaty. Two days later the Free State general election results were announced. They showed that the Collins-De Valera Pact had not worked, because of the electoral successes of other parties who supported the Treaty – a Dáil which has been split 64 to 57 in favour of the Treaty was replaced by one in which 58 Pro-Treaty, 17 Labour, 7 Farmers' Party, 6 Independents and 4 Unionists (total 92) lined up against 36 anti-Treaty Republicans who refused to recognise the new parliament. On 28 June, following an ultimatum, Free State forces began a bombardment of the Four Courts which signalled the commencement of the Irish Civil War. It is probable that in his private talks with Collins earlier in June, Churchill had warned him that if the British Coalition Government fell over the failure to make progress with implementing the Treaty, the outcome would be the return of a die-hard Conservative Government which would not arm and support the Free State but would choose its moment to intervene as Irish independence collapsed in ruins.

WINSTON CHURCHILL: When, on the night of 6 December 1921, we signed a Treaty with the plenipotentiaries of the Irish people we have every right to believe, and every reason to believe, that the Irish signatories represented the settled view of the vast majority of the Dáil and the united authority of the Sinn Féin cabinet. But we learned almost immediately that Mr De Valera and a very large number of his followers repudiated the action taken by his own plenipotentiaries, and the Treaty was only carried through the Dáil, after prolonged wrangling, by a majority of seven votes ...

We therefore pressed upon the Provisional Government the importance and urgency of an election, which alone could give them the status of a national administration and which alone could enable them to govern with native authority. Mr De Valera, knowing himself to be in a minority in Ireland, and in a small minority, set to work by every means in his power to obstruct, to delay, and, if possible, to prevent, such an election ...

The first half [of our policy] ... was to give the southern Irish every opportunity of saying freely whether they accepted or rejected the Treaty offer which we have made; the second inseparable part was to supply Ulster with the means which would prevent her from being forced to come into a Dublin Parliament unless and until she came into it − as I trust some day she will − of her own free will ...

The situation on the frontier of Ulster is also much easier. Disturbances and inroads upon the western border threatened a few weeks ago to make it necessary for us to clear up the whole position in Donegal and to break up the Republican bands which are spreading ruin throughout that county. I am very glad to say that the operations undertaken by His Majesty's Forces under the direction of the Government, in Pettigo and Belleek, have had the effect of clearing the border.

... I wish I could end here but I cannot. I should not be dealing honestly and fully with this subject if I left in the minds of the House the impression that all that is required is patience and composure. No, Sir ... Firmness is needed in the interests of peace ... Now this Provisional [Free State] Government is greatly strengthened. It is armed with the declared will of the Irish electorate. It is supported by an effective Parliamentary majority. It is its duty to give effect to the Treaty in the letter and in the spirit, to give full effect to it, and to give full effect to it without delay. A much stricter reckoning must rule henceforward. The ambiguous position of the so-called Irish Republican Army, intermingled as it is with the Free State troops, is an affront to the Treaty. The presence in Dublin, in violent occupation of the Four Courts, of a band of men styling themselves the Headquarters or the Republican Executive, is a gross breach and defiance of the Treaty. From this nest of anarchy and treason, not only to the British crown, but to the Irish people, murderous outrages are stimulated and encouraged, not only in the 26 counties, not only in the territory of the Northern Government, but even, it seems most probable, here across the Channel in Great Britain ... The time has come when it is not unfair, not premature and not impatient for us to make to this strengthened Irish Government and new Irish Parliament a request, in express terms, that this sort of thing must come to an end. If it does not come to an end, if either from weakness, from want of courage, or for some other even less creditable reasons, it is not brought to an end and a very speedy end, then it is my duty to say, on behalf of His

Majesty's Government, that we shall regard the Treaty as having been formally violated.

H C Deb 5th series, vol 155, cols
1696–1712 (26 June 1922)

141 'The clearing of the south-west'

anti-Treaty forces were quickly driven out of the Four Courts, and retreated from Dublin during July 1922. Their initial strategy was to attempt to hold a line from Waterford to Limerick, the 'Republic of Munster'. IRA activity in the North came to a virtual halt as civil war spread through the southern and western counties of the Free State. Notwithstanding the death of Griffith from a heart attack and the killing of Collins in an ambush in Co Cork during August, the control of towns and communications in the south-west was steadily reasserted by superior Free State forces. More than 500 died in July and August however, and guerrilla incidents continued in face of stern repression. Notwithstanding the desperate position of Catholics in the North at that time, the Devlinite *Irish News* of Belfast was as firm as the major southern newspapers in its condemnation of the anti-Treaty side.

With the fall of Bandon and Dunmanway in General Collins's constituency in County Cork, all the important towns in the 26 counties from Cork to Donegal are now held by National [Free State] troops. With the clearing of the south-west, the major military operations are practically ended. The Irregulars have retreated to the hills and mountains, from which harassing tactics are being carried out, but these do not affect the main military situation, which is that the military forces of the Government are now supreme throughout 26 counties ...

A new feature of the campaign is instanced in the seizure of all the finest hunting horses that came across their path. Lord Kenmare's stables were swept clear of all horses. The formation of an Irregular cavalry is ostensibly the purpose ... Irregular transport ... would seem to be a thing of the past. The motors dumped in the River Lee during the evacuation of Cork might probably be more than welcome at this juncture. The difficulties of the Irregular mountaineers will be many. Descent after descent may be made on villages and towns for supplies. But this scourge can be adequately dealt with in time by our troops ...

Irish News, 22 August 1922

142 Republicans and the rules of warfare

Though quickly losing control of all but remote mountain territories and faced with harsh treatment by Free State troops, the anti-Treaty IRA was in no mood to give up the fight during the autumn of 1922. De Valera was asked to resume the 'Presidency of the Republic' on 25 October, but he remained a follower rather than a shaper of events, and the militarists continued to dictate a 'no surrender' policy. The following letter from Liam Lynch, Chief of Staff of the Army Council of the (anti-Treaty) IRA, sent to the Speaker of the Provisional Parliament in November 1922, maintained the myth of the inviolable republic. Shortly after the letter a Pro-Treaty member of parliament was shot dead in a Dublin street, whereupon the Provisional Government ordered the execution of four imprisoned anti-Treaty IRA leaders without trial.

Sir,

The illegal body over which you preside has declared war on the soldiers of the Republic and suppressed the legitimate Parliament of the Irish Nation.

As your 'Parliament' and Army Headquarters well know, we on our side have at all times adhered to the recognised rules of warfare. In the early days of this war we took hundreds of your forces prisoners, but accorded to them the rights of Prisoners-of-War and, over and above, treated them as fellow-countrymen and former comrades. Many of your soldiers have been released by us three times although captured with arms on each occasion. But the prisoners you have taken you have treated barbarously, and when helpless have tortured, wounded and murdered them.

We have definite proof that many of your Senior Officers including members of your 'Parliament' have been guilty of most brutal crimes towards the IRA prisoners and have reduced your soldiers to a state of savagery in some areas.

Finally you are now pretending to try IRA prisoners before your make-believe courts. You have already done to death five after such mock ceremonials. You now presume to murder and transport the soldiers who have brought Ireland victory when you, traitors, surrendered the Republic twelve months ago.

Next to the members of your 'Provisional Government' every member of your body who voted for this resolution by which you pretend to make legal the murder of soldiers is equally guilty. We therefore give you and each member of your body due notice that unless your army recognises the rules of warfare in the future we shall adopt very drastic measures to protect our forces.

Irish Independent, 3 December 1922

143 Liam Deasy: '... In the best interests of the country ...'

The guerrilla war continued into the spring of 1923, with the anti-Treaty forces driven increasingly into remote mountain districts. They returned to the tactics of the war against Britain, but this time with decreasing support from the local communities on which they depended. The bitterness engendered during these months was possibly greater than at any time during the war of independence. The number of executions – 77 in six months compared to 24 under the British administration over a slightly longer period – lends support to this view. One who faced execution, following capture with arms in January 1923, was the Deputy Chief of Staff Liam Deasy. He escaped death, but such was the determination and bitterness generated by the conflict that even this appeal to his anti-Treaty comrades evoked no positive response.

HAVE UNDERTAKEN FOR THE FUTURE OF IRELAND TO ACCEPT AND AID IN AN IMMEDIATE AND UNCONDITIONAL SURRENDER OF ALL ARMS AND MEN AS REQUIRED BY [Free State] GENERAL MULCAHY ...

IN PURSUANCE OF THIS UNDERTAKING I AM ASKED TO APPEAL FOR A SIMILAR UNDERTAKING AND ACCEPTANCE FROM THE FOLLOWING:

E. DE VALERA [and 15 other names]

Signed LIAM DEASY

The [above] attachment bearing my signature will very probably be not unexpected but a general surprise: hence my reason for this covering note to you. Previous to my arrest I had decided to advocate a termination of the present hostilities ... My arrest prevented me from carrying out the intentions and it was not until I saw the development of the campaign above referred to, *viz*. taking people as hostages because of the acts of their sons or brother, that I decided to ascertain the extent to which I might go in taking action inside ...

... I was informed [that my] execution would not be suspended unless I agreed to sign what is contained in block capitals in the attached. After long consideration I decided on accepting the conditions in the best interest of the country ... In considering the whole position there are a few matters I will put before you all and simply ask that they be carefully weighed before making your decision.

(a) The increasing strength of the Free State Army as evidenced by the present response to the recruiting appeal.
(b) The decrease in strength of the IRA consequent on the numerous recent arrests.
(c) The entire defensive position of our units in many areas and the general decrease in fighting.

(d) The 'War Weariness' apparent in so many areas.

(e) The increasing support to the Free State Government consequent on our failure to combat their false propaganda.

(f) The serious situation which the executions have created: *viz*. reprisals, counter-reprisals.

Regarding (a) Undoubtedly the increase is due to unemployment, but then war like the present will only make for more unemployment; in other words more fodder for the battle fields.

Regarding (b) In many areas we are confined to the numbers at present under arms and instances of arms being dumped for want of men are not rare. More serious is the loss of fighting officers.

Regarding (c) Protection of small columns by road blocking, etc. and the impeding of railway traffic is the general rule. Ambushing, town fighting etc. is so very isolated that its effects on the general situation is nil.

Regarding (d) This is apparent in the south, and not confined to the rank and file but also among senior officers in our best brigades.

Regarding (e) Comment is needless. This may not be support, but at any rate propaganda has alienated a big percentage of genuine separatists from us.

Regarding (f) This calls for more serious consideration than the others. There is nothing to prevent the Government from continuing and naturally reprisals will follow, so will counter reprisals. Then we will have arrived at a point where the war will be waged by both sides against the people, in some cases against active people, but in the majority non-combatants, whose only crime is having a son or brother in either army, will suffer.

I should have referred to the prospect of a summer campaign which will undoubtedly be more intense than was the fight in 1921. You realise what difficulties we confronted in keeping intact during that period. I hope in the foregoing are reasons for ending the present fight ... Our advance may be greatly impeded for a time but the freedom we desire will be achieved by, we all hope, our united efforts again.

Only because I believe this fight will eventually end in negotiations do I make this appeal. A suspension of executions until 6 February is guaranteed. Your reply to the attached is expected by that date ... This note *is absolutely confidential* and is being handed enclosed and sealed by me to a courier ... I would suggest the sending of the replies in the first instance to the Chief-of-Staff [of anti-Treaty forces, Liam Lynch] and through him to me.

L Deasy, *Brother Against Brother* (Dublin & Cork:
The Mercier Press, 1982), pp 115-122

144 Dorothy Macardle: Unspeakable things done to prisoners

Increasingly a hopeless fight – if not from the beginning, at least from the Autumn of 1922 – the Republican aims and strategies during the later months of the civil war are not easy to understand. Part of it was certainly the inflexible resolve of young men of principle engaged desperately in a form of military activity which had become a way of life to them. Analyses have been constructed around class-based and region-based arguments, as well as more cynical interpretations based on personal rivalries and access to posts in the emerging Free State regime. Important, too, was the sheer impact of spiralling brutality, reprisal and counter-reprisal; the more personal sacrifices were accumulated, the harder it became to give way. Underlying it all was an analysis of the Treaty and civil war which perhaps only hindsight reveals as being wildly at odds with reality. Dorothy Macardle (1899-1958), daughter of Sir Thomas Macardle the Dundalk brewer, later became a successful historian, novelist and critic, but this extract from an early pamphlet by her illustrates clearly the distorted sense of reality, as well as the passion and suffering, which cast their shadow over a generation of young people in 1922-23.

The Terror failed. The Empire resorted to a more subtle policy – 'divide and conquer' – a motto as old as Rome.

Believing, as they were told, that it was still the Republican army, that the oath to the English king meant nothing, that England was the only enemy they would ever be called upon to fight, Irish Volunteers joined the Free State army, and took the guns and the uniform and the pay.

When, without an hour's warning, they were given English artillery and ordered to make war upon their old comrades – upon those who refused allegiance to the English king – they were in a death-trap. To mutiny was to die.

This tragedy is more pitiful than the tragedy of the men they killed. Fighting for a cause they hated against the cause they loved, hunting and killing their old comrades and leaders, dying, not a few, for their country's enemy, execrated by the people they had betrayed – what reward could the Empire offer to atone for this? Debauchery was the only refuge, the only stimulus to such work as they had to do.

Of the degradation that followed one thing only need be said. The unspeakable things done to prisoners in jails and camps and barracks and on lonely roadsides were not due to insane impulses of these drink-sodden irresponsible men. They were the fruits of a policy calculated, authorised and prompted by the government which they had to obey.

That government was subject to England, bound by oath and interest to the English king. It was pledged to do the Empire's work, and the Empire's work can only be done the Empire's way.

That way, even, wins no lasting victory. That policy was pursued, with the most concentrated vigour, in Kerry, in the Spring of 1923. And in Kerry it has most surely failed.

D Macardle, *Tragedies of Kerry, 1922-23* (Dublin:
Irish Book Bureau, 1924), pp 4-5

145 *Legion of the rearguard*

At last, following the death in action of the anti-Treaty IRA chief of staff, Liam Lynch, in April 1923 De Valera, who as political leader of the Republican movement had commanded little influence during the war, was able to call on his forces to conceal their arms and stand down.

Soldiers of the Republic, Legion of the Rearguard ... The Republic can no longer be defended successfully by your arms. . . military victory must be allowed to rest for the moment with those who have destroyed the Republic ... Much that you set out to accomplish is achieved. You have saved the nation's honour and kept open the road of independence. You have demonstrated in a way there is no mistaking that we are not a nation of willing bond-slaves. Seven years of intense effort have exhausted our people. Their sacrifices and their sorrows have been many. If they have turned aside and have not given you that active support which alone could bring victory in this last year, it is because they saw overwhelming forces against them and they are weary and need a rest ... A little time and you will see them recover and rally again to the standard ...

E Neeson, *The Civil War in Ireland*
(The Mercier Press, Cork, 1966) p 7

The establishment of the Northern Ireland state

146 Lloyd George: To force union is to promote disunion

As the struggle in the South of Ireland intensified between, first, the British Government and Sinn Féin and, subsequently, between the Free State and anti-Treaty forces, the story of the conflict in the North became increasingly distinct. The two conflicts of course remained closely inter-related, but they can no longer be contained within one narrative. The clearest dividing point is the British Government's decision at the end of 1919 to bring forward yet another home rule bill, based on six-county partition, which became the Government of Ireland Act of 1920. The policy of 'exclusion' of the North from home rule, which appeared to have been waiting in the wings since 1913, was replaced by 'partition' into two separate jurisdictions which would both have home rule. This approach was developed in a cabinet committee chaired by the Coalition Unionist Walter Long (1854-1924), and first disclosed to the House of Commons in a prime ministerial statement by Lloyd George.

The first fact of which the House will take note is that there is a Home Rule Act on the Statute Book. Unless it be either postponed, repealed or altered, it comes automatically into operation ... Legislation, therefore, is indispensable. I am sorry to say that I cannot think of any proposals that you could put forward from the box which would be in the least degree possible or practicable or acceptable to British opinion at the present moment, which have any chance of acceptance now, in the present position of Irish affairs. We must get that fact right into our minds. Therefore, we must take our responsibility, and propose what we think is fair, and just. Settlement will be found, not in the enactment, but in the working ...

Irishmen claim the right to control their own domestic concerns, without interference from Englishmen, Scotsmen or Welshmen. That is a fundamental fact ... It is also a fundamental fact that you have a considerable section of the people of Ireland who are just as opposed to Irish rule as the majority of Irishmen are to British rule. Both these facts must be taken into account ... If they unite, they must do it of their own accord. To force union is to promote disunion. There may be advantages in union – I do not deny it ... But that is a matter for those populations, and no-one else, to decide. Lord Durham attempted to force Quebec and Ontario to join ... in the same parliament ... by forcing them together you created antagonism. The moment you had separation, confederation was possible ... If Great Britain, with all its infinite resources, cannot govern a hostile Ireland, I do not see how Ireland could control a hostile North-East ...

...We propose that self-government should be conferred upon the whole of Ireland, and our plan is based on the recognition of those three fundamental facts: first, the impossibility of severing Ireland from the United Kingdom; second, the opposition of nationalist Ireland to British rule in Ireland, and third, the opposition of the population of North-East Ulster to Irish rule. The first involves the recognition that Ireland must remain an integral part of the United Kingdom. The second involves the conferring of self-government upon Ireland in all its domestic concerns. The third involves the setting up of two parliaments, and not one, in Ireland. One will be the Parliament of Southern Ireland; the other will be the Parliament of Northern Ireland. There are four alternative proposals which have been discussed with regard to boundaries. The first is that the whole of Ulster should form one unit ... The objection to that is that it would leave a large areas where there is a predominantly Catholic and Celtic population in complete sympathy with the southern population. The second suggestion is county option. The objection to that is that it would leave solid communities of Protestants who are in complete sympathy with the North-eastern section of Ireland outside, under a government to which they are rootedly hostile. It is sometimes impossible to avoid that, but it is desirable to avert it where practicable ... The next suggestion is that these North-eastern counties should form a unit. There is the same objection to that, because there are solid Catholic communities in at least two of these counties which are co-terminous with the southern population ... The fourth suggestion is that we should ascertain what is the homogeneous Northern-Eastern section, and constitute it into a separate area, taking the six counties as a basis, eliminating, where practicable, the Catholic communities, whilst including Protestant communities from the co-terminous Catholic counties of Ireland ...

We propose that every opportunity shall be given to Irishmen, if they desire it, to establish unity, but the decision must rest with them. If they agree, it will require no Act of the Imperial parliament to enable them to accomplish it. There are two proposals which we have in mind in order to attain that object. The first is that there shall be constituted from the outset a Council of Ireland, consisting of twenty representatives elected by each of the two Irish legislatures. This Council will be given the powers of private bill legislation from the outset; but otherwise we propose to leave to the two Irish legislatures complete discretion to confer upon it any powers they choose, within the range of their own authority ...

We propose to clothe the two Irish legislatures with full constituent powers, so that they will be able, without further reference to the Imperial Parliament, and by identical legislation, to create a single Irish legislature ... It will then rest with the Irish people themselves to determine whether they want union, and when they want union. The British Parliament will have no further say in the matter ... With regard to Irish representation in this Parliament, we propose to adhere to the scheme of 1914 – that is, a reduction of the number to 42 members [from 105] for all purposes ...

I next come to the powers of these two legislatures ... There will be full control over education, local government, land policy, agriculture, roads and bridges, transportation, old age pensions, insurance ... municipal affairs, housing, local judiciary, hospitals, licensing, all machinery for the maintenance of law and order, with the exception referred to of the higher judiciary and, of course, the Army and Navy.

H C Deb 5th series, vol 123, cols 1169–1178
(22 December 1919)

147 Devlin v Craig: Providence arranged the geography of Ireland?

The Government of Ireland Act became law in December 1920. Notwithstanding the increasingly disturbed state of Ireland, on the one hand, and their long record of opposition to Irish home rule on the other, the Coalition Conservatives in Parliament supported the passage of the bill. The strongest opposition to the bill came from the Irish Parliamentary Party, but being now reduced to a rump of six MPs led by Devlin, and in a parliament less sympathetic than that of the pre-war Liberal era, their arguments were both ineffectual and resigned in tone. Of more concern to the Government were the attitude of Sinn Féin (who, by ignoring it, made a nullity of the Parliament of Southern Ireland, except to use the elections to provide a renewed mandate for an expanded Dáil) and of the Ulster Unionists, who were asked to accept devolved government in place of direct rule from London, and to surrender their claims to counties Cavan, Donegal and Monaghan. Captain Charles Craig, brother of the future NI prime minister, responded on behalf of the Ulster Unionists.

(a) Part of letter from Joseph Devlin to Bishop Patrick O'Donnell of Raphoe

United Irish League

Telegraphic Address
"Tinsnaoh Dublin"

39. Upper O'Connell Street,

Dublin, 13th February, 1920.

My dear Lord Bishop,

      I am crossing to-night to London and I would be very glad
to hear from you on the situation. As far as I can see the
situation, it means that a Parliament will be set up in the North
of Ireland, and I am practically certain not for the whole of Ulster
but for the Six Counties. It is they likely they will proceed to
put the Bill into operation in that portion of Ireland that wants it,
and that Carson will establish his Parliament for the Six Counties.

  This will mean the worst form of partition and of course permanent
partition. Once they have their own Parliament with all the machinery of government and administration, I am afraid anything like
subsequent union will be rendered impossible. I propose if an
opportunity is offered to attack the Bill, and to do so from an
Ulster point of view giving reasons why we Catholics and Nationalists
could not under any circumstances consent to be placed under the
denomination of a Parliament so skilfully established as to make it
impossible for us to be ever other than a permanent minority, with
all the sufferings and tyranny of the present day continued, only in
a worse form.

ADA Patrick O'Donnell Papers, IV, 5

(b) MR DEVLIN: ... I cannot understand this bill. In my judgement the bill was conceived in bedlam and drafted by F E Smith; for anything so extraordinary I can offer no other excuse or justification ... It is a bill which proposes to permanently divide a small nation into two nations, and which not only proposes to partition Ireland, but even to partition Ulster ... There are to be two so-called parliaments. Why, they have not the powers of a wretched municipality! The over-riding body is to be a council; it is not to be called a parliament ... and this council has neither, so far as I can see, shadowy powers nor any other powers ...

... I am put under the Ulster Parliament. The Catholics in the six counties – we may take it they are all nationalists – number 430,161 out of a total of 1,250,000. I shall be under the jurisdiction of that parliament ... We shall be in a permanent minority ... I do not dislike these people [Ulster Unionists] in the least degree. On the contrary, I am as proud of my native county as they are, but what I hate about it is its intolerance, its bigotry and its refusal to recognise this [Catholic] section of the population.

The fact of the matter is that this parliament, as it is called, will be practically an enlarged edition of the Belfast Town Council ... If you have that spirit in Ulster, no Unionist will be returned for any seats in the Southern Parliament ... The controversy over this ill-treatment, either of Catholics in the Northern Parliament or of Protestants in the South, will be carried over from Ireland and will recommence all over again in this Parliament ... I said that this bill was ridiculous. I say now it is fantastic. They have created two Irelands. Providence arranged the geography of Ireland, and the right hon gentleman [Lloyd George] has changed it ...

H C Deb 5th series, vol 127, cols
1139-1149 (30 March 1920)

(c) CAPTAIN [Charles] CRAIG: With the prospect of this bill passing into law, we Ulstermen find ourselves face to face with the most extraordinary paradox. While on the one hand our hatred and detestation of home rule and all connected with it is as great as it ever was, and in fact more so owing to the action of the predominant party in Ireland today, yet on the other hand we do see in this bill the realisation of the objects which we aimed at when we raised our [Ulster] Volunteer Force in 1913 and 1914 ... Because it gives Ulster a parliament of its own, and sets up a state of affairs which will prevent, I believe, for all time Ulster being forced into a parliament in Dublin without its own consent; because it does those two things I say that the bill practically gives us everything we fought for ...

We would much prefer to remain part and parcel of the United Kingdom

... But we have many enemies in this country, and we feel that an Ulster without a parliament of its own would not be in nearly as strong a position as one in which a parliament had been set up, where the executive had been appointed and where above all the paraphernalia of government was already in existence ... We do not know how long, if we did not take a parliament, our Unionist friends in this country could hold the fort against the forces which would be brought to bear on them, and we know that attempts on our liberty would be repeated time and again, and therefore I say that we prefer to have a parliament, although we do not want one of our own ...

We quite frankly admit that we cannot hold the nine counties ... Sinn Féiners ... could make it impossible for us to govern those three counties [Cavan, Donegal, Monaghan] ...

H C Deb 5th series, vol 127, cols 985-993
(29 March 1920)

148 *The demography of partition*

The pragmatic logic of Craig's argument was irrefutable, and other mainstream Ulster Unionists, such as the Belfast journalist Thomas Moles MP (1871-1937), went out to sell the decision to their followers. Unionists in the three 'abandoned' Ulster counties of Cavan, Donegal and Monaghan (where the Protestant proportion was below a quarter) who had been included in the Ulster Covenant of 1912, manipulated the demographic arguments as best they could, but to no avail.

... It was represented that a Parliament for the nine Counties would have a Nationalist and Sinn Féin majority. Mr Moles, MP, had the hardihood to state that it would consist of 33 Nationalists and 31 Unionists. It was pointed out to him in vain that the population of Ulster was:

Protestants	890,880
Roman Catholics	690,816
Leaving a Protestant majority of	200,064

and that it was impossible a majority of 200,000 should not be able to return a majority of members.

It was further shown that at the last Election [December 1918] for the nine Counties, when the number of members to be elected was 38, the members returned were:

Unionists	23
Nationalists	15
Unionist majority	8

and that Election was held on the *present franchise*.

It was further pointed out that the new bill gives Ulster 64 members and that if there had been 64 at the last election the numbers would have been:

Unionists	38
Nationalists	26
Giving a Unionist majority	12

All was in vain. Mr Moles persisted in his estimate but gave no reasons for it except that the result of the last municipal election in Belfast was not satisfactory to certain interests there. It was insinuated that the Unionist working men of Belfast could not be depended on as heretofore, and therefore we must be cast out. This is a libel on the Unionist Labour voters in Belfast. To those who are acquainted with municipal affairs in Belfast it is not surprising that Labour should assert itself in elections for the Corporation, but to infer from that fact that the sturdy working men of Belfast are not as staunch Unionists as ever they were is not only unjust but untrue. After all why should not Unionist Labour be represented in the Belfast Corporation, and even in the Ulster Government, and why are we to be abandoned lest that should happen?

... An argument that has been used is that the three Counties contain a majority of Nationalists and Sinn Féiners. That is true. But so does Derry City, Fermanagh County, Tyrone County, South Armagh, South Down and the Falls Division of Belfast. Yet no one proposes to exclude them. The truth is that it is impossible to fix upon any exclusively Unionist area. There are more Unionists in the Southern [ie Irish Free State] area than there are Nationalists in the three Counties and no provision whatever is made for them. In their case we are told minorities must suffer, but that doctrine seems to be ignored where the minority is a Nationalist one ...

Ulster and Home Rule: No Partition of Ulster,
Statement by Delegates for Cavan, Donegal and Monaghan
PRONI Montgomery Papers, D 627/435

149 The Lisburn pogrom, 1920

In Ulster the IRA campaign was inevitably more muted than in many parts of southern Ireland. The violent episodes in the South nonetheless produced a mass Protestant backlash in the North which was most pronounced in July and August 1920, and in the early months of 1922. In Belfast, Catholics and their sympathisers in the labour movement were driven from employment in most of the large Protestant-dominated concerns, especially shipbuilding and engineering. The fragile non-sectarian industrial unity established during a major strike in 1919 was broken. Old-established patterns of residential segregation were reinforced and extended, as refugees from outlying districts (150 families on one day in August 1920) flooded into the main Catholic district of the Falls. Particularly bad incidents - indiscriminate attacks on Catholic houses and business premises, leading to wholesale evacuation – occurred in Banbridge, Co Down and Lisburn, Co Antrim after two police officers, natives of the towns, were killed by the IRA. Fred Crawford, the UVF gun-runner of 1914, described in his diary the aftermath of the Lisburn episode, in which 273 homes were burned out.

... I took Adair up to Lisburn to see the state it was. It reminded me of a French town after it had been bombarded by the Germans as I saw in France 1916. We visited the ruins of the Priests' house on Chapel Hill. It was burnt or gutted and the furniture all destroyed. When coming down the avenue I found a small pair of manicure scissors that had been through the fire. I kept them as a souvenir of the event. We called at Mr Stephenson's and had tea there. Mrs Thompson his sister was also with him. They told me of some very hard cases of where Unionists had lost practically all they had by the fire of the house of a Catholic spreading to theirs, and also of some very decent respectable families of long standing loosing [sic] everything also. But when one thinks of the brutal cold-blooded murder of Inspector Swanzie [sic for Swanzy] one does not wonder at the mob loosing [sic] its head with fury ... It has been stated that there are only four or five RC families left in Lisburn. Others say this is wrong that there are far more. Be that as it may there certainly are practically no shops or places of business left to the RCs ...

P J Buckland. *Irish Unionism 1885-1923: a Documentary History* (PRONI, Belfast, 1973), p 445

150 Belfast 1922: Unspeakable barbarity

In the South the elections of May 1921 for 'the House of Commons of Southern Ireland' were (apart from the Dublin University seats) an uncontested walkover for Sinn Féin, whose 124 representatives ignored the Act and constituted themselves as the second Dáil Éireann. In the North, elections for a 52-seat 'House of Commons' returned 40 Unionist members, together with 6 Sinn Féiners and 6 Nationalists, all of whom abstained, and a government was set up with Sir James Craig as 'Prime Minister of Northern Ireland'. The Northern Parliament's area of jurisdiction was limited to six of the nine Ulster counties (Antrim, Armagh, Down and Londonderry, which had clear Protestant majorities, and Fermanagh and Tyrone, where Catholics were slightly in the majority), which together made up the largest possible area in which Protestants could command an overwhelming majority.

Following the opening of the IRA's campaign in the North and the mass expulsion of Catholics and Labour activists from Belfast's main industrial centres in the summer of 1920, Belfast underwent a two-year period of savage local warfare. It was characterised by IRA murders of policemen and 'specials', by widespread and indiscriminate sectarian sniping by extremists on both sides, by evictions of isolated families and communities from their homes in neighbourhoods where the other side was dominant, and by 'reprisals'. These reprisals were sometimes random, sometimes targeted against individuals believed to be republican or loyalist activists or sympathisers, and occasionally directed at prominent members of the community such as William Tweddell, Unionist MP for Woodvale, who was shot dead in May 1922. The city's Catholics, roughly one quarter of the population, suffered disproportionately more, sustaining 257 out of 416 civilian deaths in the two-year period. One of the vilest, and certainly the most sensational, incident was the murder of five members of the McMahon family and an employee by an armed gang who invaded the family home during the night of 23 March 1922. Owen McMahon, his brothers and his sons, owned a string of public houses across the city and were well-known to be low-key supporters of Devlin's moderate Nationalist Party, rather than of Sinn Féin. No-one was ever convicted of the killings, although there were strong and persistent rumours, and testimony given to the Provisional Government in Dublin, that this was one of a number of atrocities carried out by a murder gang operating within the police force. The gang's alleged leader, District Inspector John W Nixon (1880-1949), was dismissed from the RUC in 1924, but later represented Woodvale as an Independent Unionist in the Northern Ireland Parliament for twenty years.

The funerals of the late Mr Owen McMahon and his three sons Frank, Patrick and Gerald, who were brutally murdered in their home ... [at] ... Antrim Road on Friday morning took place yesterday afternoon to Milltown Cemetery, amidst scenes of mourning unprecedented in the history of the city [a fourth son died of his wounds shortly afterwards, a bar manager was also killed, and a fifth son survived the attack].

Addressing the congregation ... Rev. Bernard Laverty, Administrator, paid touching and eloquent tribute to the deceased who had, he said, led exemplary Christian lives. The world, he continued, stood aghast at the terrible tragedy that had been enacted in their midst. The late Mr McMahon and his boys were inoffensive citizens who had taken no part in politics, and they had been done to death merely because they were Catholics. Many shocking crimes had been perpetrated by the Black and Tans and Auxiliaries in other parts of Ireland, but they had not been guilty of anything approaching this in its unspeakable barbarity. He referred to the terror at present prevailing in the city, and said that the Catholic people were on trial. He exhorted them to pray for peace, to practise patience and forbearance, and not to give offence and in God's good time all would be well.

The route was via Royal Avenue, Castle Street and Falls Road ... Certainly not less than 10,000 people participated in the mournful proceedings; and it is no exaggeration to say that never before has such a public tribute to the dead been witnessed in Belfast ... While the cortege was composed in the main of the working people of the Falls Road and other Catholic districts of the city, it included many hundreds of business and personal friends ... Among the laity were Messrs Joseph Devlin MP (for many years a close personal friend of the late Mr McMahon), and Mr C.J.France, a prominent American, who has been directing the White Cross relief work in Ireland for many months past, and has been responsible for the alleviation of much suffering in Belfast ...

Irish News, 27 March 1922

151 'The cleavage between the Poles and the Jews in Warsaw does not compare'

Under pressure from the British Government, and also genuinely alarmed about the level of civilian casualties, Collins as head of the Free State Provisional Government and Craig as prime minister of Northern Ireland, made two attempts, in January and again in March 1922, to reach agreement on measures to alleviate the communal violence in Belfast and other parts of the North. Much hope was pinned on the intricate peace arrangements made in March (see Document 136), but the results were disappointing. Part of the reason for this was certainly the reluctance of the new Northern Ireland Government to insist in the face of loyalist anger that its forces should act impartially. But an important additional factor, as we now know from recent research, was the fact that the continuing IRA campaign in the North down to June 1922, far from being all the work of anti-treaty irregulars, was in substantial measure an undercover operation planned with the knowledge and support of Collins himself. In June 1922 the British Government sent a civil servant, Stephen Tallents (1884-58) to report on the working of the Craig-Collins Pact, which he did in a report to the permanent secretary at the Colonial Office. His report is shrewd and fairly dispassionate, although it should be noted that this previously unknown English civil servant inspired the confidence of the NI Government sufficiently for them to accept him shortly afterwards as the link between Belfast and London, in the post of Imperial Secretary for Northern Ireland (1922-26).

Stephen G. Tallents to Sir James Masterton-Smith   4 July 1922

I am sending you separately a formal report on the working of the Agreement of 30 March [the Craig-Collins Pact], which was the definite subject of my visit of the last ten days of June to Belfast. That Agreement has come to very little and I doubt if it will be found advantageous either to attempt to revive it in anything like its original form or to enter into further discussion of the causes of its failure ...

A number of minor causes might be recited for the failure of the Agreement and some of them would be the subject of dispute. But I have no doubt that it failed chiefly because it dealt with minor issues before the major issues, which really governed them, were decided. The future of the Provisional Government [of the Free State] seemed to be in the balance; the Northern Government was not acknowledged by the Catholic minority in the Six Counties; Southern Ireland was unsettled; the Boundary Commission under Clause 12 of the Treaty loomed, and still looms ahead and the organised conspiracy of violence to make the Government of Northern Ireland impossible was intensified in May. In currents such as these the light anchors of the March Agreement were soon swept away. But it is worth noting for future consideration that the system employed in that Agreement of inviting Mr Collins virtually to act as the representative of a minority in the territory of another government both encouraged the Catholics in the North in their policy of non-recognition of the Northern Government, and exasperated Sir James Craig's supporters. He had a cold reception when he returned to Belfast with the Agreement ...

For practical purposes the Catholics in Belfast, outside the gunmen and a few irreconcilables, seem to be divided into the followers of Mr Devlin and the followers of Mr Collins. These two parties have their local points of contact, but the cleavage between the Poles and the Jews in Warsaw does not compare to the social gulf which separates both Catholic parties from the Protestants of Belfast. Bishop MacRory, who is a follower of Mr Collins ... told me ... that during his seven years in Belfast he had rarely met a Protestant of standing and that he could not recall during the last twelve months a single opportunity of talking with an intelligent Protestant. Yet before he left Maynooth to come north some of his best friends, he told me, had been Protestants. The Devlinites, to judge from those whom I met, were ready and even anxious to recognise the Northern Government, but said that their party was bound by a pact made with de Valera in May of 1921, at the time of the first elections to the Northern Parliament. Bishop MacRory told me that he would not favour recognition of the Northern Government unless it agreed to cooperate in broad general questions with the Government in Dublin ... He has gone down to Dublin partly in order to get de Valera, if he had the power, to call off or otherwise restrain the violent Catholic element in Belfast; and he told me that de Valera, who had talked to him at great length on other subjects, seemed to him to be quite *désorienté* since the Treaty ...

The present reputation of the B Specials in the Six Counties is disquieting. This force was, I am told, an invention of Sir James Craig's and he will hear nothing to its detriment. But the Catholics regard it with a bitterness exceeding that which the Black and Tans inspired in the South, and several prominent Unionist public men told me privately that this purely partisan and insufficiently disciplined force was sowing feuds in the countryside which would not be eradicated for generations. The mobilised B Special costs from £4.10s to £5 a week. It will be difficult to reduce his numbers while the present unemployment lasts and still more difficult, I am told, ever to get back his arms from him in country districts, unless he is brought quickly under proper discipline ...

I feel that the ambitious programme upon which General [Arthur] Solly-

Flood, the [Northern] Government's 'Military Adviser', has embarked, requires closer scrutiny by the British Government ... Strong and impressive measures had no doubt to be taken in order both to suppress republican violence and to reassure the loyalists. But this £5,000,000 programme has been initiated by a soldier without police experience, whose name carried no weight in the country which seems destined to finance his plans [ie Great Britain] ... I have heard my own doubts much more forcibly expressed in private by experienced loyalists with heavy stakes in the country ... I suggest that the British Government ought without delay to send over a highly qualified Commission of, say, three persons to take stock of this whole programme ...

I feel sure that the idea of holding an independent judicial enquiry into events in Belfast, though it may have been feasible at one stage, should now be ruled out. I do not think that it could secure any advantage and I am sure it would lead to a revival of propaganda about matters that are best forgotten. Inadvertently it would encourage Northern Catholics in their refusal to recognise the Northern Government.

I hope I may add without impropriety that a change in the [Northern] Ministry of Home Affairs would give, so far as I could learn, satisfaction to everyone in Ulster except the present Home Secretary [Sir Dawson Bates] and Sir James Craig, who strongly upholds him. Sir Dawson Bates has the most difficult task in Northern Ireland, and appears to be the least competent of all the present ministers to rise to the occasion. His house is, of course, carefully guarded; but the story goes the round in Belfast that this guard is an extravagance, since the Republicans long ago realised what an asset he was to them in his present position. If I had to choose a precise wish for immediate fulfilment in Northern Ireland, my first selection would be the kindly removal of the present Minister of Home Affairs to a less responsible ministry. I am inclined to think that my second would be his replacement by Lord Londonderry. [In fact Bates remained Minister for Home Affairs until 1943, while Londonderry's foray from Westminster into Northern Irish politics was a short one].

PROL, CO 906/30

152 Unionism and Labour

The relative absence of class consciousness from Ulster Protestant politics had for long been the despair of Nationalists and the delight of Unionists. The advance of trade union organisation in Ireland from 1916 onwards, coupled with the outbreak of social revolution in a number of European cities in the following three years, rather shook the faith of the

Unionist party in the permanence of this situation. A widespread strike in Belfast in the early months of 1919 seemed to confirm that the city was in danger of going the way of 'Red Clydeside' if not worse. In an attempt to stave off the expected socialist challenge, the Unionist leaders had established an Ulster Unionist Labour Association in 1918, under the chairmanship of J M Andrews, a large textile employer. This body shortly secured the election of three working-class Unionists for Belfast seats in the Westminster parliament, but made no apparent impact on party policy nor – in the long run – on its personnel. Until the reappearance of sectarian rioting in 1920 however, socialism continued to constitute something of a threat to the Unionist party in Belfast, as the following letter from Dawson Bates (1876-1949) – the leading Unionist party official who later became Minister for Home Affairs – indicates.

Dawson Bates to Sir Edward Carson   30 June 1919

The question of extending the area of the work of this [Ulster Unionist Labour] Association has given Andrews and myself a great deal of concern. You know the circumstances which led to the formation of this Association (of which you are President), and which ultimately led to three Labour [Unionist] members being selected for the City of Belfast.

The two principal Unionist organisations which exist at the present time in Ulster are the Parliamentary [constituency] Associations and the Orange Institution. Having regard to the fact that members of both these organisations comprise all classes, it is obvious that it is a practical impossibility that matters outside the question of the Union should be the subject of discussion and action. Therefore, no subjects, except those directly affecting the Union, are discussed. The working people in Belfast have felt for a very considerable time past that means should be placed at their disposal whereby domestic matters could be discussed by them under Unionist auspices. As you are aware the trade unions are practically precluded from discussing political matters other than those affecting labour questions, but while this is strictly accurate, at the same time many of the unions are controlled by officials who hold home rule views. The result has been that frequently the opinions of the working classes in Belfast on the question of the Union are misrepresented in England and elsewhere. The absence of such means as I have indicated above frequently leads to the younger members of the working classes joining socialist and extreme organisations run by the Independent Labour Party, where they are educated in views very different to those held by our body. The defect has to a very large extent been made good by the Ulster Unionist Labour Association, but at the same time it is felt that having ordinary meetings, such as they have about once a month, is not sufficient. In other words, the Association will have to extend its sphere of operations.

The matter has been discussed at several of the meetings of the

Association, and finally on Saturday last a resolution was passed, of which I enclose a copy, which puts the matter in a nutshell. If the resolution is given effect to, it means the formation of four working-men's clubs in Belfast, on the lines of the Working-men's Conservative and Liberal Clubs in England. These clubs will be kept linked with the Ulster Unionist Labour Association, and, consequently, with the Ulster Unionist Party.

I have had many talks with Andrews on this subject, and I think if this arrangement could be carried out it would do an incalculable amount of good. On the other hand, if nothing is done the Association will die, because its members will feel that it is not sufficiently progressive to meet an admittedly felt want.

Andrews you will naturally understand feels in his position, as Chairman of the Association and one of the Honorary Secretaries of the Ulster Unionist Council – in addition to being an employer of labour himself – a good deal of responsibility, and he would not be a party to extending the sphere of the existing Association without your approval.

As you are aware, there are many employers in Belfast who take the view that Andrews goes too far on labour questions, but, on the other hand, the vast bulk of thinking employers, and those who have interests of the Empire at heart, realise that Andrews' actions have been most beneficial.

PRONI Carson Papers, D 1507/1

153 The passage of the Local Government Bill, 1922

The system of proportional representation by single transferable vote was implemented for local government elections in Ireland in 1920. The result in the North was to weaken the Unionist Party, by giving more weight to dispersed and previously ineffectual Nationalist votes, and by allowing the appearance of third parties. The Belfast Labour Party had done unexpectedly well in the city in 1920 at the expense of the Unionists, while Nationalists and Sinn Féiners had won control of Fermanagh and Tyrone county councils, Derry city council (for the first time) and a number of smaller units. After May 1921 the Catholic-controlled councils attempted to ignore the newly-created Northern Parliament and continue their allegiance to the revolutionary Dáil in Dublin. Local government thus took its place beside law and order as an area in which the Unionist regime felt it imperative to establish its authority. The first step in this direction was to end the PR system of election, and in doing so the Northern Ireland cabinet, though provoking a constitutional crisis, established a very favourable precedent for the development of its relationship with the British Government.

(a) Lord Fitzalan [Lord-Lieutenant of Ireland] to Sir James Craig MP

5 July 1922

I have telegraphed today giving assent to four bills, but not to the Local Government Bill. This only reached me this morning, and it really is too short notice. There can be no reason why I should not have had a draft copy of this as introduced, and then a wire to say what alterations had or had not been made.

Moreover, I find the government here are hesitating about this bill and think it may be wise to make it a reserved bill, at any rate pending further consideration with you upon it ...

Another point I want to write about is that I have received from the [NI] Home Secretary a long list of recommendations for magistrates – there are eighteen for Belfast and some half a dozen for other counties.

There is not one Catholic. I can quite imagine this is all right, and that very likely no Catholic eligible for the appointment can be found who will consent to serve. But it seems to me to be a large order and likely to cause what may be considered a legitimate criticism if so many are now appointed without one of them being a Catholic.

I should be glad if you would wire to me, e.g. 'Please sign' and I shall then know it is your wish for the whole lot. Or if you wire 'Wait' I shall know you are writing on the subject.[1]

PRONI, Cab 9B/40/1

(b) Northern Ireland Cabinet minute 27 July 1922

The Prime Minister [of NI] indicated that Mr Churchill was withholding the Royal Assent to the Local Government Bill on the grounds that the change from proportional representation in county council elections was a matter affecting the whole of Ireland therefore one in which the Imperial Government were justified in withholding their Assent. It was agreed that this constituted a very grave step on the part of the Imperial Government and that to allow this precedent to be created would warrant the interference by the Imperial Government in almost every Act introduced in Northern Ireland. Although it was recognised that the resignation of the Government of Northern Ireland did not probably create the same crisis as would a resignation in similar circumstances of a Government in one of the Colonies,

1 Three days later Fitzalan wrote again, 'On receipt of your wire 'Please sign' I signed and returned the list of magistrates, so that is all right...'.

it was decided that this would prove the most effective course of action.

PRONI, Cab 4/50/1

(c) Winston Churchill [Colonial Secretary] to W.T.Cosgrave [Chairman of the Provisional Government of the Irish Free State]   9 September 1922

I told General Collins in my last letter to him that after exhaustive examination of the constitutional issues I have come, though most unwillingly, to the conclusion that the Local Government (Northern Ireland) Bill could not be vetoed. In view of your further memorandum on the subject I felt that the matter ought to be discussed by the British signatories to the Treaty – a view with which the Prime Minister agreed. After full discussion we came to the unanimous conclusion that for us to veto a measure clearly within the powers delegated to the Parliament of Northern Ireland would form a dangerous precedent. I have never concealed from Sir James Craig my opinion that the measure was inopportune. The same might, however, be said of other measures submitted from time to time for the Royal Assent but such considerations, if allowed to weigh, would tend to a dangerous enlargement of the prerogative. Sir James Craig assures me that the measure is in no way intended to prejudice the Boundary question ... It is useless, as I repeatedly told the House of Commons, for you or me or any one else to make predictions about what the Boundary Commission will or will not take into account ...

PRONI, Cab 9B/40/1

154 'Indecent gerrymandering'? Electioneering in a divided society

The abolition of PR for local elections, though likely to favour the Unionists as the largest party, could not entirely reverse the balance of forces in areas where Catholics possessed a local majority. But political parties were able to obtain, from the population census and from their own records, precise information on the religious distribution – and thus the likely voting behaviour – of all areas in Northern Ireland down to the level of the townland, the smallest unit of rural measurement. The drawing of electoral boundaries, therefore, frequently decided the outcome of future elections, or at least made clear how many fabricated votes would be necessary to turn the tide. In disputed areas of Tyrone, Fermanagh and elsewhere Unionist and Nationalist registration agents, usually local solicitors, were very experienced at this kind of work. James Cooper of Enniskillen (1882–1949), a member of the first Northern parliaments, was one such practitioner. Interestingly, his initial advice to Craig (a) was to retain PR for a while, though this should probably be put down to exasperation at having to overturn detailed arrangements which he had only recently made.

Although the work of 1922 greatly strengthened the Unionist grip on local government in west Ulster, these successes only served to intensify the eagerness of less fortunate Unionist parties to emulate them. The situation in the town of Omagh, Co Tyrone, was outlined in a letter (b) from Sir Charles Blackmore (1880-1967) who, as Secretary to the NI Cabinet, was a civil servant rather than a Unionist Party official, to the Minister for Home Affairs on 17 July 1934. His outmoded assertion of the political rights of property against persons echoed Bates's parliamentary declaration of 31 October 1928 that 'strong financial interests ... are entitled to preferential treatment' in the matter of voting qualifications. Bates's reply to Blackmore came in the form of a direct communication to his Prime Minister (c). He explained the technical difficulties which impeded a rapid settlement of the Omagh situation, and went on to raise the question of keeping the Unionists in power in the much larger city of Derry. In the face of mounting demographic adversity this was accomplished effectively until the local government reorganisation of the 1970s.

(a) James Cooper MP to Sir James Craig MP   9 August 1922

A remark you dropped today that we must proceed by installments and get back the old county council and rural council areas first and then proceed to revise them at a later date rather fills me with alarm.

Any such procedure would result in a fearful hash so far as the county Fermanagh is concerned. At our last county council election we were only a few votes short of three quotas in two divisions and the Nationalists just had the two quotas. So 1600 Unionist votes were thrown away for nothing. The winning of either of the seats would have won our county council and we took steps last winter and went all through these divisions and manufactured votes wholesale, so that we would have the quota at the election. The peculiar part of the thing is that our strongest divisions in votes were our weakest under PR and that it was in our strongest divisions we needed to manufacture the votes. These manufactured votes of course are useless in a straight voting system, as they are largely in areas where we already have the majority ...

Fermanagh is absolutely Unionist all over except in two or three mountain areas. The fact is Fermanagh is about the most skillfully rigged county in favour of the Nationalists you could possibly conceive. In the rural councils as they stand 50 or 60 Nationalist voters often equal a Unionist division with 400 to 500 voters. Enniskillen and Lisnaskea councils are particularly bad. Under PR they could not run away with us (though even under it the district council areas were rigged) but if we are to go back to the old system we are swamped.

Personally I have gone to very considerable trouble just over the manufacture of the new votes and then in carving up the county vote into new divisions and arranging the different areas. This meant going carefully into the composition of every townland in the county and fitting them together ... In Fermanagh we have been fighting for the last ten or twelve years and every time we came close to victory we were knocked at in some way and I very much fear if this final blow falls it will knock the heart out of the people altogether. I may also say that I called a few days ago with Mr Miller [Unionist MP] at Newtownstewart on my way here and found him plodding away on the Tyrone maps. He has a very big job to tackle and the people all over are most enthusiastic about the whole thing ...

If areas are not revised the only result of the present bill so far as Fermanagh is concerned will be to hand back to the Nationalists the county council we would have won this time under PR and probably a couple of district councils with it ...

Mr John McHugh [Nationalist] late chairman of Fermanagh County Council has already stated that of course the Unionists will revise the areas and win the county council and he and the Nationalists will be equally disappointed as they do not expect anything else. The first act of the Free State government was to abolish the only Unionist council in Donegal which had been set up by the Local Government Board as a result of the dividing of a Union between Donegal and Tyrone.

PS, I scarcely like to mention it at all owing to the difficulties which arise over the boundary question but if any opportunity arises to arrange the matter by agreement I could give you 36 townlands round the borders of Fermanagh in which there is not a *single* Protestant which or portion of which we would be quite willing to exchange for the Pettigo area of Donegal and the Unionist townland of Clyhore [sic for Cloghore] at Belleek just inside the Donegal border, in which townland the floodgates of Lough Erne are situated.

PRONI, Cab 9B/40/1

(b) Sir Charles Blackmore to Sir Dawson Bates MP   7 July 1934

Representations have been made to the Prime Minster in regard to the Urban District Council of Omagh which has for the past fourteen years been under Nationalist control, notwithstanding the fact that the Unionists pay over three-quarters of the capital rates and are owners of all the large residential and business premises in the town. The Nationalists have consolidated their position by large building schemes in the South

Ward in which they had formerly only a trifling majority, the present position being that the Unionists hold the North Ward whilst the Nationalists hold the South and West Wards.

As a result of the municipal building schemes carried on by the Nationalist Urban Council, in which it is stated over 95 percent of all the houses were given to the Nationalist tenants, they have now increased the Local Government electorate in South Ward out of all proportion to the other two wards. It is understood that in March last the Unionist Party in the town petitioned the Ministry of Home Affairs pointing out this anomaly and asking that there should be a redistribution of the wards, and they prepared and submitted a scheme whereby the Unionists would have obtained control of the Council ... In view ... of the present law the scheme will not be effective for the election next year, and even if the scheme may be adopted during the present year, the Nationalists will be left in control of the town for the next three years with ample opportunity of building and otherwise to upset the Unionist proposals.

It is pointed out that the Unionists of Omagh feel their present position very keenly and are prepared to make any sacrifices before admitting defeat, and the local Nationalists are boasting that they have already defeated the Unionists' proposals even before an Inquiry is held.

I shall be glad if you will let me have full particulars as early as possible.

PRONI Cab 9B/13/2

(c) Sir Dawson Bates to Lord Craigavon   24 July 1934

You will recollect that the Omagh people got into touch with you direct with regard to the question of the Home Office adopting a scheme for the alteration of Wards there, the effect of which would be to change the balance of power from the Nationalists to the Unionists in the Urban District.

The difficulty that arises in this case is that unfortunately the promoters of the scheme delayed coming to me until it was too late to hold the necessary enquiry, etc., giving the other side time to make representations in the meantime ...

If we had risked it and made the order, I have not the slightest doubt that the Nationalist Party would have applied to the Court for an Order restraining us from making the Order, and in my opinion, and in the opinion of our legal adviser, we would have been beaten. The result would have been held up to the charge of 'indecent gerrymandering'.

It is, of course, impossible for me to explain all this in public, but I think it well to let you know the true facts of the case. It has occurred to me, however, that, as we are introducing a Local Government Bill in the Autumn, we might consider the possibility of postponing all Local Government Elections for a year, as we did in 1923. This is a matter which we can discuss at a later date, but I just mention it to you meantime.

A similar situation, though not quite so acute, is cropping up in Derry. The Derry Unionists find increased difficulty, as is felt in other areas, in getting suitable people returned to the Corporation and therefore they are promoting a scheme for the alteration of the wards and reducing the number of members. I have discussed this privately with the people concerned, and the scheme has not yet come up to me, but I have warned them that any publicity at the present time or speeches on the subject would only add to difficulties which I must always have in dealing with the alteration of wards where the two parties are closely effective. I need hardly point out to you that in Derry, unless something is done now, it is only a matter of time until Derry passes into the hands of the Nationalist and Sinn Féin parties for all time. On the other hand, if proper steps are taken now, I believe Derry can be saved for years to come.

PRONI Cab 9B/13/2

155 Religious education: The 'humbug' of public control

Education was one area in which the Northern government attempted to deal more cautiously with the Catholic minority. Before partition, most schools had in practice been controlled by denominational managers, under the general supervision of the Commissioners of National Education, and all were funded on the same basis. There existed practically no public initiative for building the new schools which were desperately needed in Belfast and elsewhere, and no local authority control on the English model. A new structure for Northern Ireland, headed by a Ministry of Education, was inevitable. But the Lynn Committee, appointed in 1921 to draft a scheme, was boycotted by Catholic clerical and political leaders, partly because they objected to public control, partly because they were not at that stage prepared to recognise the existence of the Northern state. The 1923 Education Act provided for the continued payment of salaries and some maintenance for those schools (almost all Catholic-managed) which opted to remain outside public control, but not for any capital costs. Schools coming under public control on the other hand (which the great majority of Protestant children attended) were fully financed, but were not permitted to provide Bible instruction in school hours, nor impose a religious test for the appointment of teachers. Either of these might have been construed as *ultra vires* under the Government of Ireland Act, 1920. Protestant critics argued that in predominantly Catholic areas Nationalist councillors would control the schools of Protestants, while Catholic schools would remain outside public control.

Following a vigorous clerical campaign by the United Education Committee of the Protestant churches however, this arrangement was eroded by amending acts in 1925 and 1930 so that the publicly-controlled or state schools became effectively Protestant schools in terms of staff and religious instruction as well as pupils. Protestant clergymen thus obtained the same degree of effective control as their Catholic counterparts, without the financial sacrifice. The Catholic response, now that the Nationalist political leaders had ceased their abstention policy, was vociferous, along the lines of Devlin's bitter speech on the second reading of the 1930 bill. Following this protest, and threats by Catholic bishops to prod the British government into testing the legal validity of such proposals, the Northern Ireland Government purchased acquiescence by conceding for the future fifty per cent capital grants to Catholic schools and any others which remained under private management (this was increased in 1947 to seventy-five percent). State schools were able to consolidate their Protestantism while retaining one hundred percent grants.

Mr DEVLIN: Does the right hon. gentlemen who is at the head of the government realise that on the rolls of the public elementary schools in Northern Ireland the children of this minority which he proposes to treat with contumely and contempt, form a larger percentage of those receiving instruction than the children of any other religious denomination? Here are the figures which supply, I think, a damning indictment of the policy of religious intolerance which the present bill proposes to intensify. The Catholic children on the rolls of the elementary schools number 36.1 percent; the Presbyterians represent 32.3 percent; the Episcopalians represent 25.9 per cent ...

It is interesting to observe the way in which complete change in one respect in this Northern system, so loudly boomed as the greatest in the British Empire, was first brought about. At first it was thought that the Catholics had been dished, and that everybody else was satisfied. That was the mentality of the right hon. and hon. members opposite and of those for whom they spoke; but the militant leaders of some of the churches suddenly discovered that there was a flaw in the ministerial masterpiece. There were Protestants who were not satisfied with the provision for teaching religion that they conscientiously desired for their children, and their leaders joined with the Orange Lodges in organising an agitation for religious instruction in the schools. The Government, anxious to placate every aggrieved section of the Protestant community ... found a formula that met the wishes and needs of every section of Protestants, and therefore what is known as simple Bible teaching is introduced to meet what they regard - and I do not dissent – as the just claims of the Protestant body ...

By the Act of 1923 the Catholics had already been robbed of the rights which they enjoyed under the British regime, namely, a grant of two-thirds of the cost of the building of their schools. It might reasonably have been expected that when you were introducing an amending bill you would have at least restored that right to the Catholic body ...

... Catholics do not in the least degree object to what you are doing in the building, extension and lighting, and cleaning, of schools for the Protestant children ... and they do not desire directly or indirectly in any shape or form to interfere with Protestant schools or with the teaching of religion as they conceive it in their schools. But they do claim, and claim emphatically and justly, a similar right for themselves ...

This performance is bad enough, but the shabby pretence by which it is sought to buttress it up is in many ways worse; it is even more contemptible. That is the pretence that all this is caused by the fact that we will not accept popular control. Under the Act of 1923 you invented what is called four-and-two committees ... Under this system of so-called popular control ... four of the committee are appointed by the manager and two are chosen by the elected authority. This popular control is mere empty camouflage ...

And then the humbug of all this talk about 'we will not give public money without public control.' Without public control you are paying the teachers' salaries. I could see the consistency of your policy if you came along and said, not one farthing of public money will be paid to any school unless there is public control of that school. But they dare not do it. What they do is pay the teacher, and they pay, I think, some proportion of the equipment of the school, and of lighting and heating. But because there is no public control you are not going to give grants for building ...

NI HC Deb vol 12, cols 714–20 (9 April 1930)

156 Thomas Moles: An Irish Thermopylae

The city of Derry had in 1921 a Catholic proportion of fifty-six per cent. Its outskirts were but a mile or two east of the proposed partition line and its historic centre lay on the western bank of the River Foyle, the 'natural' frontier in the area. If the Boundary Commission was to operate at all on the lines which the Pro-Treaty Sinn Féiners predicted, Derry would be the crucial test. But the city was equally important to the political mythology of Unionism, which Ulster Unionist speakers in the Westminster debate on the Treaty provisions lost no time in making clear.

Mr T. MOLES: Let me now look at another matter. The city of Derry is historic ground. It enshrines memories that no Ulsterman, no man who loves his country, ought ever to forget. The very dust of its churchyard heaves with the immortal dead. The apprentice boys who made a stand in Derry created an Irish Thermopylae as noble and historic as the old, and they are buried there. Our cathedral is there. There too are the walls behind which a famished garrison fought disease and fought the enemy and held high the lamp of freedom and kept its flame pure and bright. There is no Ulsterman who would surrender a yard of them. The thing is impossible. It would outrage every sentiment and every feeling we have ever cherished and respected, and I tell you that if an attempt be made to deprive us of Derry you will succeed only when you have prevailed over a conquered community and a divided country ...

H C Deb 5th series, vol 149, cols 340-1
(16 December 1921)

157 Eoin MacNeill: Economic and geographical considerations

The Boundary Commission provided for in the Treaty came into existence, at the request of the Free State government, in the summer of 1924. Richard Feetham, a justice of the South African supreme court, was appointed as chairman by the British Government, who also nominated an Ulster representative J R Fisher, when the Northern Ireland Government declined to do so. The Free State Government nominated its Minister for Education, Eoin MacNeill, a distinguished Gaelic scholar and a native of Co Antrim. First meetings were held in November 1924, and hearings continued throughout border areas during the following winter, spring and summer. Notwithstanding the appointment of MacNeill, a political minister, the whole emphasis of the Commission was judicial rather than political. The Commissioners bound themselves not to take their respective governments into confidence, and while there is evidence that Fisher largely disregarded this, MacNeill appears to have been punctilious in the extreme, keeping his governmental colleagues entirely in the dark. At last, in November 1925, a detailed leak of the proposed award appeared in the *Morning Post* newspaper. Although formal confirmation of the proposals did not become publicly available until the opening of the public records in 1968, the press leak was substantially correct: the Commission's award was limited to minor adjustments and rationalisations of the long border, reducing its length from 280 to 229 miles. In all it was suggested that 180,000 acres containing 31,000 people be transferred to the Free State (notably in south Armagh), but that 50,000 acres in east Donegal and elsewhere, containing 7,500 people, be transferred to Northern Ireland. Taken in conjunction with the sharply limited scope of the Commission, the actual loss of territory was more than the Free State Government could accept. MacNeill resigned from the Commission, and the Free State leaders negotiated a new settlement with the British Government, renouncing their claim to a boundary revision in exchange for absolution from their outstanding financial obligations to Britain under the Treaty. MacNeill had not proved a very effective commissioner, but his unpublished memoir, written some years later, outlines his difficulties clearly.

As regards the partition clause, Article 12 of the Treaty, there has been a great deal of misunderstanding. The same clause appears word for word in what was known as 'Document No. 2', which Mr De Valera put forward as the proper substitute for the actual Treaty during the debate about it. From the first I regarded this clause as very faulty in some respects ...

The clause provides that the amendment of the boundary should be in accordance with the will of the inhabitants but only so far as this would appear compatible with economic and geographical considerations. The will of the inhabitants was ascertainable, but the economic and geographical considerations were left entirely to be decided by the Commission in accordance with any opinion that its members might happen to hold. Moreover it was evident that the decision of the Commission, if it came to any, would be dominated by the voice of the chairman representing the British Government One thing I was able to observe for myself in the course of the proceedings was that the chairman was very deeply impressed by the evidence brought forward on two points. One of these was the conduct of the 'B Specials' [a part-time police force attached to the Royal Ulster Constabulary, exclusively Protestant, which was used extensively during the troubles], the other was the gerrymandering of the [Ulster] constituencies ... I specially recommended that the Free State government should have recourse to the League of Nations which had made the protection of minorities a prominent part among its objects. Nothing was done in this way. My own opinion is that the [Free State] Government made the mistake of thinking that good relations could be promoted by avoiding drawing attention to objectionable features on the British side.

MacNeill Papers, cited in F X Martin & F J Byrne
(eds), *The Scholar Revolutionary*,
(Dublin: Jas. Duffy & Co Ltd, 1973) pp 269-72

Select Bibliography

General Texts

Bardon, J	*A History of Ulster* (1992)
Boyce, G	*Nationalism in Ireland* (1982, 1991)
Boyce, G & A O'Day	*The Making of Modern Irish History* (1996)
Connolly, S J (ed)	*The Oxford Companion to Irish History* (1998)
Fitzpatrick, D	*The Two Irelands, 1912-1939* (1998)
Foster, R F	*Modern Ireland, 1660-1972* (1988)
Hoppen, K T	*Ireland since 1800: Conflict and Conformity* (1988)
Kennedy L & P Ollerenshaw (eds)	*An Economic History of Ulster, 1820-1939* (1985)
Lee, J J	*Ireland, 1912-85* (1989)
Lyons, F S L	*Ireland since the Famine* (1973)
Mitchell, A & P Ó Snodaigh	*Irish Political Documents, 1869-1916* (1989)
O'Connor, E	*Labour History of Ireland, 1824-1960* (1992)
O'Grada, C	*Ireland: a New Economic History, 1780-1939* (1994)
Vaughan, W E (ed)	*A New History of Ireland VI, 1870-1921* (1996)
Ward, M	*Unmanageable Revolutionaries: Women & Irish Nationalism* (1989)

Chapter 1

Comerford, R V	*The Fenians in Context* (1985)
Davis, R	*The Young Ireland Movement* (1987)
Elliott, M	*Wolfe Tone: Prophet of Irish Independence* (1989)
Holmes, R F G	*Henry Cooke* (1981)
Kinealy, C	*This Great Calamity: The Irish Famine, 1845-52* (1994)
MacDonagh, O	*O'Connell: The Life of Daniel O'Connell, 1775-1847* (1991)
Senior, H	*Orangeism in Ireland and Britain, 1795-1836* (1966)

Chapter 2

Bew, P	*Land and the National Question* (1978)
Bew, P	*Conflict and Conciliation in Ireland, 1890-1910* (1987)
Callanan, F	*T M Healy* (1996)
Clark, S	*Social Origins of the Irish Land War* (1979)
Hoppen, K T	*Elections, Politics & Society in Ireland, 1832-85* (1984)
Loughlin, J	*Gladstone, Home Rule & the Ulster Question* (1986)
Lyons, F S L	*Charles Stewart Parnell* (1977)
Lyons, F S L	*John Dillon: a Biography* (1968)
Moody, T W	*Davitt and Irish Revolution, 1846-82* (1982)
Thornley, D	*Isaac Butt and Home Rule* (1964)
Warwick–Haller, S	*William O'Brien and the Irish Land War* (1990)

Chapter 3

Bull, P	*Land, Politics & Nationalism: a Study of the Irish Land Question* (1996)
Davis, R	*Arthur Griffith & Non-Violent Sinn Féin* (1974)
Dunleavy, J E & G W Douglas	*Hyde: a Maker of Modern Ireland* (1991)
Gailey, A	*Ireland and the Death of Kindness: The Experience of Constructive Unionism, 1890-1905* (1987)
Garvin, T	*Nationalist Revolutionaries in Ireland, 1858-1928* (1987)
Hepburn, A C	*A Past Apart: Studies in the History of Catholic Belfast, 1850-1950* (1996)
Hutchinson, J	*The Dynamics of Cultural Nationalism: the Gaelic Revival & the Creation of the Irish Nation State* (1987)
Johnston, S	*Alice: a Life of Alice Milligan* (1994)
Lyons, F S L	*Culture & Anarchy in Ireland, 1890-1939* (1979)
Mandle, W F	*The Gaelic Athletic Association & Irish Nationalist Politics* (1987)
Martin, F X & F J Byrne (eds)	*The Scholar Revolutionary: Eoin MacNeill, 1867-1945* (1973)
Maume, P	*D P Moran* (1995)
Miller, D W	*Church, State & Nation in Ireland, 1898-1921* (1973)
O'Halpin, E	*The Decline of the Union: British Government in Ireland, 1892-1920* (1987)

Chapter 4

Buckland, P (ed)	*Irish Unionism, 1885-1923: a Documentary History* (1973)
Jackson, A	*The Ulster Party: Irish Unionists in the House of Commons, 1884-1911* (1989)
Jackson, A	*Colonel Edward Saunderson: Land & Loyalty in Victorian Ireland* (1995)
Kendle, J	*Walter Long, Ireland and the Union, 1905-20* (1992)
Loughlin, J	*Gladstone, Home Rule & the Ulster Question, 1882-1893* (1986)
Lucy, G	*The Great Convention: the Ulster Unionist Convention of 1892* (1995)
Miller, D W	*Queen's Rebels: Ulster Loyalism in Historical perspective* (1978)
Shannon, C	*Arthur J Balfour & Ireland, 1874-1922* (1988)
Walker, B M	*Ulster Politics: the Formative Years, 1868-86* (1989)
Wright, F	*Two Lands on One Soil: Ulster Politics before Home Rule* (1996)

Chapter 5

Boyle, J W — *The Irish Labour Movement in the Nineteenth Century* (1988)

Keogh, D — *The Rise of the Irish Working Class* (1982)

Gray, J — *City in Revolt: James Larkin & the Belfast Dock Strike of 1907* (1985)

Larkin, E — *James Larkin, 1876-1947: Irish Labour Leader* (1965)

Morgan, A — *James Connolly: a Political Biography* (1988)

Morgan, A — *Labour & Partition: the Belfast Working Class, 1905-23* (1991)

Mitchell, A — *Labour in Irish Politics, 1890-1930* (1974)

O'Brien, W — *Forth the Banners Go* (1969)

Patterson, H — *Class Conflict and Sectarianism: the Protestant Working Class & the Belfast Labour Movement, 1868-1920* (1980)

Chapter 6

Beckett, I F W (ed) — *The Army and the Curragh Incident, 1914* (1986)

Bew, P — *Ideology & the Irish Question: Ulster Unionism & Irish Nationalism, 1912-16* (1994)

Gwynn, D. — *The Life of John Redmond* (1932)

Edwards, Ruth D — *Patrick Pearse: the Triumph of Failure* (1977)

Stewart, A T Q — *The Ulster Crisis: Resistance to Home Rule, 1912-14* (1967)

Blake, R — *The Unknown Prime Minister: Andrew Bonar Law, 1858-1923* (1955)

Jenkins, R — *Asquith* (1964)

Jalland, P — *The Liberals & Ireland: the Ulster Question in British Politics to 1914* (1980)

Mansergh, N — *The Unresolved Question: the Anglo-Irish Settlement and its Undoing, 1912-72* (1991)

Chapter 7

Martin, F X (ed) — *Leaders and Men of the 1916 Rising* (1967)

Murphy, B P — *Patrick Pearse & the Republican Ideal* (1991)

Ni Dhonnchadha, M & T Dorgan (eds) — *Revising the Rising* (1991)

Nowlan, K B — *The Making of 1916: Studies in the History of the Rising* (1969)

O'Broin, L — *Dublin Castle & the 1916 Rising* (1966)

Chapter 8

Denman, T — *A Lonely Grave: the Life and Death of William Redmond* (1995)

Fitzpatrick, D — *Politics and Irish Life, 1913-21* (1977)

Macardle, D — *The Irish Republic* (1937)

MacDowell, R B — *The Irish Convention, 1917-18* (1970)

Chapter 9

Augusteijn, J	*From Public Defiance to Guerrilla Warfare* (1996)
Barry, T	*Guerrilla Days in Ireland* (1949)
Breen, D	*My Fight for Irish Freedom* (1924)
Hart, P	*The IRA and its Enemies: Violence and Community in Cork, 1916-23* (1998)
Mitchell, A	*Revolutionary Government in Ireland: Dáil Éireann 1919-22* (1995)
Neligan, D	*The Spy in the Castle* (1968)
O'Malley, E	*On Another Man's Wound* (1936)
Macardle, D	*The Irish Republic* (1937)
MacDowell, R B	*The Irish Convention, 1917-18* (1970)

Chapter 10

Coogan, T P	*Michael Collins* (1990)
Coogan, T P	*De Valera: Long Fellow, Long Shadow* (1993)
Cowling, M	*The Impact of Labour, 1920-24* (1971)
Jones, T	*Whitehall Diary, vol 3: Ireland, 1918-25* (1971)
Pakenham, F	*Peace by Ordeal* (1935)

Chapter 11

Deasy, L	*Brother Against Brother* (1982)
Garvin, T	*1922: the Birth of Irish Democracy* (1996)
Gilbert, M	*Winston S Churchill, vol iv Companion, pt 3* (1977)
Hopkinson, M	*Green Against Green: the Irish Civil War* (1988)
O'Malley, E	*The Singing Flame* (1978)
Rumpf, E & Hepburn, A C	*Nationalism & Socialism in 20th Century Ireland* (1977)
Valiulis, M G	*Portrait of a Revolutionary: General Richard Mulcahy and the Founding of the Irish Free State* (1992)

Chapter 12

Bew, P, P Gibbon & H Patterson	*The State in Northern Ireland, 1921-72* (1979)
Bowman, J	*De Valera and the Ulster Question, 1917-73* (1982)
Buckland, P J	*The Factory of Grievances: Northern Ireland 1921-39* (1979)
Farrell, M	*Northern Ireland: the Orange State* (1976)
Hand, G J	*Report of the Irish Boundary Commission, 1925* (1969)
Harkness, D	*Northern Ireland since 1920* (1983)
Loughlin, J	*Ulster Unionism & British National Identity since 1885* (1995)
Phoenix, E	*Northern Nationalism* (1994)
Wright, F	*Northern Ireland: a Comparative Analysis* (1987)